Italian Marxism

Italian Marxism

PAUL PICCONE

UNIVERSITY OF CALIFORNIA PRESS

Berkeley • Los Angeles • London

University of California Press
Berkeley and Los Angeles, California
University of California Press, Ltd.
London, England
Copyright © 1983 by The Regents of the University of California
Library of Congress Cataloging in Publication Data
Piccone, Paul.
Italian Marxism.
Includes bibliographical references.
1. Communism—Italy—History. 2. Communism and
philosophy—Italy—History. 3. Gramsci, Antonio, 1891–1937.
4. Marx, Karl, 1818–1883. I. Title.
HX288.P48   1982   335.4'0945   82-8474
ISBN 0-520-04798-2
Printed in the United States of America

1 2 3 4 5 6 7 8 9

Contents

Introduction

Phenomena whose contours are vague and meanings ambiguous are usually difficult to capture without risking oversimplification or distortion. "Italian Marxism" is one such phenomenon. It is neither a clear-cut doctrine nor a well-defined body of ideas. Thus, the following analysis delivers at the same time both less as well as more than the title promises. It falls short of an exhaustive account since, by focusing primarily on the predominant tradition, it necessarily overlooks many lesser known but nonetheless important trends. It delivers more than it promises in that the reconstruction of the predominant tradition requires an elaboration of ideas and events only marginally related to it, yet essential for a satisfactory understanding of the genesis and structure of that tradition.

Marx's thought does not automatically systematize into Marxism—witness Marx's own disclaimer, later in life, that he was not a Marxist. Brilliant insights, penetrating critique, and painstaking analyses remain juxtaposed in different historical contexts. They successfully escape the otherwise unavoidable obsolescence by being embedded in a philosophical vision much more impervious to the corrosive effects of time. Yet, unlike the parts of a jigsaw puzzle which, properly ordered, ultimately cohere into a meaningful whole, Marx's thoughts remain a plethora of fragments occasionally in conflict with one another, disconnected, and reconcilable only through forcible fits, elimination of some parts, and extraneous introduction of still others. It is not surprising, therefore, that whenever this body of ideas is systematized into a "Marxism," the operation is usually carried out by means of a set of seldom explicitly stated organizing principles that select what features of Marx's thought are to be emphasized, arrange them in order of importance and eliminate others, while introducing still additional ones. This explains why the history of Marxism is a history of often violent debates, at times even settled with guns when those making their case could resort to power if logic and persuasion happened to fail them. This also explains why Marxism has been in crisis for over a century—from the time that Marx himself was still writing.

It is well known how Marx's own position was defeated politically by Bakunin at the First International—an event that was decisive in the eventual dismantling of that organization. The Second International was only a few years old when the "Bernstein-debate," or the "revisionism debate," once again plunged "orthodox" Marxism into a major crisis that, although organizationally managed within the Social Democratic party, was never theoretically resolved. Lenin's own break with Kautsky and the Social Democrats was precipitated by World War I and the collapse of the Second International. Far from solving any crisis, however, the launching of the Third International and what came to be known as "Marxism-Leninism" signaled the beginning of a new dogmatism and deterioration. The instrumentalization of all official Communist parties to the foreign policy of the USSR and the rapid involution of the Bolshevik regime into Stalinism were *not*, however, responsible for the explosion of new brands of Marxisms immediately after the war. Rather, it was the earlier need to modify the predominant Marxism at that time—that of the Second International—so as to allow it to explain new developments that spurred the resystematization of Marx's thought in terms of new sets of organizational principles and, thus, generated new brands of Marxism later subsumed under the heading of "Western Marxism."

After 1928, of course, Trotskyism opened a new chapter in the ongoing crisis by seeking to salvage the Bolshevik heritage from Stalinism—a task that turned out to be both theoretically impossible and politically futile. With the dissolution of the Third International and the coming of the cold war, the crisis of Marxism was intensified by silence, conformity, and repression by both Marxists and anti-

Marxists[1] so that, when it was rediscovered by the New Left in the 1960s, it did not take long to recapitulate all earlier ideological phases and rediscover the same old pitfalls.[2] By the late 1970s, Marxism had turned into an intellectual fad or simply another academic oddity. Yet, the perennial rediscoveries of the "crisis of Marxism"[3] by academics whose social amnesia cripples their memory to the immediacy of the present, cannot be explained merely in terms of the bureaucratically enforced compulsion to publish or, with Murray Bookchin, in terms of the academicization of politics—for the critique here falls prey to the very same charge[4]—but also in terms of a more general exhaustion of thought, which, in the desperate effort to hang onto a reef of pseudo-originality in a sea of conformity, exploits ambiguity and confusion to recycle worn-out ideas as fresh insights.

What gives rise to this peculiar predicament, however, is not merely a "crisis of intelligence," but the fact that the history of Marxism remains confused and ambiguous. Thanks primarily to most Marxists' bad habit of rewriting not only history in general but their own history as well, to suit immediate political needs, and most non-Marxists' reluctance to tackle these subjects seriously, the record is not clear—hence, the ambiguities, confusions and pathetic academic reiterations. Expectedly, this farcical repetition has its tragic antecedents. What can now be clearly discerned as a *permanent* crisis

1. For a recent account of "orthodox" Marxists' repression of Marxists, as well as Marxism, see Russell Jacoby, *Dialect of Defeat: Countours of Western Marxism* (New York, 1981).

2. Thus, it is ironic to find recapitulations of arguments well developed during the Bernstein debate at the turn of the century, marketed under new terminologies and with new examples, but making essentially the same points as Croce, Sorel, Bernstein, etc. See Anthony Giddens, *A Contemporary Critique of Historical Materialism* (Los Angeles, 1981); and Stanley Aronowitz, *The Crisis of Historical Materialism: Class, Politics and Culture in Marxist Theory* (New York, 1981).

3. Alvin W. Gouldner, *The Two Marxisms: Contradictions and Anomolies in the Development of Theory* (New York, 1980), pp. 26–29. To emphasize his point, Gouldner quotes Louis Althusser, Göran Therborn, Lucia Colletti, and Georg Lukács. This, however, only shows that social amnesia is an academic phenomenon more widespread than one might have initially suspected.

4. Murray Bookchin, "Beyond Neo-Marxism," in *Telos* (Summer, 1978), n. 38, pp. 5 ff.

of Marxism could reasonably appear as an accidental development—a problem associated with growth—around World War I. It was thus not strange for the new generation of radical thinkers to attempt to resystematize Marxism in a way more in accordance with the founders' original intent. Gramsci's work constitutes one of the most serious and penetrating efforts in that direction. But it was not simply a ''correction'' or a better restatement of the authentic doctrine. His resystematization was understood as a necessary reconstitution of ''the philosophy of praxis'' according to its interpretation of an ''absolute historicism.'' Its tragic aspect consists in the fact that, as the following pages seek to explain, the distinctive character of the ''Italian Marxism'' developed by Gramsci became embroiled in theoretical ambiguities and misunderstandings that linger on to this day for very specific political reasons.

The political other side of this state of affairs is that the identity of organizations such as the Italian Communist Party, which eventually appropriated the Gramscian heritage, remains clouded in a mystery usually unraveled by means of ready-made conceptual labels such as ''social-democracy,'' ''Marxism-Leninism,'' and so forth, which occlude more than they reveal. *Italian Marxism* seeks to set at least part of this record straight by locating the neo-Hegelian tradition within which Gramsci's Marxism was systematized, tracing the uneasy blend of this systematization with a poorly understood Bolshevik tradition, and indicating how, once fully translated into a political strategy under extremely difficult conditions, it lost its original emancipatory impulse.

This does not entail a Manichean contraposition of an all-pure philosophical Gramsci to a politically corruptible Togliatti, nor should it be taken as an attempt to vindicate Gramscian Marxism or any other brand as *the* correct interpretation. One of the conclusions of this work, in fact, is precisely to show, in an absolute historicist fashion, how Gramscian was inextricably tied to a historical phase of capitalism which was rapidly becoming obsolete while Gramsci himself was still writing in jail. The more modest aim is to indicate how, within the Crocean tradition, Gramsci's attempt to resystematize Marxism along lines he mistakenly considered parallel to Lenin's own efforts in that direction, resulted in an original theoretical synthesis. The more this synthesis was integrated into an Italian Communist Party in the process of rapid Bolshevization, the more it faded into mainline Third International Marxism, up to the time of Gramsci's incarceration and Togliatti's effective takeover of the party leadership in 1926.

The reconstruction stops at that point because, afterward, it became primarily a matter of *survival* while holding on to that minimal connection with the tradition allowed by the shifting requirements of Stalinist policies. Thus, the tormented figure of Togliatti is not extensively dealt with since it would have entailed *another* type of reconstruction: that of the Bolshevized Italian Communist Party which is only contingently related to the Gramscian tradition, and these relations were uneasily reestablished only after the late 1950s when Gramsci's works began to resurface and were widely discussed. While it would have been impossible to discuss Italian Marxism in any way other than from the vantage point of six decades of subsequent developments, every effort has been made to capture both the *living* meaning of events in terms of a broader understanding of the context within which they unfolded. It is thus fair to say now that whatever was original in Gramsci and therefore what here is generalized simply as Italian Marxism, faded with his incarceration and was pretty well eclipsed as a meaningful political doctrine after his death.

The particular theoretical synthesis he developed could be retained only by refragmenting it, rehistoricizing it, and therefore by fundamentally altering it. What Italian Communist Party intellectuals were subsequently able to resynthesize under the Gramscian label not only turned out to be at odds with the original version but, and what is more important, had lost most of its emancipatory thrust. Problematic as it may have been, what provided this original synthesis its explosiveness was its embeddedness in Italian neo-Hegelianism, its antipositivism, and its attempt to confront, rather than simply ignore, as other Marxist traditions have done since that time, the decisive challenges made during the revisionism debate. All these elements were either deemphasized or outrightly rejected by subsequent reconstitutions of that tradition. The neo-Hegelian dimension, identified with idealism and, consequently, with the "ideology of imperialism," was discarded and ridiculed in favor of a materialism that gradually reintroduced all the crudities of neopositivism (e.g., the School of Della Volpe and Colletti).[5] While neopositivists have usually been a minority within the party, especially before Togliatti's death, the failure to develop Marxism as *a branch of neo-Hegelianism* deemphasized the dialectic and, by default, led to a slide back into conformist theoretical positions. Lastly, the most important result of the revisionism debate, the realization of the impossibility of Marxism as a philosophy of history, was set aside by the reintroduction, as early as the late 1920s and early 1930s, of an Enlightenment belief in progress that, by placing communism at the end of the historical rainbow, reintroduced all the problems Gramsci's historicism had sought to avoid.

This is not to say that the Italian Communist Party has become nothing more than another social democratic party. What it has become, however, must not be understood so much or primarily in terms of its Gramscian heritage, but in relation to the sociohistorical events of the last half century that have decisively shaped its contemporary theoretical and political profile. But this is another story altogether. The present work only seeks to rescue from oblivion and confusion a tradition that deserves a better fate.

Paul Piccone

5. For an analysis of how this school eventually ends up giving up Marxism altogether with Colletti, see Paul Piccone "The Future of Eurocommunism," in *Theory and Society*, 10, 5 (1981) 721–732.

I

The Cultural Background

Origins of the Philosophy of Praxis

Writing in prison under his warden's careful scrutiny, Antonio Gramsci was forced to resort to using a sort of code for whatever expressions might have betrayed the profoundly political nature of his concerns. But his articulation of Marxism as "the philosophy of praxis" was more than a convenient paraphrase. It was, in fact, an accurate characterization of his theoretical perspective as part of a long-standing tradition opposed to positivist, naturalist, and scientistic deformations of Marxism.

This tradition goes back to Antonio Labriola, who first vindicated historical materialism as a "philosophy of praxis" and a "philosophy of life" against his positivist contemporaries in the Italian Socialist Party.[1] But it extends back beyond that, finding its origins in the broader nineteenth-century Neapolitan neo-Hegelianism, which, after its initial strong impact during Italy's Risorgimento in the 1850s and 1860s, faded out of sight for a couple of decades, eclipsed by the positivism that is usually uncritically associated with rapid industrialization and scientific progress. But this neo-Hegelian tradition re-emerged with a vengeance at the turn of the century to dominate twentieth-century Italian culture overwhelmingly. Thus, except for what can be described accurately as "the positivist parenthesis" in Italian culture,[2] there is an unbroken continuity between such major

1. Antonio Labriola to Georges Sorel, 14 May 1897, and 20 June 1897, in Antonio Labriola, *Socialism and Philosophy*, trans. Ernest Untermann (St. Louis, 1980), pp. 94, 126.
2. Although this is the derisive general interpretation of the period provided by the

figures in the introduction of Hegelianism in Italy as Francesco De Sanctis and the Spaventa brothers (Silvio and Bertrando, who were Benedetto Croce's uncles) and their students Donato Jaja and Labriola (who were Giovanni Gentile's and Croce's teachers), as well as Gramsci. The latter openly considered himself a Crocean as late as 1917, when he edited the short-lived journal *La Città Futura*,[3] and even a decade later, in prison, he considered Croce's work so important as to suggest that it would have been useful for a whole group of men to dedicate "ten years of activity in the writing of an Anti-Croce."[4]

This generally underemphasized heritage is significant not only because it provides useful background information;[5] it is in fact a necessary component of any understanding of Gramsci along the lines that he himself laid down for reconstructing the genesis and structure of the Italian intelligentsia. Any study of Gramsci's thought claiming continuity with his work must approach it from the dual perspective of a constantly rejuvenating *tradition* and the *specific* configuration that this takes in concrete historical situations. Gramsci's thought can be characterized as running along two main parallel theoretical tracks: a reelaboration of Marxism as the crowning point of Western thought presupposing the "Renaissance and Reformation, German philosophy and the French revolution, Calvinism and English classical economics;"[6] and a constant historicist emphasis on the particular way in which this tradition lives and is practically articulated. In this we can see why, as early as 1917, Gramsci contraposed what he took to be

---

neo-idealist schools of Benedetto Croce and Giovanni Gentile, it remains sound in spite of objections from the Left. See Sergio Landucci, "L'Hegelismo in Italia nell'Età del Risorgimento," *Studi Storici* VI (1965), 602.

3. Antonio Gramsci, *Quaderni del Carcere*, ed. Valentino Gerratana (Turin, 1975), II, 1233. Unfortunately, this part of the *Prison Notebooks* was omitted in the Quentin Hoare and Goeffrey Nowell-Smith English edition (London, 1971).

4. Ibid., p. 1234.

5. Three recent works attempting to map out the large and still growing number of Gramsci interpretations hardly mention this Hegelian heritage. See Gianfranco Albertelli, ed., *Interpretazioni di Gramsci (1957–1975)* (Trento, 1976); Gian Carlo Jocteau, *Leggere Gramsci: Guida alle Interpretazioni* (Milan, 1975); and Tito Perlini, *Gramsci e il Gramscismo* (Milan, 1974).

6. Antonio Gramsci, *Prison Notebooks*, ed. Quintin Hoare and Geoffry Nowell-Smith (London, 1971), p. 395.

Bolshevism—"the Marxist thought that never dies, which is the continuation of Italian and German idealist thought"[7]—to the sclerotic doctrines sanctified by the Italian Socialist Party; and we can see why he always emphasized the need to deal with social and political problems in their historical concreteness, as specifics that always must be given absolute precedence over any abstract categorical schemes that might be forced onto them.[8] The multidimensional specificity of life cannot be reduced to well-packaged abstractions whose conceptual elegance only temporarily hides their manifold deficiencies. Abstractions, and theoretical structures in general, remain valid only as long as they are never unchained from the social milieu where they were first born and where they must ever be re-created as mediations. This is the most fundamental trait of Gramsci's "absolute historicism" understood as "the absolute secularization and earthliness of thought."[9]

All of Gramsci's thought rotates around this axiom—from his periodic attacks on cosmopolitanism understood as abstract universalism (or, in the Italian case, as the cultural expression of an otherwise

7. Antonio Gramsci, "The Revolution against *Capital*," in Pedro Cavalcanti and Paul Piccone, eds., *History, Philosophy and Culture in the Young Gramsci* (St. Louis, 1975), p. 123. Here Gramsci extends to Marxism the Neapolitan neo-Hegelians' thesis of "the circulation of European thought" and, faithful to his historicist principles, he reconstitutes Marxism in terms of the specificity of the sociohistorical situation.

8. Thus, for example, in 1918, in a party debate concerning Esperanto, Gramsci argued against its uncritical acceptance as the official party language, as was being proposed: "Language is not just a means of communication: it is first of all a work of art, it is beauty. . . . The international language would rather be a mechanism without the agility and the expressive possibilities of a spoken language; it would be a perfect and definitive mechanism, while expression is never definite since relations of thought change continually, the ideal of beauty is always shifting and only the spoken language can find in itself, or in other languages, the new nuances, the new verbal ties adequate to the new needs: it finds them in the past that it lives as renewed." See Luigi Ambrosoli, "Nuovi Contributi agli *Scritti Giovanili* di Gramsci," *Rivista Storica del Socialismo* III, 10 (August 1960), 548. Gramsci's point was that artificial efforts to introduce Esperanto *from above* are useless since "this process can only come about freely and spontaneously. Linguistic stimulus comes from the bottom up. Books have little influence concerning changes in ways of talking." See Gramsci's "Universal Language and Esperanto," in Cavalcanti and Piccone, *History, Philosophy and Culture*, p. 32. Also relevant here is Gramsci's implicit acceptance of the Croce-Vossler identification of language and art.

9. Gramsci, *Prison Notebooks*, p. 465.

nonexistent national unity)[10] to his obsession with Croce and intellectuals in general. And it is clear why Gramsci's absolute historicism focused on the reconstruction of the Italian neo-Hegelian tradition through a systematic study of the formation of Italian intellectuals, and on a regrounding of this tradition by means of a merciless critique of its major exponent (Croce) in the *Prison Notebooks*.[11] All of this was part of Gramsci's effort to explain the failure of post-World War I European revolutions and to investigate the conditions necessary for their future realization. Considering that all of Gramsci's works, along with those of other Marxist thinkers of the time, assumed that the objective conditions for revolution were present and that the only remaining obstacle was to organize "the subjective factor,"[12] it is understandable why, in explicating the reasons for the failure, Gramsci's analysis tended to focus on the subjective domain and those responsible for its articulation: the intellectuals. But, as he well knew, even before he began his prison study of Italian intellectuals, such a project was bound to remain unfinished or, at best, fragmentary.[13] As a result, a reconstruction of Gramsci's thought entails completing this unfinished project, arriving at an understanding of the Italian neo-Hegelian and socialist traditions and the sociohistorical conditions that fertilized their hybridization in Gramsci's Marxism.

The Hegelian Heritage

Hegelianism has had a measurable influence on almost all cultures, but, with the possible exception of Poland, nowhere as massively or

10. Gramsci, *Quaderni del Carcere*, I. 133. See also II, 866, where Gramsci contraposes Trotsky, the "cosmopolitan, i.e., superficially national and superficially Western or European," to Lenin, "profoundly national and profoundly European."

11. As Garin puts it, "The problem of the intellectuals was not . . . one among various arguments in the prison problematic: it ws the nexus around which everything came to rotate." Eugenio Garin, *Intellettuali Italiani del XX Secolo* (Rome, 1974), p. 327.

12. For an excellent account of this position, see Massimo L. Salvadori, *Gramsci e il Problema Storico della Democrazia* (Turin, 1970), pp. 110 ff.

13. On this point, Gramsci wrote to his sister-in-law on 19 March 1927: "Naturally, I could only sketch out the major lines of this highly appealing argument, given the impossibility of obtaining the immense amount of material necessary." Antonio Gramsci, *Letters from Prison*, trans. Lynne Lawner (New York, 1973), p. 79.

for the same reasons as in Italy.[14] In Germany, for example, immediately following Hegel's death, his disciples split into conservative Right-Hegelians and their more liberal counterparts. Orthodox Marxists such as Georg Lukács explain this split as the rise of a Marxist alternative in the wake of the decadence that bourgeois culture fell into after its peak philosophic expression in Hegel. The subsequent late nineteenth-century retreat from Hegel in German thought is likewise seen as an attempt to avoid its inevitable Marxist outcome—an attempt that helped pave the way for fascism and Nazism.[15] Whatever shortcomings this thesis may possess, it is true that Hegelianism has had little effect in shaping German culture (the works of Ernst Bloch, Lukács, the Frankfurt School, and other relatively isolated groups were historical flashes of brilliance but did not play a determining role in German thinking). In the debates concerning Nazism, Hegelianism was both violently attacked as its source and defended as its main opposition.[16] Yet, given the authoritarian character of German political life from Bismarck to Hitler, it has been the Right-Hegelians' Hegel (if, indeed, a Hegel is at all to blame) who has had the upper hand.

In England, the situation was somewhat different. Hegelianism became popular in Britain in the late nineteenth century, precisely when it was all but dead in Germany. In 1882, William James accurately described the situation when he wrote:

> We are just now witnessing a singular phenomenon in British and American philosophy. Hegelianism, so defunct in its native soil . . . has found among us so zealous and able a set of propagandists that today it may really

14. Bronislaw Baczko, ''La Gauche et la Droit Hegeliennes en Pologne dans la Premiere Moitie du XIX Siecle,'' *Annali Feltrinelli* VI (1963), 137–163. Probably because of a similar political and historical situation, the Polish experience is almost parallel to the Italian one.

15. Georg Lukács, *Die Zerstörung der Vernunft* (Berlin, 1954).

16. For typical examples, see Karl R. Popper, *The Open Society and Its Enemies*, Vol. II: *The High Tide of Prophecy: Hegel, Marx and the Aftermath* (New York, 1962; originally published in 1945); and Herbert Marcuse, *Reason and Revolution: Hegel and the Rise of Social Theory* (New York, 1941). Since almost every German emigre of some repute felt compelled to deal with the subject of the Nazi outcome in German culture, the literature is extensive. Fromm's *Escape from Freedom*, Horkheimer and Adorno's *The Dialectic of Enlightenment*, Cassirer's *The Myth of the State*, and scores

be reckoned one of the most powerful influences of the time in the higher walks of thought.[17]

From the time of the publication of Stirling's *The Secret of Hegel* (1865) to World War I, Hegelian philosophy dominated the British scene—checkmating materialism, as Passmore put it, as well as providing a viable political philosophy.[18] During this period, the works of neo-Hegelians were so dominant that even Bertrand Russell and George Edward Moore could not resist their influence and, consequently, began their philosophical careers as Hegelians.[19] T. H. Green first and Bernard Bosanquet later were the leading political theoreticians of British neo-Hegelianism up to World War I, when the "Teutonic" foundations of their positions did not weather the ensuing British national chauvinism. Associated with conservatism by Hobson[20] and with German imperialist ideology by Hobhouse during the war,[21] British neo-Hegelianism did not survive the forced identification of the Hegelian and fascist concepts of the state during the early 1920s. It finally disappeared altogether from the English scene with the death of J. H. Muirhead and R. G. Collingwood, leaving no lasting cultural imprint.

A very similar phenomenon took place in Russia. In fact, according to Planty-Bonjour's somewhat exaggerated evaluation, "No European country has felt a Hegelian influence as durable as Russia, and no

of others fall into this category.

17. William James, "On Some Hegelism," *Mind* (April 1882); reprinted in William James, *The Will to Believe* (New York, 1898), pp. 263 ff.

18. John Passmore, *A Hundred Years of Philosophy* (London, 1957), p. 51.

19. Bertrand Russell, *The Autobiography of Bertrand Russell* (New York, 1967), p. 76. R. G. Collingwood did not exaggerate too much when he wrote that "the philosophy of Green's school might be found, from about 1880 to 1910, penetrating and fertilizing every part of national life." As quoted in Passmore, *Hundred Years of Philosophy*, p. 57.

20. J. A. Hobson, *Democracy after the War* (London, 1919). For an excellent analysis of these criticisms, see Cristiano Camporesi, "Il Neoidealismo Inglese e la 'Teoria Metafisica dello Stato,' " unpublished thesis.

21. Leonard T. Hobhouse, *The Metaphysical Theory of the State. A Criticism* (New York, 1918). In a particularly pathetic preface addressed to his son, a pilot in the British air force, Hobhouse recalls how one summer morning, while reading Hegel, he was surprised by a German air raid. It was the German bombs, he claims, that proved to him once and for all the falsity and evil character of Hegel's philosophy!

European country has been so profoundly affected by this philosophy."[22] This influence easily survived the positivist reaction to Hegel, which raced across Europe to touch Russia as well, only to succumb eventually for other reasons.[23] Even before it was ruthlessly and finally "refuted" by Stalin's well-known administrative methods, Hegelianism had run into other problems:

> In spite of the brilliant variations inspired by Hegelianism concerning the importance of the dialectic as the foundation of social practice, the individualist, nihilist, anarchist, or, from the opposite side, collectivist tendencies so lively in Russia at that time, resulted in Hegel's political philosophy failing to influence favorably the course of the Russian state.[24]

In America, Hegelianism also played an important role. Despite the dominant mythology popularized by Frederick Jackson Turner's thesis, according to which the practical needs of the western frontier conditioned all of American culture,[25] what philosophy existed during the pioneer days of western expansion (1850–1890) was mainly Hegelian or Platonist.[26] In 1859–1860, while buffaloes were still roaming the Great Plains, Henry C. Brockmeyer was tucked away in the wilderness of Warren County, Missouri, tirelessly attempting to translate Hegel's *Logic* into English.[27] (For a while he even tried to teach Hegelian philosophy to the Indians around Muskogee, Oklahoma.)[28] The first professional philosophy journal in the United States

22. Guy Planty-Bonjour, *Hegel et la Pensée Philosophique en Russie 1830–1917* (The Hague, 1974), p. 323.

23. Ibid., p. 245.

24. Ibid., p. 332.

25. This erroneous thesis is extrapolated to philosophy by L. van Becelaere in his *La Philosophie en Amerique Depuis les Origines jusqu'a Nos Jours (1607–1900)* (New York, 1904), where the low interest in Thomist philosophy is traced to the American spirit, which is "primarily interested in practical matters, so that speculative research is only of relative and secondary relevance. [Thus], its formula remains Benjamin Franklin's: these speculations can have some truth, but they will generally remain uncertain. Consequently, they are useless and it is preferable not to deal with them" (p. 160). In the introduction to the book, Josiah Royce promptly rebuffs such an interpretation (p. xiii). Ironically, the book was dedicated to W. T. Harris, a St. Louis Hegelian whose lifework violently contradicted the book's main claims.

26. Paul R. Anderson, *Platonism in the Midwest* (New York, 1963).

27. See Henry A. Pochmann, *New England Transcendentalism and St. Louis Hegelianism* (Philadelphia, 1948), p. 12.

28. William H. Goetzmann, ed., "Introduction" to *The American Hegelians: An*

was published in 1867 by the St. Louis Hegelians after W. T. Harris, its future editor, could not publish a critique of Herbert Spencer's philosophy in the fashionable *North American Review*.[29] For twenty-six years the *Journal of Speculative Philosophy* (described by John Dewey as "the only philosophic journal in the country at that time [published] by the only group of laymen devoted to philosophy for non-theological reasons") made available in English the best contributions of American and German philosophers.[30] Furthermore, far from being a local phenomenon, the St. Louis Hegelians established philosophical centers all over the Midwest and, with the Platonists, were entrenched in such aspiring metropolises as Osceola, Missouri, Jacksonville, Illinois, Dubuque, Iowa, Terre Haute, Indiana, and Cincinnati, Ohio. Chronologically located between the fuzzy New England transcendentalists of the early nineteenth century and the more practical-minded pragmatists of the *fin de siècle*,[31] William T. Harris, Brockmeyer, and Denton J. Snider in St. Louis, and Johann B. Stallo, Peter Kaufmann, Moncure Conway, and August Willich in Ohio, were generally considered leading American philosophers between 1860 and 1890.[32] Although they had died out by 1900, after Harris became U.S. commissioner of education and Brockmeyer Missouri's lieutenant governor, the Hegelians made a considerable cultural impact.[33] As Anderson puts it,

> The equalitarian attitude toward education and culture tended to break down not only barriers between classes but also barriers between the sexes. It was no mere accident that the feminist movement had greater strength in

---

Intellectual Episode in the History of Western America (New York, 1973), pp. 11, 354−355. Unfortunately, Brockmeyer failed to produce, even after several revisions over a period of forty years, a publishable translation. For a sample of his work, see ibid., pp. 355−363.

29. Anderson, *Platonism in the Midwest*, p. 3.

30. Quoted in Goetzmann, *American Hegelians*, p. 383.

31. For reconstructions of a couple of confrontations between the transcendentalists Amos Bronson Alcott and Ralph Waldo Emerson and the more philosophically sophisticated St. Louis Hegelians, see Pochmann, *New England Transcendentalism*, pp. 34−65.

32. Loyd D. Easton, *Hegel's First American Followers: The Ohio Hegelians* (Athens, Ohio, 1966).

33. Goetzmann, *American Hegelians*, p. 25.

the Midwest than elsewhere, that Sorasis of Jacksonville and Friends in Council of Quincy were two of the earliest women's clubs in the country, that the first coeducational institution in the country was in Ohio (Oberlin), that Mississippi was the first state to grant women control over their own property, that Kansas first permitted them to vote in school elections, and that Wyoming was the first state to grant complete equality in the franchise.[34]

Contrary to the superficial standard explanations for the decline of Hegelianism in the United States and England—explanations citing the basically foreign nature of this theoretical framework,[35] shifting patterns of leisure,[36] or St. Louis's loss of midwestern cultural hegemony to Chicago[37]—the social and political reasons underlying this phenomenon are considerably more complex. On the one hand, the social individuality postulated by the Hegelian theory of the ethical state could not be brought about without qualitatively altering socioeconomic relations (which explains why Left-Hegelians in Europe tended to gravitate toward Marxism): on the other hand, the successful relaunching of capitalist accumulation through imperialist expansion at the turn of the century led to a forced identification of the ideal with the real, and thus to the formulation of a conservative idealist apology. Both branches of Hegelianism soon lost their appeal. The eschatological expectations of the radical wing foundered on a sandbar of un-

34. Anderson, *Platonism in the Midwest*, p. 19. For a more systematic account of the St. Louis Hegelians' views, see Frances Bolles Harmon, *The Social Philosophy of the St. Louis Hegelians* (New York, 1943).

35. According to Harmon, the St. Louis Hegelian conceived of "a national state in terms foreign to social theory in the United States at the time." Harmon, *St. Louis Hegelians*, p. 99. Even Bosanquet himself, during World War I, felt compelled to denounce the foreign character of German philosophy. See Bernard Bosanquet, *Social and International Ideals* (London, 1917), pp. 286 ff.

36. According to Anderson, at the end of the nineteenth century, "when there was time for leisure, men wanted a less studious type than philosophical clubs could offer. . . . The result was a tremendous increase in sports. . . . Racing became a common spectator sport. . . . Interest in prize-fighting increased tremendously. . . . Baseball was well on its way . . . to becoming the chief American sport." See Anderson, *Platonism in the Midwest*, pp. 192–193. Along with vaudeville shows, P. T. Barnum's circus, and Buffalo Bill's "Wild West Show," sports also spelled the end of midwestern idealist philosophy!

37. William H. Werkmeister, *A History of Philosophical Ideas in America* (New York, 1949), p. 74.

anticipated resistance in a sea that the Left-Hegelians thought had long ago dissolved all obstacles to social change. The conservative wing, meanwhile, was reduced to providing accounts of social reconciliation that were neither credible nor, ultimately, necessary. It is not surprising that in the United States the pragmatists ended up jettisoning the speculative Hegelian framework altogether and salvaging its contents,[38] whereas in England the pop philosophies of Russell and Moore captured Oxford and Cambridge, with the few lingering tendencies toward Hegelianism in the London School of Economics turning to Marxism.

It was in Italy that Hegelianism had its most profound and lasting impact. As Landucci puts it, in Italy, "unlike in England (and France), Hegelianism was not merely an academic movement of professors but was an element of the civil life of the nation at the time of the Risorgimento."[39] Not only was Hegelianism identified with the philosophy of Italian unification, but it set the tone for the intellectual life of the next century. Unlike the struggles that unified Germany, England, and the United States—predominantly Protestant countries that had already bucked the Roman church—Italy's national unification took place against Vatican cultural and political hegemony, causing Hegelianism to become a kind of lay religion. This helps explain why, as early as 1851, Bertrando Spaventa could prefigure the Gramscian theme of cultural hegemony: "The cannon is not always enough. Maybe the Austrians will be armed matter, but the Pope, the cardinals, the priests, the friars, the Jesuits, the ignorants, and maybe even Ferdinand of Bourbon are half matter and half idea."[40] Unlike in other countries where the Hegelian theory of the ethical state, social individuality, and education did not directly clash with existing social and political realities, Italy translated Hegelianism immediately into an explosive political program. In his theories of civil society, intel-

---

38. Thus, Dewey openly acknowledged that "acquaintance with Hegel has left a permanent deposit in my thinking. . . . In the content of his ideas there is often an extraordinary depth; in many of his analyses, taken out of their mechanical dialectical setting, an extraordinary acuteness." See John Dewey, "From Absolutism to Experimentalism," in Goetzmann, *American Hegelians*, p. 387.

39. Landucci, "L'Hegelismo in Italia," p. 615.

40. Bertrando Spaventa, letter dated 8 October 1851, in Bertrando Spaventa, *Opere*, ed. Giovanni Gentile (Florence, 1972), III, 636.

lectual formation, and cultural hegemony, Gramsci is the clear heir to the Italian neo-Hegelian heritage.

Hegel in Italy

Strange as it may seem, Hegelian thought came to Italy by way of France.[41] Strange, because Hegelianism did not have much success in nineteenth-century France. Although the first French translations of Hegel—such as that of the *Encyclopedia*—were published by the Neapolitan emigré Augusto Vera[42] between 1859 and 1870 (terrible translations, but not worse than others done at that time),[43] it was not until the 1930s that Hegelian thought had a major impact on French culture through Alexandre Koyré, Alexandre Kojève, and Jean Hyppolite.[44] In the 1830s, Victor Cousin had introduced Hegel in France and discussed new developments in German thought in his

41. See Giovanni Gentile, *Storia della Filosofia Italiana dal Genovesi al Galluppi* (Milan, 1930), II, 118 ff.; Eugenio Garin, *La Filosofia* (Milan, 1949), II, 488 ff.; and Giuseppe Vacca, *Politica e Filosofia in Bertrando Spaventa* (Bari, 1967), p. 50.

42. Contrary to Hyppolite's claim that only *part* of Hegel's *Encyclopedia* had been translated by Vera, all three sections appeared. In fact, Vera was well into a French translation of Hegel's lectures entitled *The Philosophy of Religion* when the publisher's bankruptcy forced a suspension of the whole project. Hyppolite, who traces the French Hegel-revival to Lucien Herr and Jean Wahl, completely overlooks the *foreign* impact of the mid-nineteenth-century French translations of Hegel. See Jean Hyppolite, "La Phénoménologie de Hegel et la Pensée Francais Contemporaine," in his *Figures de la Pensée Philosophique* (Paris, 1971), I, 231–233. Already in 1843 Vera had introduced his account of Hegel's philosophy in France with his "Logique de Hegel," *Revue du Lyonnais* XVII (1843), 397–404. Subsequently, Vera's book, *An Introduction to Speculative Philosophy and Logic* (St. Louis, 1875), was published by the St. Louis Hegelians, after it had already been serialized in their *Journal of Speculative Philosophy*.

43. In his *Hegels Naturphilosophie und die Bearbeitung derselben durch den italienischen Philophen A. Vera* (Berlin, 1868), Karl Rosenkranz called Vera "the most rigorous systematizer Hegel has ever had, who follows him step by step with full devotion" (p. 5), and claimed that "from now on, those who have trouble understanding Hegel in German would be advised to read Vera's translations" (p. 9). Vera's translations, however, rank among some of the worst ever published. For devastating critiques, see Benedetto Croce, "Prefazione" to the Italian translation of Hegel's *Encyclopedia*, reprinted in his *Aneddoti di Varia Letteratura* (Bari, 1954), pp. 261–265; and best of all, Guido Oldrini, *Gli Hegeliani di Napoli: Augusto Vera e la Corrente Ortodossa* (Milan, 1964), pp. 147–163, 276–284.

44. Mark Poster, *Existential Marxism in Postwar France: From Sartre to Althusser* (Princeton, N.J., 1975), pp. 3 ff.

Fragmentes Philosophique. As it turned out, however, Cousin actually was much more successful in introducing Hegel to Italian intellectuals, who at that time were greatly under the influence of French culture.[45] Thus, it was through Cousin that Domenico Mazzoni learned about Hegel and, toward the end of 1835, went to Berlin to learn firsthand of the new developments.[46] Mazzoni became a Hegelian and prepared (but never published) an edited translation of Hegel's shorter *Logic*.

More typical of the first Italian Hegelians is Gianbattista Passerini (1793−1864), who was a member of a northern Italian sect seeking national unity and independence. Chased into exile by the police for "studying the well-known French philosophers, and thus aware of and imbued with their dangerous theories often claiming that man should be free,"[47] Passerini went to Berlin in 1824, where he met Hegel and where, in 1840, he translated into Italian Hegel's *Philosophy of History*, published in Switzerland the next year. A similar inspiration produced the first Italian translation of Hegel's *Philosophy of Right* in 1848 and attempts by De Sanctis and Bertrando Spaventa to translate into Italian Hegel's larger *Logic* and parts of *The Phenomenology*—attempts carried out while the former was polishing off his political and philosophical education in a Bourbon jail, where he was serving time for "subversive activities,"[48] and while the latter was escaping

45. Pasquale Galluppi, a Neapolitan philosopher who already in 1831 had translated Victor Cousin's book into Italian, wrote him in 1838 that almost all recent French philosophical works were readily available in Naples. In contrast, Spaventa in 1851 lamented that none of the recent German works by Kant, Hegel, and Schelling were to be found even in the best libraries in Florence or Turin. For a discussion of this, see Oldrini, *Gli Hegeliani di Napoli*, p. 25; and Guido Oldrini, *Il Primo Hegelismo Italiano* (Florence, 1969), p. 323. See also De Meis's letters of 12 November and 25 December 1851, to Bertrando Spaventa, in which the former jubilantly reports from Paris to have finally located Hegel's works, which, at that time, were unavailable in Turin. Reprinted in Bertrando Spaventa, *Unificazione Nazionale ed Egemonia Culturale*, ed. Giuseppe Vacca (Bari, 1969), pp. 306, 316.

46. For biographical references on Mazzoni (1783−1853), see Guido Oldrini, *Il Primo Hegelismo Italiano*, pp. 93−95.

47. From a note in the police files, quoted in Oldrini, ibid., p. 110.

48. Having become acquainted with those parts of Hegel's *Aesthetics* available in the first two volumes of *Cours d'Esthetique Analyse et Traduit en Partie par Charles Benard* (published in 1840 and 1843; the remaining three volumes did not appear until 1848−1850), Francesco De Sanctis became a Hegelian during the middle 1840s while

northward in an attempt to avoid a similar fate.[49]

Clearly,

the struggle for the triumph of Hegelianism and of classical German philosophy retains throughout the period [1840—1850] a sharp tendency to become identified with the struggle for the universal and generalized application of liberal bourgeois principles against the old particularism of the privileges of the "estates."[50]

Conservative forces opposing Italian unification also perceived Hegelian thought in this fashion. Italian Catholics in particular, with an eye on recent French and German events, readily accepted Heinrich Heine's identification of the French Revolution and German thought and saw Hegel as the precursor of atheism and socialism. According to them, "communism and socialism emerged armed from Hegel's brain in the same way as Athena did from Zeus's head."[51] (This also helps to explain why Hegelianism did not have much success in France during the same period. There the bourgeois revolution had long ago been consummated, and Hegel was seen not as a representative of the future but as part of the past, a figure who, at best, was to be regarded as a momentary fancy within the predominant eclecticism.) While in

---

studying with other Neapolitan Hegelians. Arrested in December 1850 for political activities, he spent most of the next three years in jails, where he struggled with Hegel's *Logic*. See Guido Oldrini, *La Cultura Filosofica Napoletana dell'Ottocento* (Bari, 1973), pp. 353—368. This does not mean that the Neapolitan Hegelians were free of problems with Hegel. In a letter to his brother Bertrando, in which he promises to study philosophy again, Silvio Spaventa wrote: "Here, of philosophy books, I first read Spinoza; I studied day and night. What did you expect? I had trouble understanding. I could not retain anything. Then I read Hegel's *Phenomenology* three times (would you believe it?). I desperately cried over it: I did not understand it; I did not get anything out of it; I could not retain anything." Dated 4 May 1853, in Silvio Spaventa, *Dal 1848 al 1881. Lettere, Scritti, Documenti*, ed. Benedetto Croce (Bari, 1923), p. 182.

49. Having hastily departed from Naples on 26 October 1849, after his brother Silvio was already in jail for political activities, Bertrando Spaventa published in 1851 in Turin his *Studii sopra la Filosofia di Hegel*, which is part commentary and part paraphrase of the "Preface" to Hegel's *Phenomenology*. Excerpts from Spaventa's *Studii* are now reprinted in Oldrini, *Il Primo Hegelismo Italiano*, pp. 309—345. On the circumstances leading to Spaventa's exile, see Giovanni Gentile, "Bertrando Spaventa," in B. Spaventa, *Opere*, I, 22—25.

50. Oldrini, *Gli Hegeliani di Napoli*, p. 34.

51. Quoted in Bertrando Spaventa to *Il Progresso*, 28 August 1851, reprinted in B. Spaventa, *Unificazione Nazionale*, p. 83. As Landucci puts it: "It is understandable

France socialism and communism increasingly challenged the inadequacies of the already aging bourgeois regime, in Naples the French Revolution still belonged to the future, as a hope or a threat. Thus, unlike French students of Hegel who never became Hegelians, such as Cousin, the Italian Hegelians—especially the Neapolitans—immediately incorporated Hegel into their projects of cultural and national rejuvenation. In the words of Bertrando Spaventa, who became the most articulate member of the group,

> Beginning in 1843 in Naples the Hegelian idea penetrated the minds of young cultivators of science who, as if moved by a holy love, preached it in their words and writings. Neither the suspicions already aroused in the police—instigated by religious ignorance and hypocrisy—nor threats and persecutions were able to weaken the faith of these courageous defenders of the independence of thought. . . . It was an irresistible and universal need that drove them toward an unknown and splendid future. . . . The movement had already begun, and had it not been prevented by the arrogance of material force, today we would have already seen its fruits.[52]

Spaventa's Hegelianism

At the time of Spaventa's exile to Turin (1851), most of northern Italy was still part of the Austro-Hungarian empire. Thus, Spaventa was confronted with the unenviable task of proposing as a doctrine of liberation to the subjugated what they regarded as the subjugators'

---

how that ideological prestige that made Hegelianism a national event by transforming it into a banner was the work not only of those who claimed to be Hegelians but also of its adversaries. If in Italy there were two decades of fear of Hegel, if 1861 would produce a shock in seeing Hegelianism publicly professed from university classrooms (with the civic importance that was then accorded to universities—precisely because in the past they had been the guardians of 'traditions'), this resulted from the fact that [in Italy] Hegelianism had been seen through the filters of German and French atheism and socialism considered as its consequences." Landucci, "L'Hegelismo in Italia," p. 625.

52. Bertrando Spaventa, *Studii sopra la Filosofia di Hegel*; reprinted in Oldrini, *Il Primo Hegelismo Italiano* pp. 322–323 (originally published in 1851). In 1867 Spaventa reiterated the same account: "Hegel and the other German philosophers were perhaps better known in Naples before 1848 than they are today. In addition to Galluppi, their works had also been studied, interpreted, and discussed by Colecchi, and following him by Cusani, Ajello, Gatti, and my friends Tari and Calvello. Some of these men even took these philosophers for companions and for consolation in the Bourbon jails and dungeons." B. Spaventa, *Opere*, III, 19.

own philosophy. Aware of this paradox, Spaventa even avoided calling Hegel's philosophy "German" by substituting a less well-known euphemism.[53] Furthermore, in a political context electrified by impatient nationalist aspirations, in proposing Hegelianism as the philosophy of Italian unification and cultural rebirth, Spaventa was confronted with a chauvinist philosophical tradition dating back to Giambattista Vico's *De Antiquisima Italorum Sapientia* of 1710.[54] There Vico had located Etruria as the land of Pythagorean thought and, in the context of tracing the sources of the Italian language, he had hinted at the existence of an innate Italian philosophy whose origins were buried in prehistory. This thesis, although quickly abandoned by Vico, was nonetheless picked up by Vincenzo Gioberti and a wave of lesser-known nationalists in support of their own preposterous claims of Italian philosophical and cultural superiority.[55] With the help of Theodor Mommsen's recent historical research, Spaventa rejected this chauvinist account and resurrected Vico's own arguments against it.[56] Elaborating his younger brother's (Silvio's) rejection of these nationalist claims,[57] Spaventa directly attacked the "prejudice

53. As he himself reminisced in 1867: "I did not dare use the word *tedesca* ["German"] at a time when that term was generally applied to the Austrians [*tedeschi*], who held sway not only over Lombardy and Venetia but in Tuscany as well." Bertrando Spaventa, "Logica e Metafisica," in B. Spaventa, *Opere*, III, 20n.

54. For an excellent reconstruction and discussion of this tradition, see Marcel Grilli, "The Nationality of Philosophy and Bertrando Spaventa," *Journal of the History of Ideas* II, 3 (June 1941), 346–371. See especially p. 364, where he lists a significant number of long-since-forgotten exemplars of this tradition.

55. Benedetto Croce, *Storia della Storiografia Italiana* (Bari, 1947), I, 53, and his *La Filosofia di Giambattista Vico* (Bari, 1965), pp. 146–153.

56. Bertrando Spaventa, "La Filosofia Italiana dal Secolo XVI al Nostro Tempo," second lecture, in B. Spaventa, *Opere*, II, 466–479.

57. Silvio Spaventa, *Dal 1848 al 1861*, pp. 8 ff. Silvio Spaventa joined his brother Bertrando in Naples in the early 1840s. Unlike Bertrando, who joined the priesthood for purely economic reasons (under the exhortation of his uncle Don Onorato Croce) and remained throughout his life the more philosophical of the two, Silvio was more politically involved. As Gentile put it, "It could be said that Bertrando had split functions with Silvio: always in agreement over everything, one attended to speculation and the other to practice." Gentile, "Bertrando Spaventa," p. 21. Also, Gentile wrote (p. 11) that during the 1840s "Bertrando worked while Silvio conspired." In 1844, Silvio started a journal, *Il Nazionale*, which prefigured so many of the themes elaborated later by Bertrando in Turin after 1851 that Vacca has been more than justified in suggesting that Bertrando himself had a much more active (though anonymous) col-

that [Italian] and European thought are in opposition to each other''[58] and, following Stanislao Gatti, developed his famous thesis concerning "the circulation of Italian thought" as a critique of the Church's regressive role in Italian culture.[59]

The decline of post-Renaissance Italian philosophy has been the object of many studies (such as those of Terenzio Mamiani and Gioberti), but it was never satisfactorily explained until Gatti and Silvio Spaventa identified the Church as the culprit.[60] This account fed right into a liberal-democratic political platform of Italian unification under the Piedmontese and against the Vatican. Notwithstanding its bold implications, Spaventa's project of national and cultural reconstruction did not fall on sympathetic ears in Turin, at that time still dominated by the Catholic philosophies of Gioberti and Antonio Sebarti Rosmini. Spaventa later described this cold reception:

> Needless to say, in Turin, I was a complete fiasco. . . . Yet I did not despair. Some months after I arrived I spoke at a public meeting, delivering a lecture on Giordano Bruno's practical philosophy. It was on the eve of the feast of St. John the Baptist, when all the good folks of Turin make a huge bonfire in the town square. The reception that I got was so honest and friendly that some priest in other times would not have hesitated to throw

laboration than mere sympathetic approval of that effort. What tends to reinforce this hypothesis is the fact that the prolific Bertrando was practically prevented from actively participating in these debates by his religious affiliation up to 1850 (when he finally left the priesthood) and, during this period, seems not to have written anything under his own name. See Vacca, *Politica e Filosofia*, pp. 9–84.

58. B. Spaventa, *Opere*, II, 605.

59. In his work *Della Filosofia Italiana* of 1846, Gatti had also confronted the problems of the history of Italian philosophy, but, unlike earlier chauvinist accounts, he had attributed the decline during the last two centuries specifically to the Church's repressive policies. Himself one of the leading Neapolitan Hegelians, Gatti also saw German philosophy as the wave of the future. For an excellent discussion of Gatti, see Grilli, "Nationality of Philosophy," pp. 356 ff. On the liberal and democratic sources of Spaventa's thesis of the circulation of Italian thought, see Vacca, *Politica e Filosofia*, pp. 81 ff.

60. This does not mean that there was not a variety of absurd explanations. Thus, Luigi Palmieri saw the decline as a result of the importation of foreign ideas to Italian soil. Since he recognized "the need for the commerce of ideas as well as for the traffic of commodities," he did not absolutely condemn the study of German philosophy: he simply sought an "import quota." Palmieri, incidentally, was responsible for having the police close the Spaventas' school of Hegelian philosophy in Naples in 1847. See Gentile, "Bertrando Spaventa," p. 19; and Vacca, *Politica e Filosofia*, p. 83.

me into the flames with all his heart.[61]

Undaunted, Spaventa spent the next decade painstakingly elaborating Hegelianism as the philosophy of the Italian Risorgimento, reconstructing the philosophical thread linking Bruno and Tommaso Campanella to Descartes and Spinoza, and tying Vico to Hegel.[62] Spaventa saw the universal spirit of Italian philosophy repressed so brutally by the Church in the sixteenth century that further development of it could only occur elsewhere—in Germany and northern Europe. National liberation and cultural rebirth, therefore, could take place only by going back to that tradition—not to the precise point where its development had been violently interrupted in Italy but to the point at which it had reached its highest level of articulation abroad. It was a matter of

> undoing the work of three centuries, during which the attempts were made to destroy even the last vestiges of Italian ingenuity, to develop the germs of a new civilization which in those times were suffocated, and to accept as our heritage those which have been fruitful in freer lands and which today form the substance and principle of intellectual, political, and religious life of other nations.[63]

Despite the obvious tactical value of this nationalist emphasis (a stress that later facilitated Giovanni Gentile's efforts to appropriate Spaventa as a part of fascism's heritage), it had a theoretical foundation as well.[64] Understanding philosophy as the acme of cultural

---

61. Spaventa, *Opere*, III, 23.

62. The most systematic account of this reconstruction was presented in 1861 at the University of Naples, in the wake of the liberation of Naples by Giuseppe Garibaldi's troops, in a series of lectures subsequently published by Gentile under the title *Italian Philosophy in Its Relations with European Philosophy*, in 1908. They are now reprinted in B. Spaventa, *Opere*, II, 405–678. Ironically, Spaventa succeeded Palmieri—who had earlier in 1847 sought to refute Hegelianism with the help of the police—at the University of Naples. Apparently, Palmieri never lost his knack for administrative measures. As Bertrando wrote to Silvio on 27 November 1861: "Palmieri intends to have the students petition the Ministry to throw out of the University of Naples a professor who does not profess an *Italian philosophy*. In 1847 he forced me to close my school with a recourse to Monsignor Mazzetti. Today he still thinks that we are in 1847." B. Spaventa, *Opere*, II, 687.

63. B. Spaventa, *Opere*, III, 25.

64. This unwarranted appropriation was uncritically legitimated by the "liberals" of Crocean extraction. As Vacca puts it: "The liberal reaction to the Gentilean attempt

achievement, Spaventa defended its national character in terms of concrete universality (i.e., the specific embodiment that the universality of modern philosophy receives in particular sociohistorical settings). Challenged both by chauvinists such as Luigi Palmieri, who rejected outright all "foreign" philosophies, and by orthodox Hegelians such as Augusto Vera, whose abstract cosmopolitanism failed to recognize any cultural particularities in philosophical traditions, Spaventa defended nationalism in philosophy as the specific manifestation of a concrete expression of modern thought. As he put it,

In order to see what the nationality of our philosophy may be, it is necessary to understand the meaning of the nationality of philosophical life in general. And to this end it is not sufficient to say that philosophy is the last and clearest expression of a people's life. . . . On the other hand, I am fully familiar with what some claim: "What do we care about Italian or non-Italian philosophy? We want truth, and truth has nothing to do with nationality." Of course, truth transcends nationality, but without nationality truth is an abstraction. Transplant truth as much as you want: if it has no correspondence with our national character it will remain a truth in itself, but not for us; for us it will always be a dead thing. To show that we have always lived in the heart of European thought and we have always promoted and participated in this thought, and that we have not been alone and outside of common life, is not a revelation or a diplomatic gesture, or even mere human respect, but a noble and rigorous duty for those professing philosophy.[65]

But this peculiar mode of Italianizing Hegelian thought had not escaped the attention of even sympathetic critics. As one of them wrote in 1868:

To courage and firm conviction [Spaventa] has added a certain shrewdness truly unusual in philosophers. . . . It was not unknown to him how touchy our disposition was in its commitment to old traditions. A politician as well as a philosopher, he did not come out and say: *Here is a philosophy fallen*

---

to pass off the 'ethical state' of the Spaventa brothers as both the high point of the Risorgimento's political ideology as well as the vehicle of unification of all the Risorgimento's political thought (from Cavour to Mazzini) in the direction of a linear development toward the fascist state, was to abandon Bertrando Spaventa to the fascists while defending the liberal orthodoxy of Silvio Spaventa and De Sanctis." Giuseppe Vacca, "Recenti Studi sull'Hegelismo Napoletano," *Studi Storici* VII (1966), 174.

65. As quoted in Oldrini, *Gli Hegeliani di Napoli*, p. 171.

from the sky, a foreign but true philosophy; accept it. Instead, he had the sagacity to say: Here is a wholly homemade philosophy, entirely the product of our bowels, which foreigners have stolen from us and developed. Let us take it back and make it ours once again, since it is properly ours.[66]

In carrying out this project of philosophical nationalization, however, Spaventa prefigured what half a century later were to become vital Gramscian themes, such as a pedagogical theory of the state, the Hegelian foundations of Marxism, cultural hegemony, the primacy of the intellectuals, a theory of social individuality, and a sociohistorically grounded program of national emancipation.

Spaventa's project had a very limited *immediate* success. As already indicated, from 1850 to 1860 in Turin his work did not find widespread acceptance. According to Vacca,

if in Naples the Hegelians had from the very beginning aroused the suspicions of the Bourbon police and had been thereby persecuted, in Piedmont the road was little clearer. It was not the police, though, but the closed, biased Piedmontese society and culture that put up such a fierce resistance to the penetration of [Spaventa's] ideas; thus, he remained an irregular and a rebel throughout his exile.[67]

Even his debut at the University of Naples in 1861 was not altogether triumphant. As he described the reception:

Not all those who came did so with love and good will. I realized that from the very beginning. I know that the Giobertans—I don't know what to call them: fossils, cetaceans, antedeluvians without a breath of life stirring

66. Pietro Siciliani, "Gli Hegeliani d'Italia," *Rivista Bolognese* (1868), p. 520; as quoted in Vacca, *Politica e Filosofia*, p. 211. This was more or less consciously believed. Thus, in a letter from Silvio we read: "I believe that you have understood a crucial truth: that Italians will never understand what modern philosophy is unless they derive it from their own philosophers; and there is good reason for this, since they should not be blamed if they do not understand anything of a philosophy that they see falling on their heads as if it came from the sky. And this is what truly German philosophy is for them. Thus, your work . . . could be the communication link between the ordinary philosophy in Italy and that which we would like to be there." Gentile, *Silvio Spaventa*, p. 313.

67. Giuseppe Vacca, *Politica e Filosofia*, in *Bertrando Spaventa* (Bari, 1967), p. 172.

within them—have it in for me. They would suffocate me, too, if they could.[68]

In February and March of the following year, there were Catholic-inspired counterrevolutionary riots that had to be put down by the National Guard.[69] Although he had begun to gain some international recognition, Spaventa did not succeed in penetrating Italian culture to any great extent.[70] (Doubtless, Spaventa's abrasive personality played a part in his failure to attract a sizable following and may have had something to do with his singular lack of success in finding a publisher for his works.)[71] He left many works unfinished, and others remained completely unknown until Gentile began to publish them and to popularize some of his ideas toward the end of the century.[72]

In the rapid industrialization that followed unification, the expansion in northern Italy was carried out mostly with Neapolitan capital and at the expense of the deteriorating southern agrarian economy.[73] This resulted in a political crisis that saw the Neapolitan Hegelians become ever more conservative and irrelevant as positivist views grew

68. See Bertrando Spaventa to Silvio Spavanta, 8 December 1861, in B. Spaventa, *Opere*, II, 691.

69. See Bertrando Spaventa to Silvio Spavanta, 10, 21, and 22 February, and 22 March 1862, in B. Spaventa, *Opere*, II, 700–714. For an account of these riots, see Marc Monnier, "Le Mouvement Italien a Naples de 1830 a 1865," *Revue de Deux Mondes*, 15 April 1865, p. 1038.

70. In a series entitled "Briefe über italienische Philosophie," published in Berlin in *Die Gedanke* between 1864 and 1865, Theodor Straeter wrote that only in Naples could modern philosophy find new life. He considered Spaventa's theory of the circulation of Italian thought the most effective instrument for eliminating from Italian consciousness the residue of medieval Catholicism and for constructing a modern state. Straeter even compared Spaventa to Kuno Fischer.

71. Along these lines, Russo writes: "Severe in his judgments, rigorous in his logic, sarcastic and irritable with his friends, Spaventa tended to create around himself an atmosphere of solitude and coolness, which was one of the very reasons for his greatness." See Luigi Russo, *Francesco De Sanctis e la Cultura Napoletana* (Florence, 1959), p. 122.

72. See Gentile, "Bertrando Spaventa," in Spaventa, *Opere*, I, 5. See also Benedetto Croce, "La Vita Letteraria a Napoli dal 1860 al 1900," in his *La Letteratura delle Nuova Italia* (Bari, 1954), IV, 267–355.

73. For a systematic account of the genesis of southern Italian underdevelopment—and consequent sociopolitical decay—see Edmond M. Capecelatro and Antonio Carlo, *Contro la "Questione Meridionale"* (Rome, 1973). For an accurate summary of the economic achievement of the Italian state during this period, see Gaetano Salvemini,

ever more popular.[74]

After Spaventa's death in 1883, this rising positivism and the decline of the "historical Right," with which Spaventa had been politically associated, combined to erase his memory almost completely from Italian culture. By 1897, Labriola could rightly say of the whole Neapolitan Hegelian movement:

> Every trace, and even the memory of this movement, has passed away among us after the lapse of but a few years. The writings of those thinkers are not found anywhere but in the shops of antiquarians and second-hand book dealers. This dissolution into nothing of an entire scientific school of no mean account is not due solely to the often unkind and hardly laudable vicissitudes of university life, nor to the epidemic spread of positivism, which gathers here and there the fruits of a rather *demi-monde* science, but to deeper causes. Those Hegelians wrote, taught, and argued among themselves as though they were living in Utopia instead of Naples. They held mental discussion with their *German comrades*. They replied from their pulpits or in their writings only to such criticisms as were made by themselves, so that they carried on a dialogue that appeared as a monologue to their audience and readers. They did not succeed in molding their treatises and dialectics into books that the nation looked upon as new intellectual conquests.[75]

But precisely at the time when Labriola was writing the obituary of the Neapolitan neo-Hegelians, Croce was preparing for publication some of Silvio Spaventa's papers, and Gentile, who independently of Labriola had reached similar conclusions and had arrived at almost an identical evaluation of Spaventa, was becoming interested in publishing all those writings that later became Spaventa's *Collected Works* (*Opere*).[76] What Labriola bemoaned as incomprehensible jargon was

The Origins of Fascism in Italy, trans. Robert Vivarelly (New York, 1973), chap. 1, pp. 1–18.

74. For an exhaustive analysis of the philosophical decline of the Neapolitan Hegelians during this period, see Guido Oldrini, *La Cultura Filosofica Napoletana*, pp. 517 ff.

75. Antonio Labriola to Sorel, 14 May 1897, in Labriola, *Socialism and Philosophy*, pp. 54–55.

76. Thus, in a letter dated 16 September 1897, to his former teacher Donato Jaja, Gentile writes: "Think that Bertrando Spaventa has just about in vain lectured to several generations of youth and to the best of them. How many today uphold his

but wasn't it LL.
now-Italic too?

to become standard Italian philosophical discourse for the next half-century.

Thus, Spaventa, instead of being Gramsci's acknowledged theoretical forebear, found resonance in Gramsci only indirectly, through Croce's mediation. As Garin puts it,

> De Sanctis and Spaventa were important factors in the formation of Croce and Gentile: they became among the most significant components of Italian consciousness in the twentieth century through the diffusion and the rethinking that they underwent with Croce and Gentile. [Yet], it would be a serious error of perspective to attribute to Spaventa and De Sanctis a weight that they assumed only after Croce and Gentile emphasized their relevance and forced Italians to absorb them. In other words, the resonance that they had in the twentieth century should not be confused with their actual echo in their own age.[77]

It is not too surprising, then, that only recently, triggered by the publication of some previously forgotten works of Spaventa,[78] there has been an "attempt, on the part of Marxist historicism of a Gramscian inspiration, to change the direction [of the neo-idealist interpretation] and turn against it the experience of the first Hegelianism."[79] The full Hegelian character of Gramsci's Marxism has been blurred by the traditional contraposition of the Italian Communist Party's brand of Marxism-Leninism (claiming Gramsci as its main "Italianizer")[80] to the liberal version of Croce's Hegelianism, on the one hand, and the fascist interpretation of Gentile's Hegelianism, on the other. The result has been not only a persistent underemphasis of the theoretical continuity between Spaventa and Gramsci but also a poorer apprecia-

---

thought? Almost all of them, at that time enlightened by that profound light that emanated from his words in his lectures and in his books, were not affected. The substance of his teaching did not come down to them . . . and they went back to Kant or even to pre-Kantianism." Maria Sandirocco, ed., *Carteggio Gentile-Jaja* (Florence, 1969). I, 24–25.

77. Eugenio Garin, *Cronache di Filosofia Italiana (1900–1943)* (Bari, 1966), I, 18.

78. See Italo Cubeddu, "Bertrando Spaventa Publicista (Giugno–Dicembre 1851)," and Bertrando Spaventa, "Rivoluzione e Utopia," *Giornale Critico della Filosofia Italiana* XLII (1963), 46–93.

79. Giuseppe Vacca, "Premessa" to B. Spaventa, *Unificazione Nazionale*, p. i.

80. For an account of this, see Paul Piccone, "Gramsci's Marxism: Beyond Lenin and Togliatti," *Theory and Society* III, 4 (1976), pp. 485–512.

tion of Gramsci's own work.

The trajectory of Spaventa's thought shows striking parallels with that of Gramsci's. While Gramsci experienced his "revolutionary apprenticeship" in Turin as a journalist (1917–1919), Spaventa did his in Naples as a priest (1842–1850); the period of initiation for both ended with the failure of revolutionary movements that sprang from sociopolitical crises (1848 and 1919); both spent many subsequent years explaining the failure of these insurrectionary efforts, managing to develop strikingly similar theoretical elaborations of contextually grounded revolutionary strategies; and finally, both men died a couple of decades before their writings came to be widely appreciated. Of course, the greater part of a century that separates the two thinkers makes a great deal of difference in their outlooks. But they were both vitally concerned with the Italian revolution understood as the coming into being of a new humanity along the lines traced out by the Hegelian model, and to this extent the theoretical frameworks they developed are strikingly similar.

Gramsci made few references to Spaventa in the *Prison Notebooks*, indicating that he was not well acquainted with Spaventa's work[81] and that he never considered any interpretation of it above and beyond those interpretations popular in his day.[82] But recent Gramscian interpretations of the pre-1848 Neapolitan scene tend to go beyond the traditional Crocean view regarding it simply as a liberal and progressive phase in the process of Italian unification, and surpass also the Gentilean accounts of a Spaventa in whom philosophy and politics are

81. Gerratana lists four of Spaventa's works republished by Gentile as having been known by Gramsci, but all of them through secondary sources. Gramsci, *Quaderni del Carcere*, IV, 3076.

82. As Giuseppe Berti has shown in his "B. Spaventa, A. Labriola e L'Hegelismo Napoletano," *Società* X, 4 (1954), even Croce's own interpretation of his uncles' work was superficial and beset by contradictions. Thus, in *La Letteratura della Nuova Italia*, I, 387, Croce wrote that Spaventa "had an insatiable thirst for truth and, although a Hegelian by conviction, he did not reduce the master's philosophy to a catechism to be repeated and defended for sectarian reasons, but sought to absorb it and transform it into his very own blood. He exposed it to the fire of all objections and criticisms, always ready to try to understand the adversary, whomever he might be, always concerned with those aspects of truth that could remain hidden to him." Yet, only a short year later he could downgrade Spaventa to the level of a mere epigone who "attempted to think, and he could not, so he merely repeated." See Benedetto Croce,

radically separated.[83] Recent research shows that Spaventa was not only familiar with Ludwig von Stein's *Der Sozialismus und Kommunismus der heutigen Frankreich* but that he went so far as to seek a publisher for an Italian translation of this work, which he wanted to prepare.[84] In fact, if Löwith is correct in seeing Stein as halfway between Hegel and Marx, it would be even more correct to see him as halfway between Hegel and Spaventa.[85] Unlike the Stein depicted by Marcuse on the basis of later works, where Stein's sociology translated Hegel's categories into reified sociological concepts eternalizing conflicts typical of bourgeois society, the Stein that Spaventa knew was primarily the historian of the French Revolution, seeking to operationalize Hegelianism politically.[86] Caught in the general enthusiasm associated with the French events prior to Louis Bonaparte's

"Contributo alla Critica di me Stesso," in his *Etica e Politica* (Bari, 1967), p. 346. On the whole, Croce presented a Spaventa with positivist tendencies and lingering theological concerns. But as Serra has indicated, Croce was more interested in dissociating himself from his uncle than in providing a balanced assessment. Thus, in the very same "Contributo," p. 342, Croce writes: "Spaventa came from the Church and from theology; and his main and almost sole problem was that of the relation between Being and Knowing, the problem of transcendence and immanence—the most specifically theological-philosophical problem. As for myself, having overcome the sentimental anguish associated with breaking off from religion, I soon settled with a kind of immanentism not concerned with any other world than the one in which I actually live, and not feeling primarily and directly the problem of transcendence. Thus, I never had any problem in conceiving of the relation between being and thought since, on the contrary, the problem would have been to conceive of a being separate from thought or a thought separate from being."

83. For a systematic critique of traditional Spaventa interpretations, see Vacca, *Politica e Filosofia*, pp. 63–84. The main points of the Gentilean interpretation of Spaventa, according to Vacca, focus on the "very successful schema of the historiography of Italian and European philosophy, the exponent of Hegel in Italy, the lively and polemical adversary of positivistic fashions that will invest Italian academic culture around 1870." Vacca, *Politica e Filosofia*, p. 119. All of this, however, took place *after* the militant experiences of the 1848–1851 period, completely overlooked by both Gentile and Croce.

84. For a discussion of Spaventa's relation to Stein, see Sergio Landucci, "Il Giovane Spaventa tra Hegelismo e Socialismo," *Annali Feltrinelli* VI (1964), 647–707. Landucci quotes in full an announcement placed by Spaventa in a Florence journal, *Il Nazionale*, 14 September 1850, where he briefly summarized Stein's book.

85. Karl Löwith, *From Hegel to Nietzsche*, trans. David E. Green (New York, 1967), p. 241.

86. As Marcuse himself indicates, it is only in the third edition of Stein's book, published in 1850 (Spaventa knew only the shorter second edition of 1848), that

coup d'etat of 2 December 1851, Spaventa characterized these events as the second phase of the French Revolution, which sought the social emancipation left undone after the first phase of 1789 attained *political* emancipation.

> There are already signs of a new social transformation: the ancient world has collapsed and the new one has begun to rise. The 1789 revolution destroyed the orders, the classes, the corporations, and proclaimed the principle of equality. The new revolution will destroy all social inequalities; there will no longer be noblemen, plebeians, bourgeois, or proletarians; there will be only men.[87]

He even went as far as to locate the proletariat as the new revolutionary class:

> As long as man will remain a simple *proletarian* without the means of production, he will not be truly free and equal to the owner in exercising his political rights. Thus, the law itself, which declares absolute political equality while not guaranteeing the conditions necessary to bring it about, contains a great contradiction which sooner or later results in a revolutionary movement. This contradiction is the real cause of the social struggle troubling France and is now beginning to manifest itself also within other nations in Europe.[88]

As Vacca has shown convincingly, the impact of this political upheaval, previously ignored by neo-idealist interpretations, irrefutably colors Spaventa's thought and provides the key to his later work. In fact, the theory of cultural hegemony that Spaventa developed

---

"Stein's sociology . . . set out to uphold social harmony in the face of economic contradictions, and morality in the face of social struggle." Marcuse, *Reason and Revolution*, pp. 374–388.

87. Bertrando Spavento, "I Filosofi," *Il Progresso*, 8 June 1851; reprinted in B. Spaventa, "Rivoluzione e Utopia," p. 70. Further on (p. 86), the same theme is articulated once again; "Abolished in 1847 the political importance of *ownership*, and having the people attain universal suffrage, what remains is its *social* importance. The latter, in turn, by penetrating in the political sphere, deprives suffrage itself of any truth and reality so that . . . for man to be truly free, it is necessary to guarantee him all the conditions which promote the unfolding of liberty and without which, although the law recognizes and declares him equal to another man, in fact he depends on that man, not because of accidental or particular causes, but because of the existence of an order of things that the law sanctions and justifies."

88. Bertrando Spaventa, *Il Progresso*, 7 October 1851; reprinted in B. Spaventa, "Rivoluzione e Utopia," p. 86.

during this period is based largely on the leading revolutionary role that he assigned to intellectuals (philosophers) in the creation of a new ethical state that would, when systematically taught, help constitute a new humanity. Echoing Marx's and Engels's criticism of utopian socialism (criticisms unknown to him), Spaventa railed against utopias for their failure to develop the mediations necessary to guarantee their realization.[89] Still, despite "the falsity of the system," Spaventa writes, "the need that generated [utopias] exists and manifests itself in many ways; it is a growing illness that corrodes all social orders and, if the reforms themselves may be utopian, the idea of reform itself is certainly not."[90] This is ultimately what determines the intellectuals' revolutionary role:

> The philosophers are the precursors of revolution. . . . When the social and political conditions of the life of a people do not correspond to the new principle that has developed in the world of intelligence, when the fact is in contradiction with the idea, revolution already exists as a germ in national consciousness. But then in the people the revolutionary idea is a vague, obscure, and indeterminate feeling. Philosophers transform this feeling into a determinate thought; this thought is like a mirror in which the people recognize themselves, their new instincts, their new needs; in which they find resolute the contradiction between what is and what should be. Without philosophers the revolution would be blind, indeterminate, and aimless; it would be the fury of instinct instead of the infinite power of reason; the violent power of the multitude in place of the absolute right of humanity.[91]

Caught in the crossfire between liberals and clerics in arguments

89. Since he saw systems of social philosophy rooted in "universally felt needs . . . for a general and indeterminate happiness," which is "always the same at all times and which does not differ in quality but, rather, in the liveliness of its articulation according to the diversity of individuals, epochs, and events" (in B. Spaventa, "Rivoluzione e Utopia," p. 80), the function of intellectuals and social philosophers is to elaborate these needs into concrete projects of social reconstruction. Thus, Spaventa associated utopias with "the indiscriminate use of thought which renounces its own critical function because of either its profound distress with present unhappiness or its satisfaction with the given reality, and precipitates in the vortex of abstractions transcending the real, which is thereby restored as such, no longer challenged by the need of legitimation and explanation through reason." Vacca, *Politica e Filosofia*, p. 100.

90. B. Spaventa, "Rivoluzione e Utopia," pp. 77–78.

91. Ibid., p. 69.

concerning the theory of the bourgeois state, Spaventa turned to Hegel's critique of social-contract accounts,[92] faulting them for providing a statist account of "a higher principle which would be the essence and the content of human will and without which the latter is nothing other than pure arbitrariness and accident."[93] He followed Hegel further, seeing this social-contract foundation as necessarily resulting in Jacobin terror (because it is based on *abstract* individualism). Against the liberals, Spaventa vindicated the interventionist function of the state in educating the masses, and against the clerics he defended the right to teach other than Church dogma. And while he was attacking everything from modern authoritarianism to abstract individualism,[94] he at times came within a hair of posing the question of whether "pure communism" was the ultimate goal of the social upheavals of the time.[95] Given the overwhelming Catholic hegemony that prevailed in Italy in 1850, Spaventa focused primarily on the need to win over the masses, not just the intellectuals, in order to guarantee the success of the revolution. To this end he fought those who would apply liberal principles of scholarly competition to instruction (thus ruling out vigorous state intervention in education and, consequently, accepting continued Catholic control of that social sphere).

92. According to Hegel, the French Revolution sought to provide a purely rational basis for the state. But since "it was only abstractions that were being used . . . the experiment ended in the maximum of fearfulness and terror." T. M. Knox, trans., *Hegel's Philosophy of Right* (Oxford, 1942), p. 157.

93. Bertrando Spaventa, "Sopra alcuni Giudizi di Niccoló Tommasso," originally published in 1855; now in B. Spaventa, *Opere*, II, 205.

94. Thus, Spaventa writes: "Here, then, is the genesis of authority. At the beginning man is free, and there is no right above and beyond man himself. But he must (and no one knows why) sacrifice his liberty. The sum of the sacrifices made by each man is authority. What remains of individual liberty (which before was everything) is the corpse of this liberty: private authority. Having made this sacrifice and having constituted authority, public life proceeds as follows. The authority turned a man into the chief of State. This chief generates ministers. The ministers generate a majority. The majority generates the law. The law generates the duties of all citizens. Duties generate obedience. And thus, after innumerable and unnamed generations, out comes the social State, order, and the reign of authority. What is the reason for this emanative system? Nothing more than accident or arbitrariness, when one moves from individual right considered as an abstraction in order to reach collective authority." B. Spaventa, "Rivoluzione e Utopia," pp. 74–75.

95. Vacca, *Politica e Filosofia*, p. 23.

Let us assume that fortune and courage are enough to win, and that youth flocks around some illustrious professor. And the people? And the country-side? And the holy ignorance of early youth? While you, elect few [*pleiadi*] young speakers of the public Academy, receive praise and applause in the new Berlin of your dreams, the worker, the peasant, the mother of the people's progeny will learn to distrust you, science, and civilization; they will learn to deplore the pride of human intelligence; they will learn that the sovereignty of reason, of which you announce yourselves as the confessors, is the dogma of hell, is original sin, is a rebellion against divine truth. And if in order to fight these deadly doctrines you stray too far—or, better yet, if you attack your adversaries where they are vulnerable, where you must wound them if you want to beat them—there you will find the penal code, the courts, the fines, the cops, and the fortress.[96]

Bonaparte's coup dealt a severe blow to Spaventa's rising expectations and forced him to reconsider his earlier optimistic outlook.[97] In later years, both Bertrando and Silvio acknowledged that they had embraced illusions and unwarranted hopes in this period.[98] Spaventa retreated more and more to his philosophical studies in the 1850s, but the earlier political interests remained, especially his concern with the Church's role. He spent a considerable amount of time during this period attacking the Jesuits in a ceaseless effort to demolish the Catholic stronghold on Italian culture. In a series of writings later collected by Gentile and published under the appropriate title *The Jesuit Policy in the 16th and 19th Centuries*, Spaventa exposed the Jesuits' theoretical opportunism that led them to embrace democratic principles in the sixteenth century but to support absolutism in the nineteenth.

Today's Jesuits condemn representative orders, strongly defend the *divine*

96. B. Spaventa, "Rivoluzione e Utopia," pp. 37–38.

97. In a letter dated 16 December 1851, Spaventa wrote to his friend Angelo Camillo De Meis: "There are some times when it seems that rational and necessary laws that govern the life of people are as if suspended, and the idea, the spirit, or whatever the hell it is, hides or retreats in the depths of existence and events so that it is not enough to have the sharpest intelligence and the greatest enthusiasm for speculating in order to discover it and recognize it. . . . I am in a kind of intellectual stupor, having been unable up to now to penetrate the meaning of the latest events." B. Spaventa, *Opere*, III, 851–852.

98. Silvio Spaventa's speech in Rome, 1879, in Silvio Spaventa, *La Giustizia nell'Amministrazione* (Turin, 1943), p. 32.

right of absolute principles; attack as a diabolical invention the principle of *popular sovereignty*; they want laws to be made not by the community but by one only to whom it is communicated, through heredity, an infallible wisdom; they claim that taxes must not be approved by those who pay them, but ordered at the whim of those who collect them, and so on. Those who are not of their opinion are anarchists, communists, etc.[99]

Yet, after a rapid examination of the doctrines of such leading sixteenth-century Jesuits as D. Lainez, Cardinal Bellarmino, F. Suarez, and J. de Mariana, Spaventa concludes:

Here nothing is missing: social contract, the people's inalienable sovereignty, the delegation of power to the prince, a nonhereditary monarchy, a deliberative senate, laws made by the community, taxes voted on by those who pay them, the right to change the form of government, the justice of those governed and the popular will as a condition of the legitimacy of power, the need for a national assembly to judge the tyrant, and so on. Aren't these the germs of Rousseau's doctrine and of the French Revolution?[100]

This *exposé* of Jesuit casuistry developed into a call for religious freedom as a condition for a new kind of humanity that would eventually unseat the Catholic church and put in its stead the ethical state:

The great enemy of all of them, Jesuits and absolute princes, are the people who no longer believe in the formulae of this or that scholastic, quickly explained and elaborated in the confessional by a minister of the Company, but have some consciousness of their own right in everything in life, and begin to realize that, beyond political despotism, there is an even more unbearable and iniquitous despotism that is the foundation of the first, i.e., spiritual despotism, the tyranny of consciousness. History is now at such a point where it is impossible to touch one without also touching the other; religious freedom leads to political liberty, and the political to the religious one.[101]

99. B. Spaventa, *Opere*, II, 756.
100. Ibid., p. 760.
101. Ibid., p. 811. The reason why, in the sixteenth century, the Jesuits could hold such liberal theories was that ultimately *political* hegemony was guaranteed by *ideological* hegemony: "The principle of sovereignty did not cause much trouble in the sixteenth century, and those who preached it had no reason to fear that ecclesiastic despotism could incur any danger; there was always a special reserve clause that on certain occasions could annihilate it: above the people, natural and immediate recep-

This strategy for the attainment of bourgeois ideological and cultural hegemony, however, is not based on traditional liberal assumptions but on Hegelian theory. In Spaventa's interpretation of the latter, the ultimate aim is not the uncritical elevation of the status quo to a universally valid institutional framework, as in the forced reconciliation by the older Hegel and the Right-Hegelians; rather, Hegelianism for Spaventa provided an instrumental defense of bourgeois institutions, which he saw as leading ultimately to the birth of social individuality.[102]

Contrary to neo-idealist interpretations,[103] this shift from *political* to *cultural* concerns during the 1850s extended what Vacca identifies as the three main achievements of the 1840s (i.e., the critique of the right of property as *innate*, the recognition of the central role of the masses in the revolutionary process, and a preliminary outline of a theory of the ethical state) and fed increasingly into the politics of the

---

tacle of authority, . . . there was always the power of him who is not subject to any laws or power other than the divine, of which he himself is the interpreter, organ, and administrator." Ibid., pp. 811–812.

102. Given this state of affairs, it is not difficult to see how this Spaventean concern could feed directly into the project of national independence. It is only within that context that social emancipation can truly take place under the guidance of the *national* ethical state. Thus, the problematic of nationality becomes the precondition for social individuality. Spaventa writes: "[Nationality] for us has never been a simple geographical expression, as the Austrian minister used to say. It is more than mere custom, language, art and literature, feelings and intuitions. This nationality we have already had for some time and we are not satisfied with it. Nationality is for us unity: free, powerful, and living unity as State. And why do we want this unity as a free State? Because we know that only in unity in a free State can we freely unfold all the powers of our lives; only in that can we be and know ourselves as truly ourselves. This is already an implicit confession that up to now we have not been in all forms of our existence what we could have actually been." B. Spaventa, *Opere*, II, 427.

103. Thus, Guido De Ruggiero, in his *Hegel* (Bari, 1948), p. 278, sees this shift as "an involution of the system." Elsewhere, in *Il Pensiero Politico Meridionale nei Secoli XVIII e XIX* (Bari, 1922), p. 301, De Ruggiero argues that Spaventa's "abstract rationalism" had as its outcome a fusion with "the 'patriots' ' political praxis and generated the philosophy of the Italian liberal Right. A doctrine that deduced authority and law from freedom . . . had to be useful to the historical action of those minorities who carried out unification and to which only a rationalistic fiction could attribute a title of universal representation. The energetic assertion of the State's authority, deduced from the very principles of self-consciousness, corresponded to the practice of centralization and bureaucratization."

moderates.[104] Following Gramsci's analysis of the Italian Risorgimento, Vacca bemoans the subordination of the radical elements (the Jacobins of Giuseppe Garibaldi's *Partito d'Azione*) to Camillo Cavour's more moderate program, regarding it as a diffusion of real revolutionary possibilities insofar as it restricted radical developments within the programs of the northern industrial bourgeoisie in what later was characterized as a "passive revolution" (i.e., lacking broad popular support):

> The ever higher theoretical level that Spaventa's political commitment founders upon, and to which he carries his struggle for a primarily philosophical reform, denotes Spaventa's definitive loss of democratic political battles and broader progressive struggles after unification, up to his gloomy and irascible isolation after 1876.[105]

Gramsci, however, tended to examine the Italian Risorgimento primarily in terms of his own political problematic of a potential alliance with the peasants, thus overestimating the real revolutionary options of earlier times.[106] But it is unfair to criticize Spaventa for not choosing alternatives that were never really available to him. Confronting what was to become a major issue of the next century of socialist history—the revolutionaries' attitude toward bourgeois revolutions in contexts of social and economic underdevelopment—Spaventa opted for a bourgeois *ethical* state, which, unlike the *liberal* variety based on *abstract* individualism, had as its fundamental task the creation of conditions leading to the genesis of *social* individuality. Although it is true that any mention of communism and socialism disappeared from Spaventa's later discourse, the task that remained was to create a new type of humanity. The function of the ethical state is precisely to mediate between the given civil society and a society of social individuals within a reconciled universal community of states, which Spaventa identified as Hegel's Absolute Spirit.[107] In Vacca's words:

104. Vacca, *Politica e Filosofia*, p. 46.
105. Ibid., p. 190.
106. See Giuseppe Galasso, "Gramsci e i Problemi della Storia Italiana," in Pietro Rossi, ed., *Gramsci e la Cultura Contemporanea* (Rome, 1969), pp. 305–354.
107. Bertrando Spaventa, *Principi di Etica*, originally published in 1869; now in B. Spaventa, *Opere*, I, 611–790.

It is an original form of state having an active and driving function toward civil society, in the attempt to overcome its own divisions from it, produced by civil society: a state at the basis of which is an ever-growing political participation by citizens; and whose political and pedagogical goal is the gradual development of political participation and of the material and cultural elevation of the community.[108]

Spaventa's work tended to become more and more formalistic. In his analysis of Hegel's ethics, he went so far as to consider as a universal feature of the modern state the division of labor and, consequently, class divisions.[109] Yet, he did not attempt to raise bourgeois social relations to the level of *natural* laws. The laws of political economy were for him *ethical* in character and their development was throughout subject to human determination.[110] The earlier political and philosophical thrusts of 1851 were gradually locked into a more general theory of the ethical state that appealed to no one and stood no chance whatsoever of being translated into a political project to create a new broad-based national culture. Thus, the philosophical and political rearguard action that Spaventa became entangled in during the last year of his life did not result from any theoretical failure on his part, but had its origins in a stagnant and conservative sociopolitical situation. That he was forced into a defensive position with no alternative other than to protect his historicized version of Hegelianism had nothing to do with the inner vitality of his positions.

---

108. Vacca, *Politica e Filosofia*, p. 204.

109. Thus, he writes: "*Everyone works*, and everyone *works for everyone else.* The *universality* of labor becomes *distinguished* and *particularized*, in conformity with the *particularity* of needs: the *division of labor.* . . . This *division* of public wealth (which is both cause and universal effect), although under this double aspect, could seem, in its indefinite multiplication, accidental and arbitrary, yet in its fundamental scheme is *necessary* and *rational*. Its concrete existence is the *distinctions of classes*: a distinction which in some way or other is there and will always be there, no matter what anyone says. It will no longer be there only when, e.g., the fields will yield wheat by themselves, the wheat will become flour by itself, and the flour bread; and when fish will catch themselves and fry themselves, etc. Each class has its own particular basis for subsistence, its own work, needs, satisfactions, goals, culture, customs, etc. This distinction is by no means purely *natural*; it is not a caste; the individuals belong to this or that class according to intelligence, ability, chance, etc." B. Spaventa, *Opere*, I, 767.

110. Ibid., p. 769.

Critical versus Orthodox Hegelianism

With the possible exception of De Sanctis (who, however, was mostly concerned with esthetics), Spaventa was by far the most important member of the Neapolitan Hegelians. But he was by no means unopposed within the Hegelian camp itself. After 1865, the Neapolitan Hegelians, following the German experience of a rift between left and right wings, split into an "orthodox" and a "critical" wing, although the factions in Naples did not correspond exactly to those in Germany. Spaventa's critical wing, for example, often sided with German Right-Hegelians such as Georg Andreas Gabler, Karl Fischer, and Karl Rosenkranz on many theoretical questions, such as the relation between Hegel's *Logic* and the *Phenomenology*. Still, on the whole, Spaventa provided a *Left* reading and elaboration of Right-Hegelianism against Augusto Vera's conservative orthodox wing. With Hegelianism as the official philosophy of the new Italian state— or so it came to be regarded after 1876, following its decline[111]—the orthodox and critical wings clashed on almost every significant issue that they faced during the decade or so of their theoretical hegemony. It is important to examine the positions of the orthodox wing to understand fully why Spaventa's theory took what at first sight appears to be a step backward with respect to the bold positions of 1851. Furthermore, such examination will also help explain why Hegelianism declined rapidly after Spaventa's death.

Even before the clashes with the critical Hegelians, Vera had enjoyed considerable prestige abroad as the leading Italian Hegelian.[112] While Spaventa and the critical Hegelians had been intimately involved in the political clashes of 1848 and their aftermath, Vera spent this whole period abroad, aloof from all political confrontations.[113] Up to 1848, he had been a liberal who had defended with Spaventa the correspondence between German philosophy and the

111. Landucci, "L'Hegelismo in Italia," p. 614.

112. For an excellent account of Vera's fortunes, as well as of a lot of what follows, see Oldrini, *Gli Hegeliani di Napoli*, chap. 2, pp. 164–239.

113. This political question explains also why, unlike the violent opposition met by the outspoken Spaventa and De Sanctis when they returned to Naples, Vera received such a warm welcome that many foreign observers were led to mistakenly regard him as the leading Hegelian in Naples. Ibid., pp. 164–165.

French Revolution.[114] The unfolding of events, however, quickly turned Vera into a conservative. He broke with his liberal friends connected with the journal *Liberté de Penser*, and, in an article entitled "La Souveraineté du Peuple," he violently attacked popular insurrections, universal suffrage, the "democratic principle," and other progressive measures, concluding that "the goal of social life is not the people's health, but order."[115] Unlike Spaventa, who never lost sight of the revolutionary French political model in tentatively charting the course of the Italian Risorgimento, Vera opted for Bismarck's German state, where the Hohenzollerns in alliance with the Junkers prevented the rising bourgeoisie from attaining political hegemony.[116] In doing so, Vera apparently closed his eyes to the fact that the German and Italian socioeconomic situations were qualitatively different, and that in the latter a liberal bourgeoisie, although relatively weak, was well on its way to gaining the upper hand over the whole project of national unification, under the banner of a "moderate" program.

Vera shifted the emphasis from a political to a religious revolution. The bourgeoisie need not upset existing power relations: all that was necessary was to introduce Protestantism into Italy. In his only surviving letter to Spaventa, Vera writes:

114. Thus, in 1843 Vera had written: "German philosophy should bring about in the moral and intellectual order what the French Revolution has brought about in the social and political order. Both have their reason in history and both aim at the same goal. The principle from which they originate is the same; it is the need of science and of freedom. . . . If the results obtained by the French Revolution have been more striking and rapid, it is because it functions in the world of facts and force is its instrument. Philosophy functions in the world of ideas, and its instrument is thought. Its march is slower and more painful, more silent; but its results will be more stable and decisive." Augusto Vera, "Logique de Hegel," p. 382; as quoted in Oldrini, *Gli Hegeliani di Napoli*, p. 244.

115. This essay appears in Augusto Vera, *Melanges Philosophiques* (Paris and Naples, 1862), pp. 242–266. Quoted in Oldrini, *Gli Hegeliani di Napoli*, p. 245.

116. Already in November 1859, Silvio Spaventa realized that the German model would not do, given the huge gap between the cultural sphere and its socioeconomic base. He writes: "Germany is still politically subservient, and does not amount to a true nation because, free as it is in soul and thought, it still retains the feudal principle of man's superiority over man, of group over group, and of nation over nation. . . . Feudalism, authentic son of the German spirit, has survived its universal ruin in the only country in which it was a natural and necessary result. The religious reform,

Politics is not religion and the politician cannot resolve the problem of religion. This is clear. But it is similarly clear, or so it seems to me, that this "*cannot*" shows not only the impotence of politics, but that the problem of religion dominates the political one, and that a nation that does not remake religious consciousness does not remake itself either morally or spiritually or in any other way. There will be the name and the shadow, but not the substance of a *risorgimento*.[117]

Where Spaventa theorized the absorption of the Church by the ethical state, Vera not only dreamed of a Protestant reformation independent of any socioeconomic change but even ended up challenging Cavour on the separation of church and state.[118] Afraid of the political upheavals taking place in capitalist states such as France and England, Vera opted *tout court* for the authoritarian German state.

This conservative framework clashed with the outlook of the critical Hegelians shortly after De Sanctis, the new rector of the University of Naples in 1861, appointed Vera as a philosophy professor and the question of the death penalty came to be hotly debated. In Vera's authoritarian conception, the state had primacy over and above all individuals, and he therefore had no qualms in endorsing the death penalty:

It seems appropriate to correct the false opinion that the State cannot mete out death, since it is not the source of life. The fact is that, like everything else, we owe our life to the State. Actually, when it is claimed that life comes from God, this is . . . a meaningless proposition. Although it may come from God, yet we receive it in the State, through the State and the norms, laws, and the necessity that constitute the social entity.[119]

For his part, Spaventa, who saw the individual as a concrete universal both constituted and constitutive of the state, strongly opposed the death penalty.

Of course, all of these political differences were reflected in more

---

progress in knowledge, the great political upheavals of the first half of this century, have not been sufficient to eradicate it in Germany." S. Spaventa, *Dal 1848 al 1861*, pp. 272–273.

117. As quoted in Oldrini, *Gli Hegeliani di Napoli*, p. 250.

118. Augusto Vera, *Il Cavour e Libera Chiesa in Libero Stato* (Naples, 1871).

119. Augusto Vera, *La Pena di Morte* (Paris and Naples, 1863), p. 22; as quoted in Oldrini, *Gli Hegeliani di Napoli*, p. 263.

esoteric philosophical differences. While for Vera, Hegel meant the end of all philosophy,[120] with the philosopher's task reduced to textual exegesis,[121] for Spaventa, who assigned to Hegelianism the mediational function of bringing about a new, deprovincialized society at the level of the highest achievements of European culture, what was most important was the *new*.[122] Where Vera saw the completed systematic exposition of Hegel's *Logic* and his *Encyclopedia* as the final arrival point of all philosophy, Spaventa stressed movement as primary and favored the *Phenomenology*. According to Vera:

> That the *Phenomenology* was published before the system that subsequently came out under the title of *Encyclopedia of the Philosophical Sciences* is nothing but a subjective and accidental occurrence, while the objective and essential fact is that the system preceded the *Phenomenology*.[123]

Ultimately, "the *Phenomenology* is the vestibule, not the sanctuary."[124] Following the publication of the second edition of A. F. Trendelenburg's *Logische Untersuchungen* in 1862 (originally published in 1840 but largely ignored), where Hegel's basic categories of a static 'being' and an equally static 'nothingness' are criticized for their inability to yield a 'becoming,'[125] Vera opted for the primacy of

120. Thus, Vera's claim that "Hegel's philosophy closes, in all its constituent parts, philosophy's historical cycle." Quoted in Oldrini, *Gli Hegeliani di Napoli*, p. 169.

121. According to Vera, "After Hegel we must do nothing more than repeat or mechanically comment on his deductions as if they were so many sacramental forms." Ibid., p. 170.

122. In direct reference to Vera, Spaventa writes: "If there is something that I abhor . . . it is precisely the mechanical reproduction of someone else's doctrine. In philosophers, in true philosophers, there is always something which is more than themselves, and of which they are conscious; and this is the germ of a new life. To mechanically repeat philosophers amounts to suffocating this germ, preventing it from developing a new and more perfect system." B. Spaventa, "La Filosofia Italiana," in B. Spaventa, *Opere*, II, 643.

123. Augusto Vera, *Problema dell'Assoluto* (Naples, 1872), I, 65–70; as quoted in Oldrini, *Gli Hegeliani di Napoli*, p. 173.

124. Ibid., p. 139.

125. According to Trendelenburg, "Pure being, equal to itself, is quiet; nothingness, which is also equal to itself, is also quiet. How is it that 'becoming in movement' comes out of the unity of two representations in a stasis?" Adolf F. Trendelenburg, *Logische Untersuchungen* (Leipzig, 1870), p. 38.

absolute knowledge at the expense of the process,[126] and Spaventa gave priority to movement.[127] Thus, while Vera moved closer to a Hegelianism forcibly reconciling all contradictions within the system, Spaventa increasingly emphasized the dynamism of Hegelian philosophy in an effort to salvage its emancipatory character.

The evidence is plentiful: Vera's polemics against communists (whom he labeled "modern alchemists"),[128] the regressive legislation that he sponsored as a senator,[129] or his defense of the beginning of Italian imperialism, which he unreservedly praised.[130] But the point has been made: clearly, the orthodox wing confronted Spaventa and the critical Hegelians with such a conservative outlook that the very attempt to refute their views tended to shift theoretical and political discourse considerably toward the Right.[131]

The fall of the "historical Right" in 1876 and the coming to power of the Left in Italy was by no means a progressive development. Politically indistinguishable from the Right in terms of ideology and programs, the Left launched what has come to be known as the age of

126. Augusto Vera, "Trendelenburg on Hegel's System," *Journal of Speculative Philosophy* VI (October 1872).

127. Unlike Vera, Spaventa accepted Trendelenburg's challenge: "The merit of Trendelenburg's criticism is to have . . . called Hegelians back to their duty: of having shaken them from a kind of sleep. . . . They used to say: here we are, on this peak of pure thought, and we look at the thing, which moves by itself, and we do nothing more than watch. They almost forgot that what they watched was thought itself, and that thought cannot be watched other than by thinking." B. Spaventa, "Le Prime Categorie della Logica," in *Opere*, I, 435.

128. Augusto Vera, "Les Alchemistes Modernes," in *Melanges Philosophique*, pp. 287–295. As Oldrini points out, the communism that Vera attacked is of the utopian variety (*Gli Hegeliani di Napoli*, p. 261). It is interesting, but obviously of no political significance, that after Ferdinand Lassalle visited Italy in 1861, he corresponded with Vera. This correspondence, however, has been lost.

129. Of the two pieces of legislation that Vera sponsored, one dealt with the reintroduction of religious teaching in the universities. Oldrini, *Gli Hegeliani di Napoli*, p. 231.

130. This support for imperialist adventure was not without racist overtones. In fact, one of his fellow "orthodox" Hegelians wrote a book around that time defending imperialism in terms of the racial superiority of whites. See Raffaele Mariano, *La Razza Nera* (Turin, 1869).

131. Unlike Spaventa's and De Sanctis's work, which has gained widespread popularity in the last seventy years, Vera's work, and that of his followers, was never republished and has forever fallen into a justly deserved obscurity.

"transformism," when everything changed so that everything could remain the same.[132] Characterized by rampant corruption, social unrest, and clientism, the age of transformism meant the end of the dream of social and cultural rebirth envisioned by Spaventa and the critical Hegelians. Challenged on all fronts by the increasingly reactionary thrusts of orthodox Hegelians and positivists, critical Hegelianism declined so rapidly that it was practically forgotten until the turn of the century, when Labriola's form of Marxism finally brought to their logical conclusions many of Spaventa's theoretical visions.

Gramsci's Interpretation of Italian History

When Gramsci undertook his reconstruction of Italian history in order both to explain the existing power configuration and to plot a successful revolutionary strategy, he did not pay special heed to his nineteenth-century Hegelian heritage—by that time fully appropriated and ideologically defused by Croce and Gentile. Yet, Gramsci's account follows the main lines of contemporary liberal historiography and, with the exception of his politically dubious emphasis on the unrealized possibilities of the Risorgimento, it is wholly continuous with Spaventa's general analysis.[133] The problem of Italian national unification and independence took the Hegelian form of the determination of the concrete universal. Reminiscent of Spaventa's polemics concerning nationality in contrast to the abstract universalism of Vera and the parochial nationalism of Palmieri, Gramsci identifies *Catholic cosmopolitanism* and *municipal particularism* as the two cultural forms that had to be overcome as a condition for the constitution of a new national consciousness. Thus,

> the formation of Italian national consciousness in Jews provides a valid model for the entire process of formation of Italian national consciousness, both as the dissolution of religious cosmpolitanism as well as particularism,

---

132. As Gramsci puts it: "It turns out that there has been no essential change in shifting from the Right to the Left: the mess in which the country finds itself is not due to the parliamentary regime (which merely makes public and known what before remained hidden or gave rise to libelous clandestine publications) but to the weakness and organic inconsistency of the ruling class and to the great misery and backwardness of the country." Cf. Gramsci, *Quaderni del Carcere*, III, 1977–1978.

133. Galasso, "Gramsci e i Problemi," p. 331.

because in Jews religious cosmpolitanism becomes particularism within the context of national states.[134]

All of Spaventa's polemics against Catholic hegemony were taken a step further by Gramsci, who now saw hegemony working at the broader level of international power relations. In Gramsci's analysis, the notion of hegemony gained even more importance since he saw that the economic conditions for revolution were altogether lacking in Italy. There was neither a strong and dynamic bourgeoisie nor, consequently, any significant proletariat. Thus, "the problem was not so much one of freeing already developed economic forces from antiquated juridical and political fetters, as to create the general conditions so that these forces could arise and develop on the model of other countries."[135] As opposed to the model of base and superstructure used by the Second International to explain the unfolding of events, Gramsci analyzed revolutionary struggles primarily in terms of the battle for hegemony and the formation of historical blocs.

From such a perspective, the "Risorgimento was possible only as a result of a weakening of the Papacy,"[136] since, to complicate the problem, Gramsci fully acknowledged that the forces of national unification were very weak. According to him,

> the traditions, the mentalities, the problems, and the solutions were many, contradictory, often of an arbitrary and individual nature, and thus were never seen at that time in a unitary fashion. The forces aiming toward unity were very scarce, dispersed, disconnected, and unable to establish reciprocal ties, and this was the case not only in the eighteenth century, but up to

134. Gramsci, *Quaderni del Carcere*, III, 1801. This, for Gramsci, also helps to explain why there was no anti-Semitism in Italy. The Jews' overcoming of their religious cosmopolitanism corresponded with the birth of a lay spirit that he saw as the source of national consciousness. Thus, in Italy Jews became Italians along with, if not before, everyone else. This destroyed precisely any of their "otherness" that in other countries became the target of anti-Semitism.

135. Ibid., II, 747–748. Elsewhere, in ibid., III, 2018, Gramsci writes: "From 1861 to 1876 the government of the Right had only timidly created the general external conditions for economic development—systematization of the governing apparatus, highways, railroads, telegraphs—and had taken care of the finances overtaxed by the wars of the Risorgimento. The Left . . . had continued the Right's policies with men and slogans from the Left."

136. Ibid., III, 1963–1964.

1848. The forces opposing those seeking unity (or better, tendentially unitary) were instead very powerful, united in coalitions.

Hence, the gradual shift of power took place almost as a result of the default of the dominant side under siege on other fronts:

> International factors, and especially the French Revolution, by engaging and wearing out these reactionary forces, tended to strengthen national forces by themselves scarce and insufficient. This is the most important contribution of the French Revolution, very difficult to see and define, but which can be intuited as the decisive weight in giving rise to the Risorgimento process.[137]

What Gramsci merely intuited, of course, has long since been fully corroborated. In fact, the very development of the Neapolitan Hegelianism that played such an important role in shaping Gramsci's own intellectual heritage was the direct result of attempts by progressive southern intellectuals to transpose the ideas of the French Revolution onto Italy in hopes of triggering similar events.

Given Gramsci's own negative appraisal of the chances for a revolution to develop out of national unification, one would expect him to approve of a general strategy of "war of position" aimed at gradually gaining cultural and ideological hegemony by creating conditions for the revolutionary changes that would usher in the new humanity he envisioned. This, after all, was Spaventa's strategy from the crushing disappointments of 1851 up to his death in 1883. As we have seen, what Spaventa required in addition to the establishment of a viable economic infrastructure—the order of the day, at least in the North[138]—was the simultaneous weakening of the still very strong Catholic forces. This was to be carried out through massive state intervention in education, welfare, and other social functions assumed heretofore by the Church, a sharp separation of church and state that would allow the latter to take over the spiritual functions of the former, and the constant introduction of ever-larger sections of the population into the new nation's social, political, and cultural life. In

---

137. Ibid., pp. 1971–1972.

138. For a brief but striking account of the dramatic economic progress made at that time, see Salvemini, *Origins of Fascism*, chap. 1, "Italy from 1871 to 1919," pp. 1–18.

retrospect, Spaventa's approach assumes the characteristics of a well-thought-out war of position in a situation where little else seemed more promising. As such, it is hardly justifiable to regard it merely as the strategy for a "passive revolution," as Gramsci came to characterize the Risorgimento.

Gramsci asked himself whether the first period of the Italian Risorgimento should be seen as involving a war of position, but against the thrust of his own argument he refused to answer in the affirmative.[139] Instead, he reconstructed the process by which Cavour and the moderates gradually checkmated Mazzini and Garibaldi's Action party. He points out the role the Action party played in its own undoing: in Mazzini's lack of awareness of his own political role in opposing Cavour (in fact, in the Action party Gramsci sees only Carlo Pisacane as coming close to any kind of historical self-consciousness)[140] and in the Action party's failure to develop a Jacobin strategy based on an agrarian policy that would have engaged the overwhelming majority of Italian masses—at that time still largely peasant—in the project of national unification.[141] But Gramsci's argument collapsed at this point.[142] As he himself argued elsewhere, there was little chance that the peasants would rally around a Jacobin program advanced by the Action party. The peasants were solidly under Catholic hegemony and thus strongly opposed to Mazzini's call for a preliminary religious reform.[143] Further, throughout the Risorgimento and even afterward, the peasants remained extremely conservative.[144] Given the prevailing international power relations, a Jacobin thrust in Italy would almost certainly have run up against another Holy Alliance rather than the relatively isolated Austrian regime confronted by the moderates' project.

This paradox in Gramsci—a generally liberal Hegelian reconstruction alongside an unrealizable Bolshevik interpretation—has been explained in terms of his general political and theoretical orientation.

---

139. Gramsci, *Prison Notebooks*, p. 108.
140. Ibid., pp. 110–111.
141. Ibid., p. 100.
142. Galasso, "Gramsci e i Problemi," pp. 329–330.
143. Gramsci, *Prison Notebooks*, p. 102.
144. Gramsci himself pointed this out. Gramsci, *Quaderni del Carcere*, III, 1712.

Gramsci's identification of history and politics turns all of his historical reconstructions into historical mediations meant to provide direction in contemporary political struggles. Croce's claim that all history
is present history was radicalized into present politics by Gramsci,
who then accused Croce of falling into ideology by not pushing this
axiom far enough.[145] Thus, although he was engaged in interpreting
Italian history long before he became engaged in explaining fascism,
Gramsci's analysis ends up by examining the Risorgimento in terms of
the political tasks of the 1920s. His ascribing a Bolshevik role to the
Action party reflects his more direct concerns with the problems of
political organization of his own time.[146] It is ultimately an extension
of the themes outlined in "The Southern Question" of 1925 and the
search for an adequate political formula for the revolutionary transformation in Italy.[147]

Although it is explained easily enough, this contradiction signals a
different and deeper quandary involving Gramsci's very conception of
Marxism. His Marxism is "a reform and a development of Hegelianism," but a reform and development that takes Bolshevism as its
mode of realization.[148] Gramsci's 1917 characterization of Bolshevism as the living of "the Marxist thought that never dies, which is the
continuation of Italian and German idealist thought"—a Spaventian
formulation if ever there was one—is later elaborated but never
fundamentally modified.[149] The one-sidedness of all knowledge,
which Gramsci argued for against Bukharin, hits also the Hegelian
framework, which he comes to ground as the mediational reconstructions whose scientificity is only pragmatically validated.[150] The foun-

145. In fact, Gramsci claimed that Croce and Adolfo Omodeo fell into ideology in
not seeking "to generate present political forces." ibid., p. 1984. This is consistent
with Gramsci's general theoretical framework whereby scientificity is a function of
meaningful social and political mediation. Whatever conceptual structure remains
outside of this process automatically becomes metaphysical and ideological. See
Gramsci, *Prison Notebooks*, p. 436.

146. Galasso, "Gramsci e i Problemi," pp. 351 f.

147. Antonio Gramsci, "The Southern Question," in Antonio Gramsci, *The
Modern Prince and Other Writings*, trans. Louis Marks (New York, 1957),
pp. 28—51.

148. Gramsci, *Prison Notebooks*, p. 404.

149. Cavalcanti and Piccone, *History, Philosophy and Culture*, p. 123.

150. Gramsci, *Prison Notebooks*, p. 445.

dation of Gramsci's philosophy of praxis is based ultimately on *faith*—that mankind is on the brink of a new epoch of true humanity (Hegel's Absolute or Marx's communism) and that Leninism constitutes its mode of realization. The first tenet, inherited from the Spaventian tradition, may still be viable, but the Leninist model, through which he attempted to historicize the notion of a new epoch, not only was obsolete at the time he was writing but wrought havoc whenever it ran up against the theoretical framework.

II

Marxism in Italy

The Hegelian Kernel and the Marxist Shell

Viewing Spaventa's work in the context of mid-nineteenth-century Italian sociopolitical realities helps to vindicate its emancipatory nature, but this does not mean that it was not at the same time beset by a whole series of internal problems typical of Hegelian and post-Hegelian thought. Spaventa came to recognize at least some of them, and, in trying to solve them, he made a number of significant revisions in the Hegelian framework. In so doing, however, he moved so close to Marxism that Antonio Labriola, his brightest and most loyal student, could become the first rigorous Italian Marxist merely by extending Spaventa's reasoning to its logical conclusions.

Already in 1860 it was clear that Hegelian philosophy was rapidly giving way to the new positivism, which seemed to salvage the particularity and specificity of the real against the formal construction of the system. Spaventa accepted the challenge and readily admitted that the main problem with Hegelian philosophy,

> the discredit into which it has fallen in recent times, has no other cause than this inclination to transcend the real and to persuade itself that the speculative intuition of the universe can be had only through naked concepts. To study the real and to know it all; to know all of the manifestations of nature and history: this is the absolute condition of every true philosophy.[1]

He went so far as to call himself a positivist, if by ''positivism'' was

---

1. Bertrando Spaventa, ''Carattere e Sviluppo della Filosofia Italiana dal Secolo XVI ai Nostri Tempi'' (1860), in Bertrando Spaventa, *Opere*, ed. Giovanni Gentile (Florence, 1972), I, pp. 328–329.

meant the recognition of "the infinite existence and activity of things, and especially of man."[2] Yet he remained intransigent against any objectivistic and naturalistic interpretation:

> What is positivism? If it is naturalism, it is old junk. For me, if positivism makes sense, it is because it is based on the mind's positive activity. Otherwise, it is warmed-over naturalism. But the facts, the human facts, are to be observed; they are not invented or constructed *a priori*! . . . Even natural facts themselves—which were allegedly made by God or nature or whomever, but not by man—I cannot simply observe them with my hands in my pockets *uti iacent*; but most of the time, if I want to understand them, I am forced to *produce* or *reproduce* them.[3]

The emphasis remains throughout on the active and creative moments as inextricable phases of the subject's self-becoming. The passive and abstract individuality presupposed by the positivists had to be exposed as superficial and presupposing of a more profound and emergent social individuality that alone could provide a foundation for Spaventa's still shaky philosophical framework, as well as his projects of social reconstruction.[4] As Vacca indicates,[5] Spaventa focused on the problem of *mediation* between the particular and the universal in his work on the categories of Hegel's *Logic*.[6] For Spaventa, not only did new developments have to be placed within this system but, what's more, it was necessary to show how this system itself was presupposed by the new developments. This explains why Spaventa favored the *Phenomenology* over the *Logic*: in the latter, all of the determinations of the real are systematically presented as fixed once

2. Bertrando Spaventa, "Logica e Metafisica," in B. Spaventa, *Opere*, III, 15.

3. Bertrando Spaventa to *Rivista Bolognese*, 8 May 1868; now in B. Spaventa, *Opere*, I, 499.

4. Further on, in the previously quoted letter, Spaventa writes: "To call positive only that which is there, which imposes itself on the spirit, that the spirit must accept as a superior extraneous force, which is because it is, etc. (and therefore to call positivism that mode of thinking that results in this supine resignation of the spirit), is too much! Why does the positive impose itself on us and why must we resign ourselves to it? Because we are ourselves *within* it, although this does not appear on the surface." Ibid., p. 499.

5. Giuseppe Vacca, *Politica e Filosofia in Bertrando Spaventa* (Bari, 1967), pp. 237 ff.

6. Bertrando Spaventa, "Le Prime Categorie della Logica di Hegel," in B. Spaventa, *Opere*, I, 369–437.

and for all within the already realized Absolute Spirit; in the *Phenomenology* Hegel specified the necessary historical mediations leading to the already presupposed arrival point. Yet, the conclusion of the *Phenomenology*—the Absolute Knowledge that retrospectively shows all previous stages to have been necessary—does not invalidate emergent subjectivity as the historical agency. The way is thus left open for an analysis of the real from the viewpoint of a teleological process of self-becoming.

This attempt to analyze the process of apprehending the finite, showing the possibility—or better, the necessity—of integrating new developments within the Hegelian framework, led Spaventa to articulate the problem of mediation in terms of historically constituted *forms of consciousness* presupposed by those very same new developments.[7] The problem of knowledge shifts to the process of production of the categories required for apprehending the object of knowledge, and the emphasis falls once again on the subject as creative self-becoming.

> The real subject, the actual self, is the very *process of feeling*, and is born and formed only in this process. . . . What is required in order for the individual to *feel*? Is it sufficient that he be there simply and immediately? No. He must not simply be, but must pose himself: *produce himself*, his existence (his being, his reality) is the *act* on the process of production of himself. Thus, his being is *activity*, movement.[8]

The whole account, however, remains caught within the identity of subject and object.

> The true object is both object and subject, in the same way that the true subject is both subject and object; i.e., truth, the Absolute, is the subject-object. The possibility of knowing, of knowledge in general, is based on this identity; knowledge in general would be impossible if the spirit, the subject, were a mere spectator; if what he sees, what he knows, were not himself, his own essence, but another, an absolutely other. Knowing is essentially self-knowledge (*Selbsterkenntnis*).[9]

7. Bertrando Spaventa, "Esame di un'Obiezione di Teichmüller alla Dialettica di Hegel" (1882), in B. Spaventa, *Opere*, I, 456–457.

8. Bertrando Spaventa, "L'Anima e l'Organismo," in B. Spaventa, *Opere*, III, p. 599.

9. Bertrando Spaventa, *Sul Problema della Cognizione e in Generale dello Spirito*, ed. F. Alderisio (Turin, 1958), p. 58.

But if the Absolute resolves into the subject as already achieved self-consciousness, this clashes with Spaventa's thesis concerning the subject's self-creation. Either there is *genuine* becoming, in which case the Absolute remains to be attained and the conditions necessary for its very conceptualization are not yet given (only at the end of the historical trajectory from consciousness to self-consciousness does the Absolute reveal itself as such), or the viewpoint of the Absolute has already been achieved, in which case all becoming is reduced to autobiographical details, ruling out the very possibility of qualitatively new developments. Thus, the specification of the subject as self-creation remains at odds with the all-encompassing and closed character of the *Logic*.

Spaventa was not alone in running up against the paradox. In fact, this contradiction hounds all of post-Hegelian thought, including Marxism. Even Gramsci, who succeeded in theoretically articulating it, was unable to resolve it in the end.[10] As early as the *1844 Manuscripts*, Marx confronted the problem and identified the labor process as the domain of subjective self-becoming in his critique of the Hegelian dialectic as "the movement of abstract thought no longer directed outward but proceeding only within itself."[11] But Marx's own vindication of particularity ran into the same problem. The dialectical framework he used to ground the *necessity* that made revolution the unavoidable outcome of the resolution of contradictions entailed an apprehension of the whole that was possible only from the viewpoint of the Absolute Spirit—a viewpoint that Marx had already

10. Gramsci is very explicit: "The laceration which happened to Hegelianism has been repeated with the philosophy of praxis." Antonio Gramsci, *Prison Notebooks*, ed. Quintin Hoare and Geoffrey Nowell-Smith (London, 1971), p. 396. It is significant that already in 1916 Gramsci had identified this internal contradiction in Hegel's thought and unreservedly opted for the Spaventean solution—so much so that he considered Vera's right-wing interpretation completely discredited: "In the struggle between the Syllabus and Hegel, it is Hegel who won, because Hegel is the life of thought which knows no limit and poses itself as something transient, that can be overcome, always renewable along with history, and the Syllabus is the barrier, it is the death of internal life, it is a problem of culture and not a historical fact." Antonio Gramsci, "Il Sillabo di Hegel," originally published in *Il Grido del Popolo*, 15 January 1916; now in Antonio Gramsci, *Scritti Giovanili* (Turin, 1958), p. 17.

11. Loyd Easton and Kurt Guddat, trans., *Writings of the Young Marx on Philosophy and Society* (Garden City, N.Y., 1967), p. 321.

rejected. Marx's critique of Hegel thus rules out the very possibility of Marxism understood as systematic specification of the logic of the historical process. Eventually, this led Marx to formulate the methodological reorientation that *in principle* ruled out the completion of the project of *Capital*.

In short, what both Spaventa and Marx ran up against is the problem of the epistemological foundation of the concrete totality. Without the idealist Hegelian foundation, the kind of genetic reconstruction worked out in the *Phenomenology*—and which Marx tried to parallel along materialist lines in the *Grundrisse*[12]—was no longer possible. Marx abruptly confronted the problem when he discovered that the Asiatic mode of production could not be forced into a genetic scheme of universal history leading to capital and its eventual internal disintegration. The Asiatic mode of production, which seemed to freeze the otherwise irresistible teleology driving toward capitalist relations, exploded the possibility of any *objectivistic* historical reconstruction.[13] This is why *Capital* starts out with the commodity form and attempts to unpack all capitalist relations and contradictions from that one archetypal form. But this is also bound to fail in its claim to systematic completeness, since what is required to sustain such a specification of all the determinations of the concrete totality is once again a *Geist*-like collective subjectivity whose existence the theory itself has already disdainfully rejected. Marx avoided coming to terms with this problem by writing "critiques" that allowed him to reveal

12. Karl Marx, *Grundrisse*, trans. Martin Nicolaus (London, 1973), pp. 471 ff.

13. For a more elaborate account, see Paul Piccone, "Reading the *Grundrisse*: Beyond Orthodox Marxism," *Theory and Society* II, 2 (Summer 1975), 235–255. That there was a change of plans in Marx's own work is universally recognized in Marx scholarship. But the various reasons adduced for the shift, e.g., the nature of the subject matter (Grossmann), a final proper methodological posing of the problem (Behrens), or a shift to a more appropriate mode of presentation after completing his preliminary research (Rosdolsky), all fail to come to grips with the fundamental problem within the *Grundrisse*, which may explain the change in the plan of *Capital*: that is, the impossibility of providing a systematic genetic reconstruction that at the same time shows the necessity of revolution in situations in which the revolution, which ushers in collective subjectivity and the classless society, has not yet taken place. For previous attempts to deal with Marx's change of plans, see Henryk Grossmann, *Die Akkumulations- und Zusammenbruchsgesetz der Kapital* (Frankfurt am Main, 1967); Friedrich Behrens, *Zur Methode der politischen Oekonomie* (Berlin, 1952); and

the inevitable one-sidedness of whatever he was examining at the time, but that did not require him to undertake the impossible task of setting out all of the determinations involved in constituting it. *Capital*, as yet another of these one-sided exposés of the ideological character of bourgeois thought, likewise did not require an exhaustive (and therefore impossible) spelling out of all determinations in order to fulfill its political emancipatory function. In so doing, Marx successfully sidestepped the fundamental dilemma of post-Hegelian thought—a variation of Gödel's theorem whereby one either has relevance but lacks completeness, or has completeness without relevance.[14]

It is not surprising, then, that Marx's project remained unfinished—not because he ran out of time but because the project itself could not be finished without the coming about of collective subjectivity and of the classless society.

The situation is even more complicated for Marx's followers, who stressed precisely those aspects of Marx's theory that were most problematic in their efforts to turn Marx's project into a self-contained objective science. As the young Gramsci indicated, Marx was not safe from the songs of the positivist sirens that were so popular in the late nineteenth century, and ended up "introducing positivist elements into his work."[15] The Second International was itself unable and unwilling to undertake the kind of philosophical reconstitution that Labriola (*alone* among his socialist contemporaries) demanded. Its leaders were content to view Marxism as an objectivistic positive science, in the belief that Marx and modern science had advanced way

Roman Rosdolsky, *Zur Entstehungsgeschichte des Marxschen 'Kapitals'* (Frankfurt am Main, 1968). An Adornian interpretation of *Capital* as a collection of extended and brilliant aphorisms that, however, never came together in any systematic exposition, remains to be done.

14. For a further discussion of this, see Michael Kosok, "The Formalization of Hegel's Thought," *International Philosophical Quarterly* IV, 4; and his "The Dialectical Matrix: Towards Phenomenology as a Science," *Telos*, no. 5 (Spring 1970).

15. Antonio Gramsci, "Mysteries of Poetry and Culture," originally published 19 October 1918; now in Pedro Cavalcanti and Paul Piccone, eds., *History, Philosophy and Culture in the Young Gramsci* (St. Louis, 1975), p. 18. For a more systematic and recent account, see Albrecht Wellmer, "The Latent Positivism of Marx's Philosophy of History," in Wellmer, *Critical Theory of Society*, trans. J. Cummings (New York,

beyond Hegel. But precisely because of this scientistic emphasis, the socialists of the Second International "fell back to pre-Hegelian and at times pre-Kantian theoretical positions."[16] Their misguided scientificity was no theoretical aberration or political betrayal; rather, it represented one of the two possible solutions—both equally unattractive—to the problem of systematizing Marxism in a situation where collective subjectivity was still a pipe dream. The choice was between the restoration of a transcendental foundation to Marxism, on the one hand, or objectivistic reduction, on the other. By interpreting Marxism as an objectivistic theory of social development, either the theory's revolutionary character becomes totally arbitrary and external (a moral ideal), or else it comes to be guaranteed by a theory of the crash (as resulting from the very nature of things).[17] In either case, radical social change no longer made any sense except as a mere unbroken extension of the logic of the given—i.e., reformism. Since only the powerful notion of necessity generated by the Hegelian dialectic's identification of being and thought can confidently prefigure a revolutionary outcome, once the economic system displaces the Absolute as the concrete totality, revolution deteriorates to a technical matter of further specifying *existing* determinations.[18] It is no accident that the political bankruptcy of the Second International at the beginning of World War I resulted in a rethinking of the whole of Marxist theory, including an attempted re-Hegelianization by Lenin and Western Marxists that reintroduced roughly the same split as that

---

1971), pp. 67–119.

16. Andrew Arato, "The Second International," *Telos*, no. 18 (Winter 1973–74), p. 46.

17. For an account of how this moral ideal was introduced and functioned within the Second International, see Lucio Colletti, *Ideologia e Società* (Bari, 1963), pp. 97–103; and Arato, "Second International," pp. 37–46.

18. Of all contemporary scholars defending Marxism as an objective science, Colletti has been the only one to realize fully that the price to be paid for such a theoretical choice is the abandonment of both the dialectic and any notion of revolution. Lucio Colletti, *Intervista Politico-Filosofica* (Bari, 1975). See also his earlier formulation of the problem in "Marxismo: Scienza o Rivoluzione?" in Colletti, *Ideologia e Società*, pp. 305–314. Since Marxism as a science collapses, in terms of the prevailing criteria of scientificity within contemporary philosophy of science, Colletti was eventually forced to abandon Marxism altogether. See Lucio Colletti, *Tramonto dell' Ideologia* (Bari, 1980).

which existed between Vera and Spaventa.[19]

As Gramsci realized, in a situation where the sociohistorical conditions for the full emergence of collective subjectivity are not yet given[20]—as in pre–World War I Europe—Marxism was "forced to ally itself with extraneous tendencies in order to combat the residues of the pre-capitalist world that still exist among the popular masses, especially in the area of religion."[21] The primacy of an already attained self-consciousness (*Logic*) is not reconciled with subjective self-becoming (*Phenomenology*), and both tendencies remain abstract and rooted in existing social realities: sophisticated bourgeois culture contraposed to a crude popular ideology. Those whom Gramsci called "great intellectuals" had either rejected Marxism and incorporated parts of the philosophy of praxis into reconstituted neo-Hegelian systems (Croce, Gentile), or, in choosing to remain Marxist, had subjected "the new conception to a systematic revision rather than to advance its autonomous development."[22] But in the meantime, the popular version of the theory, concerned with the didactic tasks of raising consciousness, "was combined into a form of culture which, although a little higher than the popular average (itself very low), was still absolutely inadequate to combat the ideologies of the educated classes."[23] As a high-powered philosophy, Marxism had been re-embourgeoisified, and in its economistic reduction that was meant for mass consumption, it had "become 'prejudice' and 'superstition.' "[24]

19. For a systematic analysis of Lenin's turn to Hegel, see Raya Dunayevskaya, *Philosophy and Revolution* (New York, 1973), chap. 3, pp. 95–120.

20. Of course, in his early works Gramsci had taken a much more voluntarist position—to the point of welcoming the Bolshevik Revolution as a break with traditional Marxism precisely on the ground that the collective will could short-circuit the tedious gradualism deduced from the social-democratic interpretation of *Capital*. See his "The Revolution Against *Capital*," in Cavalcanti and Piccone, *History, Philosophy and Culture*, pp. 123–128.

21. Gramsci, *Prison Notebooks*, p. 392.

22. Ibid., p. 397.

23. Ibid., pp. 392–393.

24. Ibid., p. 396. As Gramsci puts it elsewhere: "The philosophy of praxis has undergone in reality a double revision, that is to say, it has been subsumed into a double philosophical combination. On the one hand, certain of its elements, implicitly or explicitly, have been absorbed and incorporated by a number of idealist currents (one need mention only Croce, Gentile, Sorel, Bergson even pragmatism). On the other hand, the so-called orthodoxy, concerned to find a philosophy which, according to their

This is one reason Gramsci devoted so much energy to discrediting Bukharin's crude pseudo-Marxist views and to reradicalizing Crocean philosophy (the highest point of re-Hegelianized bourgeois culture) within a general project of demolishing bourgeois cultural hegemony and raising the consciousness of the masses to the highest level attained in Western civilization.[25] That a version of Bukharin's brand of Marxism-Leninism came to displace Gramsci's Hegelian Marxism after 1926 when Palmiro Togliatti took over the Italian Communist party can be interpreted only as a major theoretical regression in the face of fascism and Stalinism—a theoretical mortgage that remains to be amortized to this day.

Internationally, this same contradiction between the *system* and the *process* reappears after World War I in the clashes between Marxist-Leninists and council communists. Already in Lukács's *History and Class Consciousness* the collective subjectivity necessary to provide the epistemological foundation was projected as the main future achievement of the classless society, so that the whole theory found its justification on the pragmatic ground that its success would redeem the whole revolutionary effort.[26] But in a reductive application of the whole-part dialectic, Lukács came to entrust the viewpoint of the totality to the party—or even to the leader[27]—thus providing a sophisticated neo-Hegelian apology for Stalinism, which, under the aegis of a secularized *Geist*, reproduced relations of domination even more brutal than anything known under bourgeois rule. The council com-

---

extremely limited viewpoint, was more comprehensive than just a 'simple' interpretation of history, have believed themselves orthodox in identifying this philosophy fundamentally with traditional materialism." Ibid., p. 389.

25. This theoretical task was so important for Gramsci that it became *the* crucial element: "The proletariat will destroy the southern agrarian *bloc* to the extent to which, through its Party, it succeeds in organizing ever larger masses of peasants of autonomous and independent formation; but it will succeed to a more or less large extent in this obligatory task according to its capacity to break up the intellectual *bloc* which forms the flexible but very resistant armor of the agrarian *bloc*." Antonio Gramsci, *The Modern Prince and Other Writings* (New York, 1957), p. 51.

26. For a fuller elaboration of this problem, see Paul Piccone, "Dialectic and Materialism in Lukács," *Telos*, no. 11 (Spring 1972), pp. 105–133.

27. George Lukács, *Lenin*, trans. Nicholas Jacobs (London, 1970). Of course, Lukács's apology was neither influential nor really necessary. What it does indicate, however, is the totalitarian implication of *possible* interpretations of post-Hegelian

munists, in contrast, rejected outright the party's claim to a monopoly on consciousness, concentrating instead on popular self-becoming.[28]

Marxists in Italy likewise could not escape this problem and were forced, more than elsewhere, to confront it head-on—which may help explain the open and developing nature of Eurocommunism today. Already in Labriola, the problem was recognized and partly articulated in a call to develop Marxism into an autonomous *Weltanschauung* free of both positivist and spiritualist encrustations. One of the factors that kept this problem constantly on the theoretical and political front burner was the predominance of the Catholic church in Italy. Thus, Hegelianism and its revolutionary progeny, Marxism, became substitutes for the Protestant Reformation, which had by-passed Italy.[29] That Hegelianism was still a lively tradition in Italy rescued the philosophical dimension of political discourse from falling into the oblivion that was its fate almost everywhere else. Italy's Hegelianism, further, served to check the development of political and theoretical aberrations that became the hallmark of other European varieties of Marxism-Leninism.

Labriola's Path to Marxism

Labriola's father had known the Spaventa brothers from the pre-1848 days when Bertrando Spaventa was teaching in Montecasino's schools. Thus, it was only natural that the elder Labriola would ask his

---

philosophy.

28. For some recent discussion of council communism, see Paul Mattick, "Anti-Bolshevist Communism in Germany," *Telos*, no. 26 (Winter 1975–76), pp. 57–69; Gian Enrico Rusconi, "Korsch's Political Development," *Telos*, no. 27 (Spring 1976), pp. 61–78; Guido De Masi and Giacomo Marramao, "Councils and State in Weimar Germany," *Telos*, no. 28 (Summer 1976), pp. 3–35; Gabriella M. Bonacchi, "The Council Communists between the New Deal and Fascism," *Telos*, no. 30 (Winter 1976–77), pp. 43–72; and Franklin Adler, "Factory Councils, Gramsci and the Industrialists," *Telos*, no. 31 (Spring 1977), pp. 67–90.

29. Thus, Gramsci writes: "The intellectual and moral (i.e., 'religious') 'reform' of popular import has already occurred twice in the modern world: the first time with the diffusion of the principles of the French Revolution, and the second time with the diffusion of a series of concepts derived from the philosophy of praxis and often contaminated with the philosophy of the enlightenment and scientistic evolutionism." Gramsci, *Quaderni del Carcere*, ed. Valentino Gerratana (Turin, 1975), III, 1985.

old friend for help[30] when his son Antonio refused to enter a monastery and instead went to Naples to study.[31] Bertrando was not able to find work for the young Labriola as a librarian, but, through the intervention of his brother Silvio, he did manage to get Labriola appointed as a police officer in December 1863. This employment enabled Labriola to continue his education at the University of Naples,[32] where in Labriola's own words thirty years later, he quickly became familiar with "all Hegelian and post-Hegelian philosophy."[33] Labriola fully absorbed Spaventa's critical Hegelianism, fought the same cultural battles, and, after Spaventa's death in 1882, brought this line of thinking to its logical conclusion by embracing Marxism. As Garin puts it, "The relation between Labriola and Spaventa, the dialectical coexistence of Hegelianism and Herbartism in Labriola, as well as his harsh and polemical attitude toward positivism, cannot be understood independently of Spaventa's teachings from 1862 on."[34]

Already, at the age of nineteen, Labriola showed exceptional ability.[35] In one of his earliest philosophical studies, he not only defended Hegelian philosophy against Edward Zeller's neo-Kantianism, which was just beginning to emerge in Germany, but he did so by stressing the same active elements that Spaventa was simultaneously elaborating. Labriola acknowledged the stagnation within the Hegelian

30. It was Antonio Tari, another Neapolitan Hegelian, who wrote Labriola's letter of introduction to Spaventa, wherein the young Labriola is described as "a potential philosopher of the first rank. Young as he is, he already has first-hand knowledge of Aristotle, Spinoza, and Kant, and devours and assimilates whatever of Hegel falls into his hands." As quoted in Luciano Cafagna, "Profilo Biografico e Intellettuale," *Rinascita* XI, 4 (April 1954), 257.

31. In fact, in 1861 Spaventa found a gymnasium teaching job for Labriola's father in Naples, where the whole family moved. C. Fiorilli, "Antonio Labriola," *Nuova Antologia*, March 1906, pp. 59−60; as quoted in Luigi Dal Pane, *Antonio Labriola* (Rome, 1935), pp. 437−438.

32. In a letter dated 13 June 1863, Spaventa described Labriola to his brother Silvio as a "youth of great talent"; in a subsequent letter of 7 July that year, he called him a youth "with much talent, what can really be called talent." Silvio Spaventa, *Lettere Politiche (1861−1893)* (Bari, 1926), pp. 45, 56.

33. To Engels, 14 March 1894; now in Karl Marx and Friedrich Engels, *Corrispondenza con Italiani (1848−1895)*, ed. Giuseppe del Bo (Milan, 1964), p. 525.

34. Eugenio Garin, "Introduzione" to Antonio Labriola, *La Concezione Materialistica della Storia* (Bari, 1965), p. xxix.

35. Dal Pane, *Antonio Labriola*, pp. 34−35, claims that the following description

camp, but he located the problem in "the school and not in the principle." The problem resulted from the excesses of the school when it dogmatically attempted to reduce all new developments to the already given articulations of an all-encompassing system. Thus, "by *absolute knowledge*, Hegel understood that knowledge is in itself all that is *knowable*; but what is knowable certainly is not now *actually* all *known*."[36] The same argument resurfaced in 1872 when Labriola reviewed Vera's *Philosophy of History* and chastised "orthodox" Hegelianism for suffocating particularity within what he called a *philosophia pigrorum*, which reduced everything to the empty formula of "the idea is all, and all is idea," and which was rapidly becoming historically irrevelant.[37]

Movement and self-becoming took precedence over the system for Labriola, helping to explain his later predilection for Spinoza and Johann Herbart, not as replacements for Hegel but as means for making Hegel's system more concrete. What Labriola regarded as significant in Spinoza was the advantage his theory had "of not presupposing anything other than man as natural power, without the

---

provided by Taine may very well have been of Labriola: "I have seen a young man twenty-one years old who has worked all alone and by himself, and who knows Sanskrit, Persian, a dozen languages, who knows very well Hegel, Herbart, Schopenhauer, Stuart Mill, and Carlyle, who is up to date on all our French writings and all new German developments, all that pertains to law, philosophy, and linguistics. His erudition and understanding are those of a forty-year-old man." See Hyppolite Taine, *Voyage en Italie* (Paris, 1898), I, 93. Although Giovanni Mastroianni, in his "Un Jeune Homme de Vingt et Un Ans," reprinted in his *Da Croce a Gramsci* (Urbino, 1972), pp. 135–146, shows convincingly that the young man described by Taine was not Labriola but someone else, the fact that there has been so much doubt is sufficient indication of Labriola's clearly exceptional credentials.

36. Antonio Labriola, "Contro il 'Ritorno a Kant' Propugnato da Eduardo Zeller," in Antonio Labriola, *Scritti Varii di Filosofia e Politica*, ed. B. Croce (Bari, 1906), p. 33. Consistent as ever, twenty-five years later Labriola would extend this formulation as follows: "All the knowable may be known; and all the knowable will be known in an infinite time; and beyond what is knowable, within the field of cognition, it has no importance for us." See Antonio Labriola, *Socialism and Philosophy*, trans. Ernest Untermann (St. Louis, 1980), p. 112 (translation modified).

37. Originally published in *Zeitschrift für exacte Philosophie im Sinne des neuern philosophischen Realismus* X, 1 (1872), 79–86; reprinted in Labriola, *Scritti Varii*, pp. 120–127. Among other things, in this review Labriola took exception to Rosenkranz's bunching of Spaventa and Vera into the same general philosophical category of "Neapolitan Hegelians."

metaphysical presupposition of the good as something substantial, and without the pretension of preaching morality where the law of nature speaks.''[38]

This apparent shift to naturalism does not in the least entail any kind of concession to those positivist fashions that Labriola's contemporaries succumbed to—especially in the face of the growing theoretical sclerosis of "orthodox" Hegelianism. Since for "critical" Hegelians the validity of Hegel's thought consisted primarily in its ability to provide adequate determinations for particularity, psychology came to take on added significance in a context where the breach between the allegedly fully determined whole seemed increasingly to contradict the still-developing parts. This is why Labriola contraposed the *genetic* to the *dialectical* concept: in Hegel "it is not a matter of having the ideas ready-made to subsequently see how they manifest themselves, unfold, or are applied, but the very unfolding of history in its reality and concreteness is the revelation of the ideal human goal."[39] Thus, the emphasis falls on the *source* of ideas and on what Labriola calls the "psychology of peoples," whose task is:

1. to trace historically the origins of ideas and to substitute for the problems of individual psychology the broader problem of social psychology; 2. to find the primitive psychological data whence the ideas governing history develop and proceed through interconnections and fusion; 3. To explain the psychological conditions of social cohesion.[40]

Understandably, this parallels Spaventa's work on psychopathologies, written around the same time (1872), which sought to vindicate a theory of *emergent* consciousness against either *reductive* or *dualist* solutions.[41] It was a matter of fighting the same old battles against the abstract universalism of spiritualists, on the one hand, and the equally abstract particularism of positivists, on the other, by elaborating a notion of self-constituting collective subjectivity whose unfolding trajectory had as its arrival point a socioeconomic framework: Marx-

38. Labriola, *Scritti Varii*, p. 86.
39. Quoted in Dal Pane. *Antonio Labriola*, p. 118, from Labriola's examination of 1871 on the theme, "Whether the Idea Is the Foundation of History."
40. Ibid., p. 123.
41. Bertrando Spaventa, "Sulle Psicopatie in Generale," in B. Spaventa, *Opere*, II, 321–404.

ism as a philosophy of praxis.

From Herbart, Labriola appropriated a theory of psychology, ethics, and pedagogy, but *not* in order to *displace* Spaventa's Hegelianism, but to *ground* it better within the sociohistorical dimension.[42] This explains why Labriola never gave any thought to Herbart's metaphysics. Although it had served Herbart well enough as his whole theoretical apparatus, it turned out to be redundant for Labriola, who, after all, sought to remain within the general Hegelian framework but avoid the vacuous universalism of the (orthodox) Right-Hegelians. The tension between the system and the process for which it provided a structure remained in Labriola's thinking, but the emphasis shifted from the level of abstract reconciliations within a preordained philosophical framework to a more concrete plane involving sociohistorical conflicts. Far from constituting a break in Labriola's intellectual development, his attraction to Herbart's thought turned out to be a major step in the *politicization* of his critical Hegelianism, even though Labriola himself considered this a break with Hegel.[43] In time, this "social psychology" became "class consciousness."

Throughout this period, not only were Labriola and Spaventa in full theoretical agreement—as can be seen from the voluminous correspondence between the two after 1873, when Labriola finally secured a university post in Rome[44]—but they also shared the same political views. Thus, while Spaventa was writing about psychopathologies in order to show that their foundation existed neither exclusively in the

42. Thus, Croce writes: "What did Labriola actually appropriate from Herbart? For some time he followed the ethics and the pedagogy: but the metaphysics, which is the foundation of the system, seemed to remain foreign to him, so much so that he never discussed it." Benedetto Croce, "La Filosofia di Herbart," *La Critica* VI (1908); as quoted in Eugenio Garin, *Cronache di Filosofia Italiana (1900–1943)* (Bari, 1966), I, 180–181.

43. Thus, in a letter dated 2 January 1904, exactly a month before his death, Labriola writes Croce: "In 1869 . . . I was already outside that order of ideas. . . . Bertrando . . . has tolerated that I, as his friend and associate for about 24 years, was not his follower." Antonio Labriola, *Lettere a Benedetto Croce (1885–1904)*, (Naples, 1975), p. 373. Since, however, Labriola was reacting to Gentile's recycling of Spaventa, these words are to be taken with a grain of salt.

44. Giuseppe Berti, "123 Lettere Inedite di Antonio Labriola a Bertrando Spaventa," *Rinascita* X, 1 (January 1954), 65–87.

"soul" nor in purely physiological causes but in the psychophysical organism (and therefore in *social* psychology), and Labriola was entering his psychologistic, Herbartian phase in order to provide *genetic* content to the empty dialectic of orthodox Hegelianism, both men were becoming more and more disillusioned with Italian political life. While it is undeniable that there were strong internal strains necessitating an increasing concretization of their critical Hegelianism, what was even more decisive in determining the direction of their ideas in this period were the political events they witnessed. As Ragionieri points out: "Labriola's essays on the materialist conception of history turn out to be absolutely incomprehensible unless considered also as the arrival point of his political experiences."[45] And Ragionieri's claim holds true for Labriola's entire career: philosophy and politics were intertwined throughout.

The year 1872 was critical in Naples. The reactionary Bourbon and clerical forces almost succeeded in regaining control of the city in the face of the complete ineptitude and corruption of the liberals and the moderates.[46] This development can be explained in large part by the shift to the North of all political initiative, which occurred after the initial enthusiasm for Italian unification had subsided and the general Neapolitan social and economic climate had begun to deteriorate. The original project of instituting a new secular cultural hegemony had failed. As Labriola said in 1887, "The State made a very grave mistake: it did not pay as much attention as it should have to the

---

45. Ernesto Ragionieri, *Socialdemocrazia Tedesca e Socialisti Italiani* (Milan, 1976), p. 337.

46. Between 28 June and 2 August 1872, Labriola published ten letters in Florence's newspaper *La Nazione*, where he bitterly analyzed the political situation: "The reproach which outside of Italy has been made of Italian *liberalism*, i.e., of having been able to negate, but of being unable to sow the seeds of a new religious life in the country, can be reasonably applied in Naples as in no other part of the country. . . . Thus, in Naples it has happened that the liberals have split into so many factions that become increasingly fragmented, and that outside of these factions all the rest of the population has closed in a passive opposition in which it is impossible to distinguish the Bourbon from the cleric, the cleric from the religious ones, the religious liberal from the irreligious liberal." Antonio Labriola, "Lettere Napoletane," *Cronache Meridionali*, 4 August 1954, pp. 558–584. See also Giuseppe Berti, "Lettere Inedite di Antonio Labriola: Alcune Lettere a Ruggero Bonghi," *Rinascita*, XI, 3 (March 1954), 217–228.

culture of the masses.''[47] This collapse of the liberal program just about shattered any lingering hope of realizing the dream of the Hegelian ''ethical state.'' As Croce recalled in his 1904 eulogy for Labriola:

> Once he told me of having come to socialism through the critique of the idea of the State. When the ethical State, fantasized by German popularizers, turned out to be a utopia, and the antagonistic interests of the various classes appeared to him as the harsh but sole reality, he found himself in the arms of Marxism.[48]

Labriola eventually came to ridicule the Hegelian ethical state as a ''metaphysical transubstantiation, so much in vogue among German philosophers, e.g., the State as the *Idea*—the State-*Idea* which unfolds in history, the State as the full realization of personality and other such-like mush.''[49]

Labriola himself identified the events in Naples as decisive in the development of his political philosophy and in the stagnation of the Italian state. Describing the shambles of the Italian state in 1887, Labriola traced the blame back to the Neapolitan developments fifteen years earlier: ''This movement to take over municipalities and subsequently University positions and even Parliament—in order to hold back the democratic movement—began in 1872.''[50] And, if we are to believe his account, he came to an understanding of the critical nature of this period much earlier: ''Already in 1873 I wrote against the

47. Antonio Labriola, ''Contro la Conciliazione,'' in Antonio Labriola, *Scritti Politici (1886–1904)*, ed. Valentino Gerratana (Bari, 1970), p. 109. This is the text of a lecture given by Labriola at the University of Rome, 12 June 1887.

48. Benedetto Croce, ''Antonio Labriola, Ricordi,'' originally published in 1904, now in Labriola, *Scritti Varii*, pp. 498–504. Labriola's critique of the ethical state became considerably more harsh with the passing of time.

49. Antonio Labriola, *Essays on the Materialist Conception of History*, trans. Charles H. Kerr (Chicago, 1903), p. 187 (translation slightly modified). Elsewhere, and in a similarly harsh tone, Labriola writes: ''Particularly in Germany, the old feudal customs, the hypocrisy of Protestantism, and the cowardice of a bourgeoisie that exploits favorable economic circumstances without bringing to them either intelligence or revolutionary courage, strengthen the existing state by preserving the lying appearance of an ethical mission to be accomplished. (With how many unpalatable sauces this state ethics, Prussian in the bargain, has been served up by the heavy and pedantic German professors!)'' Ibid., pp. 132–133.

50. Labriola, ''Contro la Conciliazione,'' in Labriola, *Scritti Politici*, p. 110.

guiding principles of the liberal order."[51] From that point on, his politics became more and more radical and, as Gerratana puts it, Labriola seemed to "tread backward the political path followed by Bertrando Spaventa from radicalism to moderatism."[52] His political evaluation of the Italian situation also became more severe, even in his letters to Spaventa: "I keep asking myself whether in Italy there are a dozen people who feel the responsibility of the State; to put an end to the empty forms of freedom, and to re-establish the seriousness of life."[53] In another letter of the same period he writes: "I have much more faith in the 19 million illiterates than in all of our schools; because you can adjust and remake them a hundred thousand times, and they will remain what they are." His disgust with official political life and the universities became so intense that he began to lecture to workers: "I now teach workers. I hope to succeed better than in the University since the frank sense of the multitude is now preferable to all of our fictitious worlds of bureaucratic science."[54] By 1879 he was totally discouraged: "Once I believed that the moderate side was at least a party of government; but how is it to be explained that now it does not know how to do anything? Who will be able to straighten things out?"[55]

Notwithstanding his dissatisfaction with developments in postunification Italy, Labriola's path to Marxism was slow and deliberate. As he repeatedly stressed in his voluminous correspondence, his philo-

51. Antonio Labriola, "Del Socialismo," a lecture originally delivered in Rome, 20 June 1889, now in Labriola, *Scritti Politici*, p. 185. Here, of course, he was referring to his work "Della Libertà Morale," originally published in 1873, now in Antonio Labriola, *Opere*, ed. Luigi Dal Pane (Milan, 1962), III, 1–110. Among other things, in this essay Labriola argued for the secularization of the religious spirit.

52. Valentino Gerratana, "Introduzione" to Labriola, *Scritti Politici*, p. 31.

53. Written during the summer of 1875, now in Berti, "123 Lettere," p. 73.

54. To Spaventa, 10 February 1876. Ibid., p. 74.

55. To Spaventa, summer 1879. Ibid., p. 82. However, Spaventa's own evaluation of the situation was not much more encouraging. Although his correspondence with Labriola has been lost, an idea of his sarcastic attitude toward the general drift of Italian politics can be obtained by skimming through his correspondence with his friend De Meis. Thus, 13 July 1880, he writes: "The balloon has gone up and it has come down. But before deflating completely, if it is possible, allow the poor balloonist to undertake still another little flight, close to the ground, from swamp to swamp, puddle to puddle. Don't you think that our fish fries and spaghetti with clams [typical Neapolitan cuisine—referring to preunification Neapolitan culture] were better than the lasagna,

sophical heritage contributed to his acquisition of Marxism almost as much as his direct political experiences. Thus, in his introductory letter to Engels of 3 April 1890, he writes:

> Very few of my countrymen are able to understand how a man dedicated for many years with indefatigable energy to abstract philosophy, precisely through philosophy could gradually turn to socialism to the point of even participating in practical propaganda. Since you not only dominate all of contemporary culture, but have also made a distinguished contribution to the development of the socialist idea, you will not judge it contrary to the nature of things that a scholar, from the heights of Kant's moral philosophy and passing through Hegel's philosophy of history and Herbart's psychology of people, could reach with conviction the need to publicly profess socialism as if it were his natural mission.

Labriola goes on to mention contributing political factors: "The gradual and uninterrupted approach toward life's practical problems, the disgust with political corruption, the acquaintance with workers, gradually changed my abstract socialism into an active one."[56] Yet, the emphasis remained on Hegelianism and on what he called rigorous

---

these pumpkins and omelets [typical northern Italian cuisine—referring to postunification Italian culture] and . . . these knaves which we are forced to swallow and digest in this modern Italy, always Catholic and, furthermore, Neapolitan and everything else . . . except Italian? . . . Thus, let us go. . . . What more can we do here? Go—hell! I am here and here I stay. It is not that I hope to see this scum treated by events and by fate as it deserves: I don't fool myself—time is on their side. But I stay to say what it is, i.e., a scum *sic et simpliciter*, unconditionally, unqualifiedly, without reserve, pure scum, the ideal and the real scum, the absolute scum. And as I get older, the closer I get to the point when, if nothing else, I will at least have the good fortune of no longer dirtying my feet among them: as it grows bigger and wider and triumphs, the more advances and grows in me the courage to call it scum. . . . I have no illusion or hope." Quoted in Giovanni Gentile, "Bertrando Spaventa," in B. Spaventa, *Opere*, I. 141, 145.

56. Marx and Engels, *Corrispondenza con Italiani*, pp. 358–359. A very similar evaluation can be found in a letter to Turati, 5 June 1897, subsequently published in Labriola, *Socialism and Philosophy*, pp. 116–118. "By a fortunate accident of my life I gained my education under the direct and straight influence of two great systems, which marked the close of that philosophy that we may now call classic. I mean the systems of Herbart and Hegel, which brought to its extreme culmination the antithesis between realism and idealism, between pluralism and monism, between scientific psychology and phenomenology of the spirit, between specialization of method and an anticipation of every method by omniscient dialectics. The philosophy of Hegel had already blossomed out into the historical materialism of Karl Marx, and that of Herbart

"scientific studies."[57]

In 1876 Labriola wrote Spaventa that he was "about to become a socialist,"[58] but Gerratana has shown this claim to be an exaggeration:[59] it was essentially based on Labriola's one lecture in the Roman League for the Instruction of the People, whose meetings were attended even by the city's mayor and other high officials. Only in 1886 did Labriola finally enter the political arena, for a while even entertaining the idea of running for office.[60] But his general perspective remained limited to modernizing Italian politics in a way that would, by establishing a solid two-party system, pull the nation out of the corrupt practices of transformism. His open adherence to socialism up to 1889 entailed little more than advocating the extension of liberal institutions: the completion of the *political* revolution already carried out with a *social* revolution.

> Political liberties are not to be rejected but completed. It will not be a matter of a step backward, but of several steps forward in political democracy. What is sought here for popular sovereignty is the economic sub-

---

into empirical psychology which, under certain conditions and within certain limits, is also experimental, comparative, historical, and social." Thus, it is understandable that he could boast of his Marxism as the result of a long preparation: "Before I became a socialist, I had the inclination, leisure, time, opportunity, and obligation to square my accounts with Darwinism, Positivism, Neo-Kantianism, and so many other scientific questions that developed around me and gave me occasion to develop among my contemporaries. . . . When I turned to Socialism, I did not look to Marx for the abc's of knowledge: I did not look to Marxism for anything except what it actually contains, namely, the determined critique of political economy, the outlines of historical materialism, and its proletarian politics, which it proclaims or implies. Neither did I look to Marxism for a knowledge of that philosophy which is its premise and which it, in a way, continues after having inverted the dialectics of that philosophy. I mean Hegelianism, which flourished in Italy in my youth and in which I had been brought up, as it were."

57. Thus, to Wilhelm Liebknecht, 23 March 1890, Labriola writes that he "came only through scientific studies, and unfortunately very slowly and late, to socialist convictions." Leo Valiani, "Lettere di Antonio Labriola ai Socialisti Tedeschi e Francesi," in *Questioni di Storia del Socialismo* (Turin, 1958), p. 377. In another letter to Engels, 14 March 1894, he writes: "Maybe—rather certainly—I have become a communist through my (rigorously) Hegelian education." Marx and Engels, *Corrispondenza con Italiani*, p. 525.

58. Berti, "123 Lettere", p. 74.

59. Gerratana, "Introduzione" to Labriola's *Scritti Politici*, p. 40.

60. His electoral program is in Labriola, *Scritti Politici*, pp. 105–107. Thus, in a

stratum, and that the economy be raised to the level of morality; what is sought is a *new right* which would be justice truly equal for all. . . . Socialism seeks to resolve the problems that skeptics ignore, liberals postpone indefinitely, and demagogues exploit. *No man slave of another man, no man a tool of another's wealth.*[61]

Such a program, so reminiscent of Spaventa's politics of 1850, culminated with a demand for four rights: "*the right to existence; the right to culture; the right to work; the right to full compensation for the work produced.*"[62]

Less than a year later Labriola gave up this gradualist program in favor of a revolutionary socialism calling for a qualitative break between the liberal and the socialist state: "Between *bourgeois politics* and *socialism* (two distinct periods of history!) there is such a decisive break that no ingenious device will be able to derive the one from the other as if by means of the magic of legislative provisions."[63] His earlier position was implicitly rejected as an "insidious means of *embourgeoisifying* part of the workers at the expense of the proletariat's solidarity." Between 1886 and 1890, Labriola had undertaken serious studies of economics,[64] the philosophy of history, and the French Revolution.[65] This last topic was the subject of his 1888–1889 course and turned out to be a devastating critique of liberalism

letter to Croce, 22 March 1886, he writes: "I am in a quandary. The elections are around the corner. I would have some hope for success if I move fast enough. And even if I failed, I feel a great desire to say my part." On 16 April of that year he writes: "In the second district of Perugia where I would run as the opposition candidate (but this is not yet fully established) there are 4,000 well-disciplined radicals with whom one must come to grips." But by 10 May it was all over. "In Perugia's second district nothing has come through. The *radicals* seem to want to vote for one *name only*, and have not come to an understanding with other elements of the opposition." Labriola, *Lettere a Croce*, pp. 12–14.

61. Ibid., p. 75.

62. Ibid., p. 180.

63. Ibid., p. 223.

64. As he repeatedly indicated, economics always posed problems for Labriola. Thus, in *Socialism and Philosophy*, p. 94, he writes: "While Marxism did not offer any difficulty to me so far as the intrinsic and formal outlines of its conceptions and method were concerned, I acquired its economic content only by dint of hard work."

65. In a footnote omitted from Kerr's English translation of Labriola's *Essays on the Materialist Conception of History*, Labriola writes in 1895: "For some years— eight to be exact—in the University courses that I called either *genesis of modern*

and liberal institutions. It had such a broad political impact that it was followed closely by the local newspapers and became associated with Labriola's political activities,[66] which, during this period, were quite intense.[67] Following riots by unemployed construction workers whose cause had won Labriola's sympathies in early 1889,[68] Labriola's course in the university was disrupted by conservative protesters from 9 February to 16 March.[69]

To understand why Labriola perceived this period as politically explosive, it helps to recall that a year before, in 1888, Filippo Turati split the Democratic Association—a political group espousing nebulous democratic, radical, and socialist ideas—and began to work for the formation of an autonomous Socialist party. Labriola came to see the proletariat organized in this fashion as the historical agency for social reconstruction, and began to study feverishly the works of Marx and Engels. At this point he also began his correspondence with Engels and undertook his new "Marxist" phase.

A German Lost in Italy

By the late nineteenth century, Italian culture had come under the spell of positivism, and Italian radicals were in the thrall of anarchism. As late as 1890, even scholars as distinguished as Labriola—in other regards extremely well informed on developments abroad—were not likely to have been exposed to most "classical" Marxist texts. These texts had not received wide distribution or attention even in Germany or England, and toward the end of the century most of them had long been out of print. There were a few mediocre Italian translations, but

---

socialism or *general history of socialism*, or *on the materialist interpretation of history*, I have had time to appropriate this [Marxist] literature." Labriola, *Concezione Materialistica*, p. 9n. Outlines of Labriola's university courses from 1887 to 1893 are reprinted in Dal Pane, *Antonio Labriola*, pp. 510–520.

66. Dal Pane, *Antonio Labriola*, p. 201.

67. In a letter to Turati, 24 July 1892, he writes: "You are wrong when you think that I do not live in contact with workers. From 1888 to 1 May 1891, I led in Rome a very agitated and noisy life—I made some 200 speeches and have taken part in at least as many meetings—I have organized circles, federations, and cooperatives—I have donated thousands of lire and opuscles—" In Alessandro Schiavi, ed., *Filippo Turati attraverso le Lettere di Correspondenti (1880—1925)* (Bari, 1947), p. 91.

68. For an account of the events, see Dal Pane, *Antonio Labriola*, pp. 473–475.

69. Ibid., p. 455.

most of the main texts were unknown.[70] In 1897, Labriola mentioned the trouble he had had finding some of these texts:

> And how rare are many of these writings, and how hard are some of them to find! Are there many who, like myself, have had the patience to hunt for years for a copy of *The Poverty of Philosophy*, which was but very recently republished in Paris, or of that queer work, *The Holy Family*; or who would be willing to endure more hardship to secure a copy of the *Neue Rheinische Zeitung* than a student of philosophy or history would endure under ordinary conditions in reading and studying all the documents of ancient Egypt? I have the reputation of being a practiced hand in seeking and locating books, but I have never run into more trouble than I did in the quest of that paper. The reading of all the writings of the founders of scientific socialism has so far been largely a privilege of the initiated![71]

In 1891, Labriola had written to Engels that there was only one copy of Marx's *Kritik der politischen Oekonomie* in Rome,[72] and said he had to resort to borrowing *The Holy Family* from Frederick A. Sorge

---

70. As Michels writes: "It was difficult in Italy during that period to obtain Marx's works. With the exception of Cafiero's hard-to-find summary and some other summarizing pamphlets published by another Southern scholar, Pasquale Martiguetti of Benevento, those Italians who sought to consult Marx were forced (unless they could read the original German) to have recourse to the French translation of the first volume of *Capital*, published in 1875. Still, in 1887 Filippo Turati could complain that Marx's and Engels's writings either were defective or else unavailable in Italian versions. True, in 1886 Boccardo had published in the *Biblioteca dell'Economista*, an Italian translation of *Capital*, but this was inaccessible to those of modest means, and the translation tasted both of French and German." Robert Michels, *Storia Critica del Movimento Socialista Italiano Dagli Inizi Fino al 1911* (Florence, 1921), p. 135. See also Dal Pane, *Antonio Labriola*, p. 454.

71. Labriola, *Socialism and Philosophy*, p. 67. In a letter to Croce, 16 May 1895, Labriola provides a similar testimony. Describing Croce's efforts to locate some classical Marxist texts as a "desperate case," he writes: "Two years ago I read *Die Heilige Familie* [The holy family] and made a long abstract of it, of a sample loaned to me from England with 500 florins of insurance. Finally I found a copy of it in Vienna (with someone inexperienced) for *twenty* florins. I left its pages uncut—because I have not re-read it. Of *Misère de la Philosophie* [The poverty of philosophy] I had two copies, one of which I recently traded in Vienna for another rarity. And if I were to tell you the whole story of my researches in this area, it would take a whole chapter on literary curiosity." Labriola, *Lettere a Croce*, p. 69.

72. To Engels, 21 February 1891, in Marx and Engels, *Corrispondenza con Italiani*, p. 370.

through Engels's intervention.[73] Yet, by 1902, when Labriola reviewed the four volumes of Marx, Engels, and Lassalle's *Nachlass*, published by Franz Mehring, he could boast that, of the documents contained in the 1,477 pages, he was already familiar with all but Marx's doctoral dissertation on the differences between Epicurus's and Democritus's philosophies—and even Engels himself lacked a copy of that work, which had up until then been thought forever lost.[74]

Even before he studied the classics of Marxism, Labriola was already widely recognized as "among Italians, the one best acquainted with German philosophy,"[75] and had been called the "Italian Lassalle."[76] Italian socialists, who regarded him as their leading theoretician, chose him to write their official address to German socialists meeting in Halle.[77] But, as Dal Pane points out:

Labriola's position represented an exceptional case, almost unique. In brief, he mastered the fundamental principles of economics, simultaneously studied the history of proletarian and socialist movements, became up-to-date concerning the most lively questions of various countries' proletarian classes, and entered into relations with the men most representative of international socialist culture. In 1890 he was already in Italy the most conspicuous socialist theoretician, even though he had written little, and

73. Engels to Sorge, 30 December 1893: "Labriola is a rigorous Marxist. To this end he has acquired all of the necessary publications, but he has never succeeded in seeing *The Holy Family*, even though in announcements published in 'Bulletin for Libraries' of Leipzig and elsewhere he declared himself prepared to pay whatever price." *Briefe und Auszüge aus Briefen von J.P. Becher, J. Dietzgen, Friedrich Engels, Karl Marx und andere an F.A. Sorge und andere* (Stuttgart, 1906), pp. 405–406. Another letter from Labriola to Engels, 5 November 1894, indicates that Labriola was also to obtain from Vienna a copy of *The Holy Family* in trade for an extra copy that he had of *The Poverty of Philosophy*. Marx and Engels, *Corrispondenza con Italiani*, p. 569. The same information is to be found also in a letter to Croce, 16 May 1895. Labriola, *Lettere a Croce*, p. 69.

74. Antonio Labriola, "L'Opera Postuma di Marx," originally published 3 December 1902, now in Labriola, *Scritti Politici*, pp. 500–502.

75. *Frankfurter Zeitung*, 3 April 1890, as cited in Dal Pane, *Antonio Labriola*, p. 443.

76. *Parti Ouvrier*, 8 October 1890, as quoted in Dal Pane, *Antonio Labriola*, p. 243.

77. This address is now in Labriola, *Scritti Politici*, pp. 248–250.

that little could not be praised for clarity or logical coherence.[78]

In fact, Labriola did not write much. On several occasions he indicated his disdain for systematic writing, preferring instead the spontaneity of the spoken word.[79] As Croce has implied, however, this predilection tended to conceal some of his theories' internal difficulties. Labriola's reluctance to put his thoughts in written form may have shielded him from those quandaries that inevitably emerge only when ideas are put on paper.[80] Gramsci (who was unaware of the extent and high quality of Labriola's correspondence) was right in emphasizing that to understand Labriola's thought, it is inadequate simply to focus on his written works. "One must also keep in mind the elements and fragments of conversations reported by his friends and students," Gramsci wrote.[81] As Procacci argues,

Labriola's correspondence is qualitatively different from many other correspondences. In fact, not only did Labriola continue in writing to friends and colleagues the discourse and meditations which he had fixed in his major writings, but he gave full expression to that dialectic of conversa-

78. Dal Pane, *Antonia Labriola*, p. 243.

79. Thus, in Labriola, *Socialism and Philosophy*, pp. 151–152, he writes: "To tell the truth, I have never had any great inclination for public writing, and I have never acquired the art of writing in prose. I have always written things as they came to me. I have always been and still am passionately fond of the art of oral instruction in every form. And attending to this work with great intensity, I have long lost the gift of repeating in writing the things that I used to express spontaneously in ready and flexible speech as befitted the occasion, pregnant with side issues and full of references. And who can really repeat such things from memory? Later when I was born again in spirit and accepted Socialism, I became more desirous of communicating with the public by means of booklets, occasional letters, articles, and lectures, and these grew in time almost without my being aware of it." The same problem arises even in the correspondence with Engels. Thus, in a letter of 9 November 1891, Labriola writes: "But I have the annoyance of having many things in my hands, besides being by nature more inclined to talk than to write." Antonia Labriola, *Lettere a Engels* (Bari, 1963), p. 38.

80. Thus, Croce writes: "Having observed him for some time, I knew of the problems and obstacles that Labriola encountered when, from the heat of discussion and from the incisive outlining of his thought in lectures, he sought to shift to writing. Maybe the reasons for this were in the very proficiency of his oral discourse, which can easily conceal to the speaker himself the lacunae in the *iunctura rerum*, inexorably revealed to those who attempt to write." Benedetto Croce, *Materialismo Storico ed Economia Marxistica* (Bari, 1973), pp. 258–259.

81. Gramsci, *Quaderni del Carcere*, II, 1060. This methodological point in deal-

tionalist that so fascinated his students, especially in his correspondence destined abroad, to which can almost be attributed the value of political documents. . . . At any rate, one gets the distinct impression that as a correspondent Labriola never let himself go and that he attributed to parts of his correspondence a character more official than familiar. Certainly, in this there was a modicum of naivete and also of presumption, as if he sought through his many correspondents to carry out a directing function in relation to the Italian labor movement.

In a nutshell, Labriola's correspondence is absolutely indispensable in reconstructing not only his "biography in the strict sense, but also his intellectual biography."[82] Only such a broadened account can show how Labriola in both political activity and theoretical work almost independently reached its outer limit: the inability to provide a consistent genetic reconstruction that could "scientifically" demonstrate the necessity of the revolution. Unlike his contemporaries in the Second International, Labriola did not rush to any easy but false solutions. He had the intellectual integrity to recognize the severity of the problems and to leave them open.

Labriola's description of himself as "a German lost in Italy" was more appropriate than he may have liked to admit.[83] His unusual intellectual formation and political leanings explain his enthusiasm for active socialist politics from 1889 to 1893,[84] when he hoped to transpose into Italian social life an idealized version of German social

---

ing with Labriola has been made by nearly all those who have studied his work. Thus, already in 1906, his student Giovanni Amendola could write that "the spiritual unity of Antonio Labriola was much more in his lively personality than in his various scientific productions," so that the study of his fragments and correspondence "provides the complete sensation of the author much better than do studies of more specialized subjects published during the course of his scientific career." Giovanni Amendola, "Scritti Postumi di Antonio Labriola," originally published in *Rivista di Roma*, 25 March 1906, reprinted as "Appendice II" to Labriola, *Lettere a Benedetto Croce*, p. 404.

82. Giuliano Procacci, "Antonio Labriola e la Revisione del Marxismo attraverso l'Epistolario con Bernstein e con Kautsky (1895–1904)," *Annali Feltrinelli* III (1961), 265.

83. This is how Labriola described himself to Engels, 22 August 1893. Marx and Engels, *Corrispondenza con Italiani*, p. 499.

84. On 27 May 1894, Labriola wrote: "Up to last year I was wholly in the party and all for the party." Antonio Labriola, "Lettere a Costa," ed. Giovanni Bovio, *Quarto Stato* IV, 10–11, p. 45.

democracy, which at that time, after its 1890 electoral success, the fall of Bismarck, and the abolition of the extraordinary antisocialist laws, enjoyed considerable popularity in European radical circles. In a fashion reminiscent of Spaventa's thesis concerning "the circulation of Italian thought" (whereby Italian philosophy picks up not where it left off during the Counter-Reformation, but at the heights of German idealism), Labriola projected a similar operation with regard to socialist politics. As Ragionieri puts it, in Labriola's thought, "German social democracy occupies the same place that classical German philosophy had occupied in Bertrando Spaventa's thought."[85] And Labriola himself was not unaware of this analogy. In *Socialism and Philosophy*, immediately after criticizing his Neapolitan Hegelian teachers for carrying on "a dialogue which appeared as a monologue to their audience and readers," he quickly adds:

> This unpleasant and unattractive recollection came to my mind when I began writing the first of my two essays on historical materialism. . . . But then I asked myself quite often: How shall I go about it to say things which will not appear hard, foreign, and strange to Italian readers?[86]

Labriola from the very beginning understood his task of introducing rigorous Marxist theory into Italy in terms of the assimilation of the German social-democratic experience. In 1890 he writes:

> Let us by all means quicken the pace; so that we can avoid repeating what happened to us in the sixteenth century when, having provided the weapons of our intellect and of humanism to the civilized world, we fell precisely at the rise of the new Europe. Today also, as in 1520, the signal of the new history comes from Germany![87]

Again in 1896, even after political disappointment and retreat, he defines his task in roughly the same terms:

> For now I feel, *first of all*, the duty of placing Italians in a position to know what scientific socialism is. To this end simple polemics are not useful, nor are translations from foreign languages sufficient. What is needed is the

85. Ragionieri, *Socialdemocrazia*, pp. 250–251.
86. Labriola, *Socialism and Philosophy*, p. 92.
87. To Alfredo Baccarini, published in *Il Risveglio*, 9 March 1890; now in Labriola, *Scritti Politici*, p. 202.

assimilation from the visual angle of the national brain.[88]

Only the general disillusionment with German social democracy (in relation to the Eduard Bernstein debate and the so-called "crisis of Marxism") gradually cooled Labriola's enthusiasm. After 1893, Garin says,

> his battle becomes primarily limited to the level of ideas, to illustrate, clarify, and defend that critical communism that he had appropriated, to *translate it* into Italian, to tie it to national culture, to use it to understand the history of Italy and its future.[89]

The Difficult Birth of the Italian Socialist Party

Labriola's project of transposing the model of German social democracy to Italy never got off the drawing board, owing to, among other things, the great differences in the development of capitalism and in the social composition of Italy and Germany. As Werner Sombart indicated in a series of articles written before 1895 as preparatory studies for a never-completed book on the Italian labor movement (and while he was still sympathetic to socialist ideas), Italian industrial underdevelopment made unlikely the growth of a labor movement comparable to the one existing in Germany.[90] Werner Sombart, who was one of the very few foreign writers in Italy to have earned Labriola's praise,[91] estimated that Italian industrial develop-

---

88. To Karl Kautsky, 23 March 1896, in Antonio Labriola, "Lettere a E. Bernstein, L. e K. Kautsky (1895–1904)," *Annali Feltrinelli* III (1961), 294.

89. Garin, "Introduzione," p. xlv.

90. Sombart, of course, had studied in Pisa and was very familiar with Italy and its language. His four articles entitled "Studien zur Entwicklungsgeschichte des italienischen Proletariats" appeared between 1893 and 1895 in the *Archiv für soziale Gesetzgebung und Statistik*. Sombart published during the same period a number of articles on Italian matters in several other German journals, particularly *Sozialpolitisches Zentralblatt*. For an excellent analysis of Sombart's work on the Italian labor movement, see Ragionieri, "Werner Sombart e il Movimento Operaio Italiano," in his *Socialdemocrazia*, pp. 359–390.

91. Labriola to Engels, 9 November 1892, in Marx and Engels, *Corrispondenza con Italiani*, p. 453. See also Labriola's article, "La Situazione del Partito Socialista Italiano," originally published in *Leipziger Volkzeitung*, 4 May 1895, now in Labriola, *Scritti Politici*, p. 366. Sombart, too, eventually expressed admiration for Labriola, whom he called "der geistwollste der Orthodoxen," in his *Sozialismus und Soziale Bewegung* (Jena, 1905), p. 273.

ment in the 1890s was comparable to that of Germany in the mid-nineteenth century, and to that of England at the end of the eighteenth century. Furthermore, the uneven pattern of industrial development in northern and southern Italy ruled out any *homogeneous* labor movement. If socialism took root anywhere, Sombart predicted, it would be in agrarian areas.

Labriola, too, was aware of these obstacles.[92] In November 1891, he wrote Engels that "in order for socialism to be born and develop in Italy, many conditions are needed which are now lacking."[93] In August 1892, he was even more pessimistic:

> Nowadays political action in Italy is not possible. It is necessary to write books in order to instruct those who want to be teachers. What is lacking in Italy is half a century of science and of experience of other countries. It is necessary to fill these lacunae.[94]

This backwardness of the Italian political situation in comparison to that in Germany became a source of constant frustration for Labriola, and periodically, whenever his Italian socialist collaborators failed to live up to the high German standards of political practice, this led him to consider—especially in his private correspondence—repudiating political involvement in favor of purely theoretical pursuits. Disgusted with the course of radical politics, in 1891 he threatened Filippo Turati that he would denounce all Italian socialists because of their incompetence and ignorance.

> Thus, I retire from everything and I am awaiting the appropriate occasion to declare in public that I return to be what I was already many years ago

---

92. Needless to say, Labriola was not altogether convinced by Sombart's argument. In fact, in a letter to Engels, 7 April 1894—shortly after Sombart had visited Labriola in Rome—Labriola writes: "He believes that the development of capitalism will be more rapid in Northern Italy, but he does not have much faith in the consistency of Italian socialism. . . . Is Sombart a socialist? He knows Marx very well, as can be seen from his articles against Wolf. But to me he showed himself as a *monarchist* convinced that the monarchy still has that certain social *Beruf* of which they have so boringly spoken in Prussia for the last 50 years. I cut the conversation short with some spicy jokes. Sombart is convinced that in Germany it is time to cut out the revolutionary talk: which, without saying any more, is the old story of state socialism." Marx and Engels, *Corrispondenza con Italiani*, p. 529.

93. Ibid., p. 408.

94. Ibid., p. 443.

without anyone else knowing it, i.e., a *philosopher of socialism*, and that I have nothing in common, either theoretically or practically, with those who in Italy declare themselves to be *socialists*.[95]

The political differences separating Labriola from the rest of Italian socialists—particularly Turati—were rooted in the contradiction in Labriola that arose from trying to base a rigorous vision of politics on both German political philosophy and the history of struggles, and at the same time trying to approach politics from a pluralist, eclectic view more concerned with immediate practicalities than with principles or internal discipline. This divergence is not surprising considering the immense intellectual gulf separating Labriola from the rest of the leading Italian socialists at that time. While Labriola had gradually and painstakingly worked his way toward a careful study of the French Revolution, economics, and the study of socialism, Turati and his friends were the product of precisely the positivist pseudoculture that Labriola had spent so much time combating.[96] As Arfé puts it:

> The Marxism from which such a position derived its organicity and its cutting edge was certainly very different from that of the Herbartian and Hegelian Labriola. In Turati and his friends it was broadly characterized by an honest Lombard positivism, not lacking a strength and a decor of its own, but certainly far from the theoretical rigor typical of the school—the Hegelian one of Naples—from which Labriola came.[97]

No matter how "honest" Turati's "Lombard positivism" may have been, his theoretical vision remained confused, not at all or-

95. Schiavi, *Filippo Turati*, p. 82. In a similar tone, Labriola writes to Engels, 30 March 1891: "Our workers will certainly not be *the heirs of classical German philosophy*, precisely because this philosophy has hardly even passed through the brain of a solitary Italian philosopher. The new generation knows only the positivists, who to me represent the cretin degeneration of the bourgeois type." Marx and Engels, *Corrispondenza con Italiani*, p. 379.

96. As Croce puts it in an article appropriately entitled "Concerning Italian Positivism": "Italian democracy was, no one knows why (other than maybe because of the tendency of popularity, which is almost an irresistible evil in all democracies) positivistic; and my stomach refused to digest it until it took on some spice from Marxist socialism, which, as is now well known, is impregnated with classical German philosophy." Quoted in Garin, *Cronache di Filosofia Italiana*, p. 186.

97. Gaetano Arfè, *Storia del Socialismo Italiano (1892–1926)* (Turin, 1965), p. 11.

ganic, without any "cutting edge." It could not help but be irritating to a thinker of Labriola's caliber. Robert Michels's evaluation of Turati's efforts during this period provides some idea of the prevailing intellectual poverty:

> Those who re-read Turati's articles during the period between 1893 and 1898 remain surprised by the continuous contradiction in his evaluations. If Turati occasionally qualifies Marx's work as untouchable and inviolate, at other times he complains against the stupid fanaticism of the "Pure" for whom Marx was a God and Engels his prophet, and who labeled as deserters whoever disagreed with them (1895). Thus Turati, always impulsive and a lover of somewhat improvised beautiful thoughts, the "literate" Turati, every now and then put aside his cult of Marx in order to take the pleasure of pinching some other faithful follower of the master.[98]

Although both Labriola and Turati may have been speaking about "socialism," they meant qualitatively different things by the term.

The first and most significant disagreement between the two came in 1890, after Turati and Labriola had begun to collaborate in an effort to salvage an autonomous Italian Socialist Party out of the shambles of a radical democracy deemed by both to be a political dead-end. Labriola preferred the German model of a *proletarian* party based on a well-defined program; Turati was in favor of a much less restricted organization, one he thought more appropriate to the backward conditions of Italian society. As early as April, Labriola outlined for Turati his notion of the party, involving spontaneous class organization and the attainment of self-consciousness through the catalytic role of theoreticians, including Labriola himself:

> The *labor party* must constitute itself through the spontaneous action of workers placed in opposition to capitalism by the actual conditions themselves, and by a wisely conducted propaganda effort. We, shall we say, theoretical socialists, can offer the more general and common weapons, but we cannot and should not disturb the proletarian movement with anticipated, premature, and abstract proposals. Yet, we must never refuse to discuss any act or political provision which implies a social interest, since it is desirable that the bourgeois become persuaded that we are the embryo of the future socialist party, and so that the proletarians become used to this

98. Michels, *Storia Critica*, p. 139.

for, if *social democracy* excludes leaders in the jacobin sense of the word, it does not exclude teachers. On the contrary![99]

It was as if Spaventa's old political project of cultural renovation had finally found a social agency able to realize it through the development of objective socioeconomic conditions and the inculcation of a new cultural hegemony based on the highest achievements of Western civilization, providing direction and self-understanding to the new emancipatory forces. But this notion of political organization—a notion peculiar to Italian Marxism from Gramsci to Togliatti up to the present—did not have much popular appeal when Labriola formulated it. As Gerratana notes:

> Turati was convinced that it was first of all necessary to be armed with infinite tactical patience. In Labriola, he had recognized a strong head with clear ideas, but to organize a mass movement in a country where capitalism was scarcely developed as in Italy he held that one had to make allowances for feebler minds with more confused ideas: if, for this, one had to sacrifice some clarity, it was worth the price, which could be compensated by organizational activism. In Labriola's refusal to accept this tactic, Turati could see only doctrinaire obstinacy, or even professional pride.[100]

Unwilling either to accept a heterogeneous organization embracing too broad a spectrum of views and groups, or to compromise, Labriola refused to participate in the new party's founding congress in Genoa, despite Turati's change of mind at the last minute, coming around to Labriola's position calling for a well-defined program and a disciplined socialist party uncontaminated by anarchist and other extraneous elements. Labriola saw Turati's sudden change of heart as a mere extension of the same opportunism that Labriola had so systematically opposed. He writes to Engels:

> I encouraged him [Turati] to choose a path, to decide, to adopt a doctrine and a line of conduct. And he replied by calling me a Marxist, a German, an idealogue, an ignoramus, a logic-lover. Things proceeded in this fashion up to the 25th of July, when I refused to go to Genoa, since Turati and others from Milan kept writing me that a clearly defined program was

99. Schiavi, *Filippo Turati*, p. 74.
100. Valentino Gerratana, ''Realtà e Compiti del Movimento Socialista in Italia nel Pensiero di Antonio Labriola,'' *Annali Feltrinelli* XV (1974), 588.

impossible; that it was convenient to mix with anarchists, socialists, and pure workers; that Italian workers were not mature enough for politics; that it was important to attend; that I should go to Genoa to defend *my* ideas.

Events in the following few days, however, changed the political climate, and Labriola's position became predominant. To his dismay, the results were not encouraging:

> The rest has been a *pasticcio* of the Italian variety, with the usual comedies and bad jokes, and with a good dose of bad faith. The *opportunists* of the day before suddenly turned "Marxists, Germans, and logic-lovers," abandoned their own program to that of their adversaries, and overnight they became the founders of the socialist party by means of an *amendment*.[101]

In spite of his stubborn abstentionism, Labriola was not entirely negative in his appraisal of the new party. "There is the embryo of something. . . . Maybe the suddenly risen small party and its program haphazardly voted on could nurture love of discipline and the decency of responsibility," he wrote to Engels. The point throughout was to have a principled party that, however small, would pose the proper political tasks so that, when the subsequent growth of Italian capitalism would swell the ranks of its potential members, there would be no serious organizational obstacle to the revolutionary outcome. Labriola was in no great rush. He fully recognized that proper political organization took time: "The concept that the socialist party is a political party cannot be forced into workers' minds with a mandate. It is a matter of experience, tactics, education, and instruction, and therefore

101. Marx and Engels, *Corrispondenza con Italiani*, pp. 447–448. See also Labriola's letter to Ellenbogen, 11 September 1894, where, in a similar vein, he writes: "Precisely in those days Turati published an enthusiastic article on Bakunin in *Socialismo Popolare* of Venice and (in a letter) called me crazy for wanting to introduce the *political principle* in the Italian *workers' party*. Others called me idealist, doctrinaire, *Marxist, Germanophile*. At any rate, there was a conversion: the class struggle was proclaimed and all became Marxists in a day." "Lettere di Antonio Labriola a L. Mariano e J.Guesde a V. Adler e W. Ellenbogen a G.V. Plekhanov (1892–1904)," *Annali Feltrinelli* V (1963), 456. Of course, Labriola had on many occasions complained of Turati's duplicity. See his letter to Croce, 14 January 1896: "Turati writes to you and to me contradictory things in one and the same day. I have known him for some time to be neurotic. He has always done this. In the past I have often received his letters that said precisely the opposite of what he had written the very same day in *Critica*, and even the opposite of what, again on the same day, he had written to others here, e.g.,

of time.''[102] Labriola pointed all this out later in a letter to his friend Pasquale Villari, dated 13 November 1900—a letter that Togliatti was particularly fond of quoting since it seemed to capture so well the outlook of the Italian Communist Party in the post—World War II period.

> I have never dreamt that Italian socialism could be a lever to overthrow the capitalist world. No one in the civil world believes this, and first of all, the socialists of other countries don't believe it. I have always understood Italian socialism as a means: 1. to develop the political sense of the multitudes; 2. to educate that part of the workers who can be educated into the class organization; 3. to oppose to the various *camorre* that call themselves parties a strong popular front; 4. to force the government representatives to undertake economic reforms useful to all. The rest of socialist propaganda, in the specific sense of the word, cannot have a practical effect in Italy other than for generations yet to come.[103]

The argument that Italian conditions were not conducive to the formation of a proletarian organization appropriate only to a higher stage of capitalist development was made again and again—and in vain. Labriola's reply throughout was to insist on the need for a *small* embryonic party with limited but principled objectives, uncompromising in its outlook. In a letter to Turati dated 4 August 1891, he makes all of this very clear:

> I would be even more happy if there were already the embryo of a socialist workers' party, which is not now the case, and does not seem likely to be the case for some time in the future. The general causes, always brought forth and repeated, concerning underdeveloped capitalism, industry being in its infancy, etc., precisely because they are too general, explain very little. There are others, all specifically Italian, which prevent even the birth of that *small* party, which would nowadays be possible even in Italy. And I do not understand why it is not possible to belong to a small party, when one is aware of being absolutely in the truth.[104]

DiFratta and Colajanni—and we had a good laugh.'' Labriola, *Lettere a Croce*, p. 94.

102. Schiavi, *Filippo Turati*, p. 93.

103. Palmiro Togliatto, ''Dopo Settanta anni,'' *Rinascita*, 13 October 1962; and *Rapporto dell'VIII Congresso del PCI, Atti e Risoluzioni* (Rome, 1957), pp. 60–61. Labriola's letter is now in Labriola, *Scritti Politici*, pp. 463–464.

104. Schiavi, *Filippo Turati*, pp. 84–85.

Spaventa's earlier strategy for the renovation of Italian thought in the face of Vera's abstract universalism and Palmieri's crass nationalism, meant to raise Italian culture by elaborating the highest achievements of German philosophy within Italian traditions and character, found its concrete political counterpart in Labriola's theory of the party. A somewhat idealized version of the German social-democratic model was adapted to the Italian context, where different socioeconomic conditions required a scaling-down of immediate objectives within a general strategy of rapid modernization of Italian society.[105] Labriola turned the charge of ignoring the existing Italian state of affairs against Turati, whose realpolitik seemed to sacrifice the theory to expedience, intensifying rather than remedying existing shortcomings. In another letter to Engels, this one dated 21 May 1892, Labriola writes of Turati that

> he knows the *real Italy* very little, and the remedy that he proposes is worse than the disease. It is the old Bakunian song of putting together a gang of misfits from the bourgeoisie, a few malcontents by temperament, and a few pessimists by envy, in order to form a socialist party that would then mean only a politicians' clique.[106]

Such a heterogeneous mess could generate only a vague program, resulting in the demand for the "right to work," whose political outcome, at best, could only be the kind of *state socialism* that Labriola had constantly attacked.[107] This is why Labriola not only violently opposed agitation for the right to work, which meant that the state would become ultimately the employer of last resort, but also

105. Among other things, this explains Labriola's support for rapid capitalist expansion, since, as he writes in 1897, "there cannot be any progress by the proletariat where the bourgeoisie is unable to progress." This very same line of reasoning was what led him, following in Marx's steps, to legitimate imperialist expansion. Antonia Labriola, "Per Candia," in Labriola, *Scritti Politici*, p. 433. One of the things that continually upset him was the inability of Italian capitalism to fully develop. Thus, in a letter to Croce, 22 November 1898, he writes: "The strange thing is that Italy, which has such a great number of petty crooks who try to reciprocally screw each other, is not able to put together one of those great companies of grand style crooks, which in other countries have succeeded in creating those so-called great forces of civilization such as capitalism, colonialism, the conquest of the market, etc. It is manure that, not used as fertilizer, fouls the air." Labriola, *Lettere a Croce*, p. 313.

106. Marx and Engels, *Corrispondenza con Italiani*, p. 435.

107. Thus, in Labriola, *Materialist Conception of History*, p. 39, he writes: "From

worked feverishly to organize around the First of May demonstrations in support of the eight-hour workday. By directly challenging the class of owners, this demand sharpened the social contradictions rather than falsely reconciling them.

> How beautiful are the effects of demagoguery! Take the *right to work* as an example! It is undoubtedly a concept of the doctrine of *socialism*, i.e., *of the doctrine which assumes the means of production to have already been socialized*. But today, while the capitalist system remains, while the owners of the means of production are a few, and both the State and City Hall are forms of bourgeois power, if the unemployed workers—without associations, without party, and without discipline—call for the right to work, they persuade employers even more that the market for the commodity man is very large, and that if Europe is not enough, hungry proletarians can be sent to Africa or to the New World. Something else altogether is the principle of the First of May demonstrations for eight hours, i.e., the *right to idleness*, which would balance out the sad effects of competition.[108]

The objective, once again, was to emphasize the ultimate irreconcilability of the class struggle and to pose the political tasks that could translate into a revolutionary project as soon as capitalism itself created a proletariat large enough for the task.

Unfortunately, Labriola's own worst fears that "Italian socialism is not the principle of a new life, but the *extreme manifestation of political and intellectual corruption*," turned out to be better grounded than he thought.[109] As he reported in *Der Sozialdemokrat*—

---

the time of its appearance, this new communist doctrine carried an implied criticism of all forms of State socialism from Louis Blanc to Lassalle. This State socialism, although mingled with revolutionary doctrines, was then summed up in the empty dream, in the abracadabra of the *Right to Work*. This is an insidious formula if it implies a demand addressed to a government even of revolutionary bourgeois. It is an economic absurdity if by it is meant to suppress the unemployment which ensues upon the variations of wages, that is to say upon the conditions of competition. It may be a tool for politicians, if it serves as an expedient to calm a shapeless mass of unorganized proletarians. This is very evident to anyone who conceives clearly the course of a victorious proletarian revolution that cannot proceed to the socialization of the means of production by taking possession of them, that is to say, which cannot arrive at the economic form in which there is neither merchandise nor wage labor and in which the right to work and the duty of working are one and the same, mingled in the common necessity of labor for all."

108. Labriola to De Martinis, 28 April 1890, in Labriola, *Scritti Politici*, p. 217.

109. Schiavi, *Filippo Turati*, p. 83. A similar bitter judgment reappears in a letter

a German paper for which he wrote from time to time—the demonstration of 1 May 1890 was a great disappointment:

> It was ridiculous and at the same time sad to see how in Rome, the First of May, while many foreigners had run away from the city and a great many gentlemen had escaped to the countryside, while many stores were closed and all public buildings, banks, etc., were occupied by a strong police force, while the majority of the workers either had stayed home or were at work, 14,000 soldiers, in addition to the armed police, were ready in battle gear to protect State and society from an imaginary revolution that did not even want to explode—and they ran from place to place to disperse small groups of obstinate demonstrators who, altogether, were at most 1,000 people.[110]

The following years things went even worse, with deaths, injuries, and hundreds of arrests, and in 1892 the effort collapsed completely.[111] As Labriola reports to Engels:

> Even the pubs usually frequented by workers were deserted. It was a spectacle of reciprocal fear. I walked for miles and met only buses and newspaper reporters seeking news that was not there. Every now and then there were rumors or explosions, meetings, etc., and one P.G., who often speaks at anarchist meetings but who is really a confidante of the chief of police, negotiated very well this false news with alarmist reporters.—This spectacle of Rome governed by fear, fruit of ignorance, and intrigue, has given me real sadness.[112]

Although sporadic subsequent events, such as the uprisings in Sicily (*Fasci Siciliani*), were welcomed by Labriola as "the first great

---

to Engels, 31 July 1891: "All bourgeois corruption, happy and scatterbrained in a typically Italian fashion." Marx and Engels, *Corrispondenza con Italiani*, p. 397. Of course, Labriola's correspondence is full of similar pessimistic evaluations of Italian Marxism and the proletariat of that time. Thus, he writes to Viktor Adler, 7 May 1893: "The Italian proletariat moves very slowly, incoherently, and often inconclusively. It is full of mistrust and has suffered much intimidation. 'Marxism' does not gain a foothold in Italy: and what looks like Marxism is a *new phrase* applied to old ideas, feelings, and needs. The Italian bourgeoisie does not yet fear socialism." "Lettere di Antonio Labriola," p. 437.

110. Antonio Labriola, "Il Primo di Maggio e il Movimento Operaio in Italia," in Labriola, *Scritti Politici*, pp. 229–230.

111. For an excellent account of this event, see Gerratana, "Realtà e Compiti," pp. 597–600.

112. Marx and Engels, *Corrispondenza con Italiani*, p. 433.

fact of Italian socialism,"[113] and he wrote about them with enthusiasm,[114] he was becoming increasingly isolated. As Gerratana puts it:

> It is not difficult to understand how *this* Labriola so pungent, with his instinctive impatience for political improvisation, would create a vacuum around himself. All of his efforts to reestablish relations of active collaboration with the organizers of Italian socialism (in particular with Andrea Costa in 1896, and with Turati in 1899, after the reactionary storm of 1898) are received with diffidence and allowed to fall through.[115]

Around this time, Labriola discovered Sorel's new journal, *Divenir Social*, and on 27 April 1895, he wrote the famous letter that forty years later Croce fixed as the birth of theoretical Marxism in Italy.[116] Although politically "defeated," during the next three years Labriola laid the theoretical foundations of the Italian Marxist tradition, which was to become the most viable alternative to both the classical social democracy of the Second International and the Marxism-Leninism of Russia and China.[117]

113. Labriola to W. Ellenbogen, 15 November 1891, in "Lettere di Antonio Labriola," p. 443. Labriola, of course, was careful to contrapose these spontaneous events to the paralysis of the official socialists. In another letter to Ellenbogen, 11 September 1894, he writes: "This instinctive, diffused, uncertain, and colorful ferment is not to be confused with the official socialist party, with headquarters in Milan, which has neither elasticity nor enthusiasm of force of expression and persuasion, and if it continues on this path, it will end up as a sect of pedants." Ibid., p. 456.

114. Thus, in an article entitled "Sui Fasci Siciliani," originally written for Ellenbogen's *Volkstribune* of Vienna (now in Labriola, *Scritti Politici*, pp. 308–309), Labriola—more diplomatic than usual toward the official Socialist party—describes the Sicilian events as follows: "The leaders, the agitators, the propagandists of the Sicilian movement have always written, spoken, and operated as convinced and precise socialists. Their direction is at one with the Party of the Italian workers, which after the Reggio congress can be considered definitely unified. There is nothing of hurried, anarchic, and inconsiderate behavior in their conduct. They speak and operate with the intentions and the ideas of the *class struggle*. . . . Given the nature of these agitators, Sicily's hot temperament, the stringent conditions of the Sicilian proletarians, in all this agitation there is something vibrant, solemn, strong, and *ursprünglich* which reflects on all of Italy." The same passage appears in a letter to Ellenbogen, 22 November 1893, now in "Lettere di Antonio Labriola," p. 445.

115. Gerratana, "Realtà e Compiti," p. 606.

116. Benedetto Croce, "Come Nacque e come Morì il Marxismo Teorico in Italia (1895–1900)," in Croce, *Materialismo Storico*, p. 253.

117. Ivanoe Bonomi writes in *Avanti!*, 13 March 1911, in an article entitled "Per l'Etica del Socialismo": "The Marxist conception, transported to Italy in its freshest

Stitching Together Western Marxism[118]

In a 1937 account that Togliatti called laughable,[119] Croce located the trajectory of theoretical Marxism in Italy between Labriola's letter announcing a willingness to collaborate with Sorel's new journal and the publication of Croce's own essays on Marxism in book form.[120] Adding insult to injury, Croce accused Labriola of promoting the crisis-of-Marxism debate that at the turn of the century engaged the best Marxist theoreticians, from Bernstein to Karl Kautsky, from Sorel to Rosa Luxemburg.[121] Although Croce's thesis concerning the rise and fall of Marxism in Italy, along with his generally superficial remarks about Labriola's allegedly discontinuous intellectual forma-

---

and most primitive form, was well able to generate a mystical idealism in the youth of the time: a period of sacrifice and pain, a frightening misery among the working classes, a liberating catastrophe shaking the injustices of the past, and finally the salvation of humanity, once and for all emerged from a pre-human era. With such an outlook, how was it possible not to construct a kind of religion to which the first persecutions gave a new flood of light? But this period, in which the neo-Christian socialists' inclinations would have found their proper environment, is rapidly succeeded by a second one. No longer persecutions and mystical awaitings of liberating catastrophes; no longer the agitating and messianic spirit of the origins; but the repetition of some formulae drawn from the baggage of positivistic democracy and grafted onto the trunk of socialism. The philosophical concept of socialism becomes identified with the concept of natural evolution; the proletarian movement is an episode of the struggle for existence; the collectivist society is the result of the victory of the best adapted to natural selection. The philosophy of the petty bourgeois class, gathered in mass around the flag of the new socialism, is summarized in the triad Darwin-Spencer-Marx.'' Quoted in Garin, *Cronache di Filosofia Italiana*, p. 203.

118. This is how Labriola described his own work to Croce, 25 May 1895: "Things would have the appearance of simply being *angereiht* [stitched together] while a few notes here and there would provide unity. A brief introduction, half serious and half joking, should explain the title *Fragments* (because Italy is all torn up and fragmentary!)." Labriola, *Lettere a Croce*, p. 73.

119. Palmiro Togliatti, "Per una Giusta Comprensione del Pensiero di Antonio Labriola," *Rinascita* XI, 4 (April 1954), 254.

120. Croce, *Materialismo Storico*. With this volume, originally published in 1900, Croce thought he had buried Marxism. Thus, on page 162, he writes: "I have gathered in one volume . . . all my writings on Marx and have laid them down as if in a casket. And I believe that I have closed the Marxist parentheses in my life." As Garin points out, however, Croce must have been an awful undertaker, since he had to continue burying the cadavers of Marx and Hegel throughout the rest of his life! See Garin, *Cronache di Filosofia Italiana*, p. 210.

121. Croce, *Materialismo Storico*, p. 289. Croce, who never said anything only *once*, reiterated in 1925: "As soon as the Marxist doctrines in Italy attracted the

tion,[122] have not withstood the corrosive effects of criticism,[123] it is still true that one type of Marxism was dealt a fatal blow at the turn of the century. Three decades later, when Gramsci sought to reconsider the foundations of Marxism, it was no accident that he insisted on a systematic critique of Croce as a prolegomenor to all future Marxist theoretical discourse.[124]

Croce's "burial" of Marxism was the result of what he saw as the definitive rejection of its key notions: "Historical materialism appeared to me doubly fallacious, both as materialism and as the conception of the historical course according to a premeditated design, a variation of the Hegelian philosophy of history."[125] At best, histori-

---

attention and the passion of men from liberalism and culture, such as Antonio Labriola—the leading Italian Marxist—a serious examination began and, with it, their disintegration: under the blow of the criticism of those men who had approached Marxism with faith and love, one after the other fell the theory of value and surplus value, that of the falling rate of profit, that of history as class struggle, and of historical materialism." On the very same page, Marxism is defined as "substantially, a theological and medieval vision, strongly colored by Judaic apocalypticism." Benedetto Croce, *Cultura e Vita Morale* (Bari, 1955), p. 286.

122. According to Croce, Labriola's intellectual development was more like "a series of jumps than a progressive path." Accordingly, Labriola "as a youth was Hegelian, but subsequently he abandoned Hegel to pass on to Herbart; but of Herbart he failed to absorb the metaphysics and the logic; and he finally turned to the somewhat spurious Hegelianism of Marx and even more that of Friedrich Engels." Benedetto Croce, "Note sulla Letteratura Italiana nella Seconda Metà del Secolo XIX," Part II: "Giovanni Bono e la Poesia della Filosofia," *La Critica* V, 417–418; as quoted in Garin, "Introduzione," p. xv.

123. Thus, Garin's "Introduzione," pp. i-lxv, is an extended refutation of Croce's authoritative interpretation. In order to appreciate fully why Croce's bogus interpretation was able to dominate for so long, it should be remembered that he was not only the most illustrious student of Labriola but also the one who had been closest to him during the last twenty years of his life. The letters of Labriola to Croce alone during this period consist of 456 items and run a good 377 pages. At any rate, when in December 1896, Labriola wrote to Croce that "I have some other friends besides you, but no one can even come close to you"—which Croce proudly quoted—it was certainly not an exaggeration. Labriola, *Lettere a Croce*, p. 172.

124. It was not at all arbitrary for the editors of the original series of books comprising the *Prison Notebooks* to entitle the theoretical part *Historical Materialism and the Philosophy of Benedetto Croce*. With typical insensitivity, the English translators have kept the first part and neglected to translate the part more directly concerned with Croce, with the result that the English version appears utterly one-sided and misleading.

125. Croce, *Materialismo Storico*, p. 275.

cal materialism amounted to a *heuristic principle* requiring "historians to pay attention . . . to the economic activity of people's lives and to the imaginations, ingenious or fictitious, originating from it." A similar fate awaited Marxist economics, whose fundamental concepts of value and surplus value were regarded by him as "the consequence of an elliptic comparison between an abstract society assumed as the prototype in which all are workers, and a society with private capital."[126] Thus, Marx was denied status either as a philosopher or as a scientist, and was reduced to a "vigorous political genius, or rather a revolutionary genius who had given impetus and consistency to the labor movement by arming it with a historiographic and economic doctrine made especially to fit it."[127]

Although Croce's critique was very effective against shoddy pseudo-Marxist works such as those of Paul Lafargue[128] and Achille Loria,[129] it was completely off the mark as far as Labriola's work was concerned. As has been repeatedly pointed out,[130] Croce's sharp distinction between theory and practice—typical of the *contemplative* viewpoint[131]—was from the very beginning inclined to "deny the theoretical validity of historical materialism precisely because of its practical political origin."[132] But for Labriola and even more for

126. Ibid., p. 277.

127. Ibid., pp. 281–282.

128. Already in 1895, Croce had severely criticized Lafargue's work on Tommaso Campanella, which had appeared in a series entitled "History of Socialism." Croce's essay (now in Croce, *Materialismo Storico*, pp. 165–201) primarily pointed out numerous factual distortions and oversimplifications.

129. Croce's essay entitled "Le Teorie Storiche del Prof. Loria" was written a year later, in September 1896. Labriola, in a letter to Croce, of 5 December 1896, called this essay "a small masterpiece," shortly thereafter asking for forty copies of it to distribute among his friends in order further to discredit Loria's pseudo-Marxism; by the twentieth of December he offered Croce a long list of possible additions to the Loria essay for future reprintings, so as to render it a more effective polemical piece. All this, of course, further supports Croce's claim that Labriola "deluded himself for some time that he had found in me his collaborator and successor in the custody and defense of the genuine Marxist tradition." Croce, *Materialismo Storico*, p. 274.

130. See, e.g., Emilio Agazzi, *Il Giovane Croce e il Marxismo* (Turin, 1962), p. 98.

131. Georg Lukács, *History and Class Consciousness*, trans. Rodney Livingstone (London, 1971), pp. 156 ff.

132. Carlo Carini, *Croce e il Partito Politico* (Florence, 1975), p. 29.

Gramsci, "scientificity" boiled down precisely to the successful mediation of social reality. On closer examination, it turns out that Croce had by no means refuted Labriola's Marxism but, to quote Carini, had simply extended "Labriola's polemic against the dogmatic sclerosis of official Marxism" by considering that reductive aberration "as the only possible interpretation of Marxism." Thus, "what for Labriola was a necessary polemical phase to help spread an adequate conception of materialism, in Croce becomes the only possible way of understanding Marxism."[133]

Labriola violently criticized *vulgar* materialism as that doctrine according to which "*matter* indicates something below or opposed to another higher or nobler thing called spirit," and "that literary habit which opposes the word materialism, understood in a disparaging sense, to all that, in a word, is called idealism."[134] For Labriola, as Croce well knew, historical materialism explained forms of thought in terms of forms of being—not for purely intellectual reasons but to provide the political and social mediations needed to solve the contradictions of capitalist society. This, Labriola asserts, "is the revolutionary assumption and the scientific aim of the new doctrine which *objectifies* and I might say *naturalizes* the explanation of historical processes."[135] This mediational function of historical explanation makes "knowledge of the past . . . useful and interesting only in so far as it throws light upon and explains the present."[136] Historical materialism, therefore, is "the discovery of the *self-criticism* that lies in the things themselves."[137] In other words, historical materialism is the attempt to reconcile the *system* and the process, in terms of the post-Hegelian problematic that remains latent in Labriola. But here the old contradiction rears up again, inasmuch as the process already *presupposes* the full realization of the system, thus ruling out the possibility of grounding the latter in the former. Eventually, Labriola's entire mediational framework collapses under the weight of this burden.

133. Ibid., p. 30.
134. Labriola, *Materialist Conception of History*, p. 97.
135. Ibid., pp. 102–103 (translation slightly modified).
136. Ibid., p. 89.
137. Ibid., p. 169.

The source of the difficulty was in the initial assumption that Marxism is a philosophy of history.[138] This allowed Labriola to specify the logic of the *genetic* process and subsequently to reconstruct *social morphology*, the awareness of which mediates the coming of that social revolution necessary to generate the *collective consciousness* needed to sustain the whole theoretical edifice. Although Labriola came to abandon the interpretation of Marxism as a philosophy of history[139] and to affirm that Marxism was still at its beginnings as a philosophy of praxis or as a world view,[140] his whole account by then had come apart at the seams. This, more than any of Croce's specific criticisms, was what exploded Labriola's initial interpretation of Marxism and required its reconstitution—a task Labriola was able to outline but, unfortunately, could not carry out. Without a philosophy of history as its foundation, his account of the theory of value collapsed along with the *genetic method* and the *social morphology* that were the two cornerstones of his preliminary reconstruction of historical materialism.

138. Labriola's initial interpretation of Marxism as a philosophy of history is not only documented by his essay on the *Manifesto* but also by his students' notes on his courses at the time. For excellent summaries of these notes, see Dal Pane, *Antonio Labriola*, pp. 286 ff. Of all historians of Marxism, Kolakowski is the only one to have noticed and emphasized Labriola's rejection of the Marxist theory of history. To the extent, however, that Kolakowski does not treat Labriola's thought as developing over time but, rather, as a self-contained totality given once and for all, he misses the full impact of this crucial element not only in Labriola but in the ensuing tradition. Thus, Labriola's account is presented as "imprecise" and generally not sufficiently rigorous—especially when measured against Kolakowski's positivistic hypostatization of the natural sciences as models for various brands of Marxism. Leszek Kolakowski, *Main Currents of Marxism: Its Rise, Growth and Dissolution*, Vol. II: *The Golden Age* (Oxford, 1978), pp. 175–192.

139. Thus, having jettisoned Marxism as a philosophy of history, in his last work he was forced to recognize the necessarily fragmentary character of what remained: "These last chapters remain as fragments. He who should blame me for that should tell me what path he, the severe critic, would follow to overcome this fragmentary state of our cognition at the present time so as to integrate it into the totality of a perfect vision. The wisest and most relevant objection put forth against every *system* of the philosophy of history is Wundt's: we do not know where history will go. Which means that, if I understand it rightly, we never have it all under our eyes as something already accomplished." Antonio Labriola, "Da un Secolo all'Altro," in Labriola, *Socialism and Philosophy*, pp. 201–202.

140. Labriola, *Socialism and Philosophy*, pp. 66, 94–95.

Unlike customary Marxist interpretations of value as an ideal type (*ein Gedankenbild*, as Eduard Bernstein called it) within "a theory of general equilibrium" (Paul Sweezy),[141] as a valid induction from all human productivity (Maurice Dobb), or as a "real activity" presupposed by "all useful or concrete labor" (Lucio Colletti),[142] Labriola saw value as "a typical premise,"[143] which, along with other similar premises, provided an account of the morphological structure of capitalist society.[144] But what is a "typical premise"? On closer examination, it turns out to be the specification of a necessary moment in the unfolding of the philosophy of history that is initially explicitly advocated and subsequently retracted within Labriola's account. The labor theory of value projected the *particularization* of the yet-to-be-attained collective consciousness onto present capitalist society, where it would generate those contradictions whose resolution would culminate in that already presupposed totalization. With the phasing out of Marxism as a philosophy of history, Labriola could no longer defend his account of the theory of value.

When Croce, following the so-called "Austrian School,"[145] rejected the theory of value as an unwarranted abstraction from an ideal society of homogeneous workers, Labriola could point out that such a critique was a result of Croce's uncritical assumption of a neo-Platonist viewpoint sharply separating the *ideal* and the *real*, the *pure*

141. Paul M. Sweezy, *The Theory of Capitalist Development* (New York, 1942), p. 53.

142. Colletti, *Ideologia e Società*, p. 117. In a typical example of what Adorno called "identity theory," Colletti projects what is obviously a highly elaborate abstraction back into reality and then takes it as the criterion of all concrete economic manifestations. Notwithstanding Colletti's pretensions to materialism, this is *objective idealism* at its worst.

143. Thus, Labriola writes: "The *theory of value* . . . does not represent an *empirical fact* drawn from vulgar induction, nor a *simple category of logic*, as some have chronicled it, but it is the *typical premise* without which all the rest is unthinkable." See Labriola, *Socialism and Philosophy*, pp. 72–73 (translation modified).

144. Ibid., p. 73.

145. Croce's predilection for the "Austrian School," of course, was a consequence of his fundamental metaphysical assumption of an unbridgeable gap between science and politics, theory and practice, whereby one is historical and particular, and the other ahistorical and formal. But, as Labriola puts it in his reply, "The Austrian school is merely a variety of theoretical interpretation for the same empirical facts of modern economic life, which have always been the object of study of so many other

and the *applied*.[146] But because of Labriola's own limitations described above, he never undertook a detailed defense or a better elaboration of the theory of value. In fact, Labriola was never all that interested in economics. On 21 May 1898, he wrote Croce that "economics is all to be reconsidered" and that he was not about to undertake the task.[147] Less than three months later he derided economics as "a discipline in which, for various reasons, a great deal of silly and contradictory things can be said."[148] And shortly thereafter he admitted that he had dealt with the theory of value only "accidentally and because of an incidental characteristic of the texture of *Capital*."[149] Although Labriola, as Croce pointed out, "did not speak anymore of the economic theory of surplus value,"[150] this had nothing to do with Croce's alleged refutation, but was rather a result of his reconsideration of Marxism as a philosophy of history.

A similar fate awaited Labriola's *genetic* method. Superficially it

---

schools. . . . It strives to make more evident the psychological stages that accompany the economic processes and relations. . . . It is not entirely superhistorical, although it often stages characters like Robinson Crusoe, whom it tries to hide afterward under the cloak of subtle individualistic psychology. Indeed, it is so little superhistorical that it assumes from actual history two concepts and molds them into theoretical extremes, namely the liberty to work and the liberty of competition, which have been carried to their maximum as hypotheses." Labriola, *Socialism and Philosophy*, pp. 166–167.

146. Thus, in a letter of 25 December 1896 (which Croce himself quotes in *Materialismo Storico*, p. 279), Labriola writes: "I take this opportunity to tell you that you have gone too far in asserting the existence, even if hypothetical, of a pure economics. And then, why not pure law, pure esthetics, pure lie? And history, where does it go? On this road one comes to Plato's ideas or to Scholasticism." Very patiently, Labriola tried repeatedly to shake Croce out of his *contemplative* trance, but to little avail. Thus, in a letter of 9 October 1898, he writes: "Let me point out only one thing: you must free yourself from the mania of reasoning from outside on concepts, as if they were *little things*. Concepts must be *conceived* with respect to a determined order of things, as *living functions*. If you, e.g., become accustomed to conceive a series of facts (e.g., chemical) as explained by certain *concepts* (*functions*) (e.g., atoms), it is useless that you attempt subsequently to put yourself above your brain and ask yourself: what is the *meaning* of this concept? This is how one goes crazy or ends up uttering silliness." Labriola, *Lettere a Croce*, p. 303. Exactly the same criticism reappears in a letter written a month before Labriola's death, dated 2 January 1904. Ibid., pp. 375–376.

147. Ibid., p. 282.

148. Ibid., p. 294.

149. Ibid., p. 304.

150. Croce, *Materialismo Storico*, p. 293.

resembles the positivists' deductive model in its account of the particular, which starts by examining the conditions that gave rise to it and with reference to mediation of general laws understood as empirical generalizations.[151] But Labriola explicitly rejected this comparison with positivism.[152] His method, understood as a way of "going from the conditions to the conditioned, from the elements of formation to the thing formed,"[153] was meant "to reconstruct by methodical thought the genesis and the complexity of the social life which develops through the ages."[154] It sought nothing less than to grasp the same totality that Lukács designated as the category "that governs reality" (*die eigentliche Wirklichkeitskategorie*).[155] As in Lukács, this account presupposed a secularized version of the Hegelian *Geist*: the grasping of the totality of social reality presupposed a subject that is itself a totality.[156] Unlike Lukács, however, Labriola could not count on a fully constituted proletarian class able to function as the subject-object identity that was needed to fulfill such a global epistemological function: he could see the proletariat in Italy as only at the beginning of its formation as a class.[157] Lacking such a foundation, he had to give up any claim to Marxism as "a general social science"[158] able to relate those "facts which were artificially torn from the whole" by means of "the connections binding them to the social complex."[159]

Marx never discussed this problem at length in his works, but he must have been keenly aware of it since, unlike Labriola, who several

151. Modified and refined, the deductive model remains the neo-positivists' paradigm. For the best restatement of this model, see Carl G. Hempel, *Aspects of Scientific Explanation* (New York, 1965), pp. 333 ff.

152. Labriola, *Materialist Conception of History*, pp. 17–18.

153. Ibid., p. 98.

154. Ibid., p. 99.

155. Lukács, *History and Class Consciousness*, p. 10.

156. Ibid., p. 28.

157. Labriola, *Socialism and Philosophy*, pp. 160 f.

158. Labriola, *Materialist Conception of History*, p. 149.

159. Ibid., p. 150 (translation modified). Less than a quarter of a century later, in a less pessimistic—in fact, overly messianic—context, Lukács reproposed the same project, "which sees isolated facts of social life as aspects of the historical process and integrates them in a *totality*," so that "knowledge of these facts" becomes "knowledge of *reality*." Lukács, *History and Class Consciousness*, p. 8.

times undertook brilliant genetic reconstructions,[160] Marx always began with the immediately given or the simple and only subsequently articulated its determinations. *Capital,* for example, starts out with the "commodity" and goes on to reconstruct its determinations—thus generating an account of the inner structure of capitalist society. In the one somewhat confused and inconclusive writing on method—the "Introduction" to the *Grundrisse*—Marx explicitly rejected beginning with a chaotic conception (*Vorstellung*) such as "population," and opted for "more simple concepts" (*Begriff*), "the simplest determinations."[161] In short, there is no genetic method in Marx, for whom "human anatomy contains the key to the anatomy of the ape," not vice versa.[162] This approach avoided the epistemological embarrassment of presupposing a yet to be achieved collective subjectivity, but the cost was dear: it ruled out any coherent systematization of revolutionary theory. Marx's thought cannot be translated into Marx*ism.*

Labriola resisted these conclusions at first. In June 1894, after rereading Engels's *Anti-Dühring*, he must have sensed some discrepancies between his "genetic method" and Engels's "dialectical method," since he went out of his way to reduce the matter to a "question of words":

> You use the dialectical and the metaphysical methods as antithetical terms. To say the same thing here in Italy, instead of *dialectical* I would say *genetic*. The word dialectic has been degraded by common usage. . . . I think that the designation of *genetic conception* turns out to be clearer: and it certainly turns out to be more comprehensive since it thus envelops the

160. Dal Pane (*Antonio Labriola*, p. 257) is correct in claiming that one can see in Labriola the development "of a new vision of history, richer, more diversified, more complex, and more critically exact than Marx's and Engels's own conception." But Labriola could do so only by overstepping the epistemological limits of Marx's own theory, thus falling back into the Hegelian dilemma of presupposing the full realization of the system that could subsequently sustain the required philosophy of history.

161. Marx, *Grundrisse*, p. 100. But, even then, the objective idealist trap of confusing concepts with living reality is not automatically avoided. Ultimately, only the *successful mediational function* of these concepts, and not any of their purely formal features, can guarantee their *scientificity*. Of course, this is precisely the meaning of Marx's eleventh thesis on Ludwig Feuerbach.

162. Ibid., p. 105.

real content of things in the process of becoming. . . . With the word dialectic only the formal aspect is represented (which, for Hegel as an ideologue, was all). And by saying genetic conception, both Darwinism as well as the materialist interpretation of history, and every other explanation of things that become and form themselves, take on their place. What I mean is that the expression *genetic method* leaves unprejudiced the empirical nature of each particular formation.[163]

But this is easier said than done. It presupposes such a complete view of the historical process that it must allow the univocal specification of each and every multicausal pattern: it is possible only for the historian as the embodied *Geist*.

In a letter of 31 July 1894 (lost, but cited in Labriola's reply to it), Engels must have pointed out something along these lines, since Labriola came back to it in his letter of 11 August:

When I say genetic I have precisely in mind the first volume of *Capital*. As far as a method of thinking is concerned, there is nothing so perfect. Not in only one form, but in all forms. The concrete genesis (e.g., English accumulation); abstract genesis (the analysis of commodities, etc.); the contradictions which force the moving out of a concept or of a fact (e.g., the formula *Geld-Ware-Geld*), etc. The difficulty of Marx is precisely in his form of thought. The naked results, popularly exposed by Deville and Kautsky, seem almost obvious. I do not ignore the often scatterbrained use that has been made in German of the word genetic. . . . And what was not done with the Hegelian dialectic? The *sprachvergleichende Logik* is not only an indispensable discipline (already *in nuce* in Herbart, and subsequently developed by Steinthal, but always with some residue of ideological phantasmagoria) but it is the "key to finding the cause," i.e., the origin of the whole (metaphysical) derivation of thought. This is clear in Plato, who is the father of *metaphysics*. The *concept*, just occasionally found (Socrates) as a function of concrete discourse, turns *sprachlich* into its own *hypostasis*.[164]

But what is the genetic reconstruction other than, at best, a *necessary* hypostatization whose necessity can be guaranteed only by a fully realized collective subjectivity that is still not an accomplished fact? Prior to its attainment, the reconstruction must be *instrumental*, i.e.,

163. Marx and Engels, *Corrispondenza con Italiani*, pp. 536–537.
164. Ibid., p. 547.

grounded solely in *praxis* as successful mediation, but must forfeit any claim to exhaustiveness and, therefore, to a *definitive* status. At any rate, Marx's first volume of *Capital* does not provide a genetic reconstruction of capitalist society, but merely a series of extended aphoristic critiques, which, starting from simple universals (commodities, machines, etc.) attempt to provide a necessarily incomplete account of the proposed determinations. Labriola eventually saw the problem and came to the Adornian conclusion that *particularity* in each "particular formation" could be safeguarded only by doing history as *art*.[165]

In his first of the four essays on Marxism, appropriately entitled "In Memory of the *Communist Manifesto*," Labriola undertook a fairly accurate reconstruction of Marx and Engels's doctrine, distinguishing between history as a totality and its structure (or, as he called it, its social morphology),[166] which is constituted by the economy[167] and which, in turn, generates social contradictions and the proletariat as the agency meant to resolve these contradictions with the instauration of the classless society.[168] Far from being merely an epigone's vulgarization, from the very beginning Labriola's account sought to reaffirm the *revolutionary actuality* of the *Communist Manifesto*, and to confront the main question that was to be also the starting point of the next generation of Hegelian Marxists in the immediate post—World War I period: Why had the revolution not come? In doing so, Labriola anticipated the explanations of Karl Korsch, Lukács, and Gramsci. And, what is more, he managed to see through the fundamental flaw of that very way of posing the question of Marxism, coming very close in the process to Theodor Adorno's position (although not in quite so pessimistic and stultifying a fashion).

Thus, in Labriola we find already prefigured not only Adorno's famous thesis of the necessarily *fragmentary* character of revolutionary thought, and of art as the only means whereby social theory can grasp particularity and avoid the cancer of Western thought—identity

165. Labriola, *Materialist Conception of History*, p. 229.
166. Ibid., p. 23. The English translation, unfortunately, translates "*processo interno, ossia morfologico della società*" as "the internal or organic process of society," thus phasing out one of Labriola's key concepts.
167. Ibid., p. 32.
168. Ibid., p. 61.

theory—but also the full awareness and preliminary elaboration of that *problem of constitution* that Negt has correctly seen as the key problem in the relaunching of Marxist theory,[169] and that Adorno could never begin to formulate properly because of his total and stubborn miscomprehension of Husserlian phenomenology.[170] The theoretical trajectory that Western Marxism traced during the almost half a century separating the publication of *History and Class Consciousness* and *Negative Dialectics* is already outlined and partly transcended in Labriola's seminal work. This state of affairs sets the stage for the prefiguration of a Marxist model qualitatively different from both traditional social democracy and Marxism-Leninism—one, however, that has been suppressed historically or, at best, cleverly instrumentalized.

The Dissipation of Labriola's Marxism

Labriola, writing in a context exhibiting "all the vices of parliamentarism, of militarism, and of finance without at the same time having the forms of modern production,"[171] did not need either Lukács's theory of reification or Gramsci's concept of hegemony to explain why the revolution had not come yet. In the Italy of 1890, the main struggle was not against whatever weak bourgeois cultural force existed, but instead was still largely a matter of conquering "peasant stupidity" by means of "the elimination and the capture of domestic industry by capital, the ever more rapid passage of agrarian industry into the capitalist form, the disappearance of small proprietorships," etc.[172] Ultimately, this limit took its toll on Labriola. Granted, he did pose the problem of class consciousness (which, following Herbart, he called "social psychology") as the mediator between "the underlying economic structure" and historical events,[173] and his critique of

169. Oskar Negt, "Theory, Empiricism and Class Struggle: On The Problem of Constitution in Karl Korsch," *Telos*, no. 26 (Winter 1975–76), pp. 120–121.
170. For a critique of Adorno's interpretation of Husserl's phenomenology, see Guido Neri, *Prassi e Conoscenza* (Milan, 1966), pp. 136–148; and Paul Piccone, "Beyond Identity Theory," in John O'Neill, ed., *On Critical Theory* (New York, 1976), pp. 129–144.
171. Labriola, *Materialist Conception of History*, pp. 66–67.
172. Ibid., p. 65.
173. Ibid., p. 111. As Labriola puts it: "This social psychology, by its nature

historical factors[174] prefigured Lukács's theory of reification by contraposing Marxism as the philosophy of praxis, which grounds a general social science,[175] to contemplative bourgeois throught, which is unable to transcend the level of immediacy—"of *abstractions* . . . as simple aspects of the whole."[176] But Labriola never came to theorize any "identical subject-object of history."[177] He did not see the need, since to explain how an increasingly alienated proletariat could suddenly attain the perspective of the whole was not yet a problem for him. He therefore left unsolved the problem of the genesis and constitution of the historical subject of this revolutionary process. But, in so doing, he spared himself the embarrassment of having to account for a metaphysical fiction such as the identical subject-object, which ultimately contributed to the collapse of the theoretical edifice of *History and Class Consciousness.*

While Labriola cannot be faulted for failing to provide a Marxist account of the possibility of overcoming the debilitating effects of a Taylorism that had not yet appeared on the horizon (although its equivalent had been discussed in Marx's own works, on which Lukács based his reconstruction of the labor process), he could be expected to explain the backwardness of Marxist theory in 1890 in relation to the achievements of the doctrine's two founders. In confronting this problem, Labriola outlined the main points of the subsequent periodization of the history of Marxism undertaken by Korsch. According to this approach, the decline in the quality of Marxist theory toward the end of the century occurred because

> the workers' movement at that time formally adopted "Marxism" as its ideology; yet although its effective practice was now on a *broader basis* than before, it had in no way reached the heights of general and theoretical achievement earlier attained by the revolutionary movement and proletar-

---

always circumstantial, is not the expression of the abstract and generic process of the self-styled human intellect," but "is the fruit, the outcome, the effect of certain social conditions actually determined—this class, in this situation, determined by the functions which it fulfills, by the subjection in which it is held, by the domination which it exercises."

174. Ibid., pp. 140–155.
175. Ibid., p. 149.
176. Ibid., p. 145 (translation modified).
177. Lukács, *History and Class Consciousness*, p. 197.

ian struggle on a *narrower basis*.[178]

Had Korsch read Labriola a little more carefully and not recorded him as just one more orthodox Marxist of the Second International,[179] he would not have mistakenly claimed that the periodization of Marxism had "not been broached by anyone else," since Labriola had developed a roughly similar account.[180] In fact, to the question, "Have we not lost in intensity and precision what we have gained in extension and complexity?"[181] Labriola answered: "The rhythm of the movement has become more varied and slower because the laboring mass has entered the scene as a distinct, political party, which in fact changes the manner and measure of this action and consequently its movement."[182]

Given the Hegelian matrix of Labriola's Marxism, it is not difficult to find even more parallels between his work and that of the post—

178. Karl Korsch, *Marxism and Philosophy*, trans. Fred Halliday (London, 1970), pp. 103–104.

179. Although in his *Die materialistische Geschichtsauffassung. Ein Auseinandersetzung mit Karl Korsch* (Leipzig, 1929), Korsch took the time to differentiate Labriola from Bernstein, who had sought to appropriate Labriola's thought in support of his revisions, and in an unpublished manuscript entitled "Gutachten über Antonio Labriola und seine Bedeutung für Theorie und Geschichte des Marxismus," dated 3 October 1929, he tried to differentiate Labriola from the rest of the Second International theorists on the ground that "Labriola's orthodoxy and the still developing Marxist theory in Italy—which is inextricably bound to him—is explained in part by the still unfinished revolution in Italy" (Karl Korsch, *Politische Texte*, ed. Erich Gerlach and Jürgen Seifert [Frankfurt am Main, Cologne, 1974], p. 317n.), Korsch read Labriola very superficially as a kind of Italian George Plekhanov who developed the "Hegelian philosophical trend." Korsch, *Marxism and Philosophy*, p. 95. Interestingly enough, Labriola regarded Plekhanov's work "a little below the level of a dissertation." Labriola, *Lettere a Croce*, p. 294. Plekhanov actually read the French version of Labriola's first two essays and wrote a very favorable review of them in the "legal" Marxists' journal *Novoje Slovo*—now included in George Plekhanov, *Les Questions Fondamentales du Marxisme* (Paris, 1947), pp. 197–233. Since it was only in the third essay (*Socialism and Philosophy*) that Labriola rejected Marxism outright as a philosophy of history, and undertook to outline his original interpretation, it is not at all surprising that Plekhanov took Labriola for a fairly standard orthodox Marxist. For more details on the Russian reception of Labriola, see Valentino Gerratana, *Ricerche di Storia del Marxismo* (Rome, 1972), chap. 4, "Sulla 'Fortune' di Labriola," pp. 145–169.

180. Korsch, *Marxism and Philosophy*, p. 95.

181. Labriola, *Materialist Conception of History*, p. 55.

182. Ibid., p. 58. But where Korsch's superficial account may be explained by his

World War I generation of Hegelian Marxists. Some examples: Marxism as a method;[183] ascribed proletarian class consciousness that regards "the proletarians [as] those who will resolve the present antithesis, whether they know it or not";[184] the stress on mediation as the decisive theoretical task;[185] etc.

But while Labriola was in the midst of carrying out his reconstruction of historical materialism, he was also teaching courses in the philosophy of history at the University of Rome. More specifically, he was grappling with the problem of determinism, leading him to abandon Marxism as a philosophy of history (and here Croce's criticism may have had some impact).[186] This necessitated a reconsideration of most of the theses that he had outlined in the first essay; thus, in the series of letters to Sorel published as *Socialism and Philosophy* (the third and last completed essay), his emphasis changed.

The self-confidence and enthusiasm of the first essay gives way to a more cautious approach: "We must confess that all the serious, relevant, and correct things that have been written do not yet make a complete theory which has risen above the stage of first forma-

---

being out of touch with any sustained discussion of the subject, the same cannot be said of Giacomo Marramao's similar analysis in his *Marxismo e Rivisionismo in Italia* (Bari, 1971), p. 117, when he writes: "*Both from a political as well as a theoretical viewpoint*, and notwithstanding the greater amount of critical perspective in his interpretation of Marxism with respect to that of his contemporaries (Kautsky included), Labriola is a Marxist of the Second International, who does not transcend the limitations of a *positive* comprehension characterizing the theoreticians of that generation."

183. Labriola, *Materialist Conception of History*, p. 135.

184. Ibid., p. 170 (translation modified).

185. Ibid., p. 154. Labriola writes: "It is not merely a matter of opening the eyes and of seeing, but of a maximum effort of thought directed at overcoming the multiform spectacle of immediate experience, in order to reduce its elements to a genetic series" (translation modified). In *Socialism and Philosophy*, p. 94, Labriola further clarifies the social character of this mediational process: "This brain work, which makes itself known in our own consciousness as a fact concerning only our individual personality, is going on in each one of us only in so far as we are beings living together in a certain environment that is socially and therefore historically developed."

186. Thus, Dal Pane, *Antonio Labriola*, pp. 377–378, writes: "In 1895–96, Labriola discussed the doctrine of determinism as a special case of a more general doctrine consisting in the application of the genetic method to psychology and ethics. . . . In the courses of 1897–98, 1898–99, and 1899–1900, Labriola went back to and dealt with the doctrine of determinism in various ways." Labriola himself writes in 1900: "Not one of my past courses of philosophy of history will ever be lost

tion.''[187] Furthermore, the whole doctrine, as "a *philosophy* . . . , i.e., as a general conception of life and of the world, does not seem to me that it can enter among the articles of popular culture.''[188] Cautiously but unmistakably, Labriola even criticized Engels for having played down the philosophical dimension in a situation where the incomplete and still preliminary state of the doctrine made that dimension all the more important.[189] Thus recognizing the doctrine's incompleteness, Labriola places increasing importance on immediately political questions: "Henceforth no one can be a socialist, unless he asks himself every minute: What is the proper thing to think, to say, to do, under the present circumstances, for the best interest of the proletariat?''[190]

Given Marxism's metamorphosis from a philosophy of history to a

---

for me. . . . I have roamed for years over various fields. Once, Vico clothed in a very modern science, another time a methodological comparison between history and philology. One year I stopped to illustrate the shifting relations between *Church and State*, another to re-examine Morgan's *pre-history* in relation to the most recent studies. Twice I dealt with the history of modern socialism from Babeuf to the International, in a documentary way; and in another case I illustrated the origins of the Italian bourgeoisie and the conditions of Italy toward the end of the thirteenth century. I discussed various times the French Revolution—the only point in history in which I feel . . . to have a specific competence—so to give, in a summary, a beginning to the correct cognition of what constitutes the essentials . . . of *modern society*." Labriola, *La Concezione Materialistica*, pp. 320–321.

187. Labriola, *Socialism and Philosophy*, pp. 65–66.

188. Ibid., p. 66 (translation modified). As Gramsci, in a similar way, pointed out, the impossibility of *popularizing* Marxism is a consequence of it not having yet achieved the kind of full systematization that neither he nor Labriola considered attained: "If the doctrine in question has not yet reached this 'classical' phase of its development, any attempt to 'manualize' it is bound to fail, its logical ordering will be purely apparent and illusory, and one will get, as with the 'Popular Manual,' just a mechanical juxtaposition of disparate elements that remain inexorably disconnected and disjointed in spite of the unitary varnish provided by the literary presentation." Gramsci, *Prison Notebooks*, p. 434.

189. Labriola, *Socialism and Philosophy*, pp. 88, 106. See also Labriola to Engels, 13 June 1894, where he already indicates uneasiness with Engels's thesis of the disappearance of philosophy into the special sciences: "It is very true what you say, that philosophy as a whole in itself is destined to disappear, except for logic and the dialectic (which means the doctrine of the forms of knowledge). . . . On the other hand, this has always been the genuine part of philosophy." Marx and Engels, *Corrispondenza con Italiani*, p. 538.

190. Labriola, *Socialism and Philosophy*, p. 83. This general position explains

not yet fully developed *Weltanschauung*, it is understandable that Labriola's focus shifted to the problem of *constitution* (although he did not employ this term, which came into use only later under the influence of Husserlian phenomenology), and that he stressed the *instrumental* rather than the *realistic* interpretation of key concepts typical of the objectivistic orthodox Marxism of his time.[191] Thought comes to be seen as labor,[192] and production becomes the apprehension and articulation of the things themselves.[193] In passages that have been used erroneously to support the stereotype of Labriola as "a Second International thinker," he praises Engels's *Anti-Dühring* not for its backsliding into positivism—as it has primarily come to be read—but for its attempt to avoid empty "dialectical" formulations lacking any real basis in life.[194] In fact, *Anti-Dühring* is seen as an antidote to the metaphysical way of thinking: that mythologizing tendency, implicit in the very nature of languages, whereby fixated

why, in the face of Bernstein's critique of orthodox Marxism, Labriola was more concerned with practical political questions than with any specific doctrinal point. Thus, in a letter to Bernstein, 1 January 1899, he asks: *"Willst du weiter auf die deutsche Partei wirken oder willst du von der Partei ausscheiden?"* Labriola, "Lettere a E. Bernstein," p. 320.

191. Although some of Husserl's work had appeared during Labriola's lifetime, he never encountered it other than through seeing some references. In fact, in a letter to Croce, 17 September 1903 he writes: "You who knows everything, can you tell me who is the philosopher Husserl?—I have found citations to his *Logische Untersuchungen* and nothing less than to page 708 of the second volume. This leads one to suppose that it is a work of at least 1,400 pages. If such a logical whale had passed through the waters of Löscher [Rome's best bookshop], I would certainly have seen it—notwithstanding my present book-phobia. The book must not have reached Rome." In another letter, three days later, he adds: "I would hope that this Husserl, who has the courage to write 1,400 pages, is not the follower of that idiot Brentano, ex-priest, Austrian, money-monger, author of invented theories, and who spent two years in the insane asylum where he deserves to remain." Labriola, *Lettere a Croce*, pp. 367–368.

192. Labriola, *Socialism and Philosophy*, p. 87. Also, in a letter to Kautsky, 29 August 1897, he writes: "You are wrong in distinguishing those who are at the treadmill (*Tretmühle*) of practice (as you see yourself) from those who are only in the theoretical field—as in my case. *For us*, it seems to me, theory and practice are only one thing. *It is always a matter of knowing what would be appropriate to do.*" Labriola, "Lettere a E. Bernstein," p. 312.

193. Labriola, *Socialism and Philosophy*, p. 110, where he discusses "science itself as work."

194. Ever since his previously discussed 1872 review of Augusto Vera's work, Labriola had become reluctant to use *dialectical* in any positive sense.

words become projected as fixated reality.[195] And this was precisely the main positivist sin, which even tended to mythologize Marx himself.[196] The aim was throughout to develop a Marxism able to mediate the new situation without falling into metaphysical, opportunistic, or reductionistic traps.

But this theoretical reconstitution was easier to state than to carry out. Procacci is correct in claiming that Labriola

> has the clear perception that the new situation poses new tasks, he is aware that these new tasks can be resolved only by holding firm to the fundamental point of the unity between theory and practice and, therefore, of the historical and organizational continuity of the socialist movement. Yet, he fails to see what the newness of the situation consists of and the tasks that it postulates.[197]

Furthermore, Labriola did not always carry his rejection of Marxism as a philosophy of history, nor his new stress on the need to constitute theoretical mediations, to its logical consequences. As a result, at the same time that he was vindicating the philosophical dimension, defending the necessarily fragmentary character of revolutionary theory, prefiguring the process of historical reconstruction as art, and arguing for the autonomy of theory,[198] he uncritically retained the genetic method, a notion of historical inevitability—at least regarding the genesis of the present[199]—and a notion of historical continuity,[200] all of which betray lingering doubts on many fundamental questions.

195. Labriola, *Socialism and Philosophy*, pp. 101–102.

196. Ibid., p. 120.

197. Procacci, "Antonio Labriola e la Revisione," p. 277.

198. Thus, in closing his series of letters to Sorel, which constitute *Socialism and Philosophy*, Labriola writes, after lengthy theoretical detours: "I hear a small voice of protest coming from those comrades who are so ready to raise objections. And this voice says: 'All this is sophistry and doctrinarism. What we need is practice.' Certainly, I agree with you, you are right. Socialism has so long been utopian, scheming, off-hand, and visionary, that it is well to repeat now all the time that what we need is practice. For the minds of those who adopt socialism should never be out of touch with the things of the actual world, should continually study their fields, in which they are compelled to work hard for a clear road. But my supposed critic should take care not to become doctrinaire himself. . . . If historical materialism does not hold good, it means that the prospects for the coming of socialism are doubtful and that our thoughts of a future society are a utopian dream." Labriola, *Socialism and Philosophy*, p. 159.

199. Ibid., p. 127.

200. Labriola, *Materialist Conception of History*, p. 237: "Need we remind the

This same situation obtains in Labriola's politics, where the biting criticism of socialist policies and programs remained caught in a unilinear vision that not only considers full bourgeois growth the condition for all further socialist development but ends up totally dismissing the peasantry as historical ballast,[201] and even supporting imperialist expansion as a necessary stage in the modernization of the non-Western world.[202] The awareness of the problems does not automatically guarantee ready solutions. But while "the crisis of Marxism" as a symptom of changing social conditions necessitating new interpretations shook the faith of even the best Marxists of the period, Labriola stubbornly insisted on a reconstruction of historical materialism to meet the new needs. Thus, in a letter to Croce of 8 January 1900, he writes:

> Socialism is now entering into a pause. This confirms historical materialism. The economic-political world has been complicated. That cretin Bernstein can believe to have played the role of Joshua, that good man Kautsky can delude himself as playing the role of the custodian of the sacred ark. . . . That Sorel can believe he has corrected what he has never learned. . . . But tell me, what is the *really new* feature of the world that in the eyes of so many has made evident the imperfections of Marxism? This is the point. Reality cannot be grasped with reasonings—but through perceptions.[203]

---

reader that writing was never lost, although the peoples who invented it disappeared from historic continuity? Need we recall again that we all have in our pockets, engraved in our watches, the Babylonian dial, and that we make use of algebra, which was introduced by those Arabs whose historical activity has since been dispersed like the sands of the desert? It is useless to multiply these examples because it is sufficient to think of technology and the history of discoveries in the broad sense of the word, for which the almost continuous transmission of the instruments of labor and production is evident. And after all, the provisional summaries which are called universal histories, although they always reveal, in their aim and in their execution, something forced and artificial, would never have been attempted if human events had not offered to the empiricism of the narrators a certain thread, even though subtle, of continuity." See also Labriola, *Socialism and Philosophy*, p. 118n.

201. Labriola, *Materialist Conception of History*, p. 65.

202. In a famous interview of 13 April 1902, Labriola came out explicitly in favor of Italian imperialism (now in Labriola, *Scritti Politici*, pp. 491–499). This position, however, was typical of many leading socialists of the time, and Labriola had consistently held it at least since 1897. Gerratana, "Introduzione," pp. 92–97.

203. Labriola, *Lettere a Croce*, p. 337.

Already in 1896 Labriola had come to realize that traditional Marxism was not up to the task of making sense out of the new historical phenomena: "The Marxist theories themselves (and here I mean the *true* ones) are nowadays partly inadequate to explain the new economic and political phenomena of the last two decades."[204] A year later, in a letter of 29 August 1897, he confides to Kautsky:

> It is certain that in the socialist and labor movement of the whole world there is an *increase of extension* which does not correspond to the intellectual unity of the leader and of the writers. And it is furthermore also certain that in international relations what dominates are equivocations, illusions, and occasionally lies. In our whole press there has been the introduction of a habit of conventionalism, diplomacy, and of stereotyped phrases: to which does not always correspond *that faith that justifies illusions*, since they rather hide a lukewarm skepticism.

And further on in the same letter, he asks:

> How is it that new intellectual forces do not come to help? How is it that from the whole mass of doctors and academics no new forces move toward socialism. . . . How is it that, especially in Germany, there is such a colossal growth of anti-socialist literature that remains *almost* without an answer?[205]

The pessimism increased with time. Thus, by 8 October 1898, Labriola's skepticism about the international role of German social democracy was even more explicit: "It seems to me that German social democracy is increasingly becoming *only an internal German matter* which, on the other hand, corresponds very well to my opinion that socialism will undergo a long pause in its general development."[206] And by 3 January 1903, he was totally disgusted with the socialist movement in Italy, which he saw as tamed and incapable of any revolutionary initiative: "The government is happy with the social peace, since it has domesticated the socialists. . . . This situation will last a long time, since the experiment seems to have succeeded."[207]

---

204. To Romeo Soldi, 31 August 1896; quoted in Gerratana, "Introduzione," p. 89.
205. Labriola, "Lettere a E. Bernstein," pp. 312–313.
206. Ibid., p. 317.
207. Ibid., p. 336.

Politically defeated, theoretically still in a state of transition, and personally isolated, Labriola died on 2 February 1904, in a situation that was even worse than his darkest premonitions. He left no followers even close to his stature. Croce, his closest friend, had long ago left no doubts about fundamental disagreements with Labriola. Given his unusual background as well as the context in which he lived, he was able before anyone else to come to the frustrating realization that the *systematization* of Marxism, which he had attempted, either tended to destroy the revolutionary thrust of the doctrine (as was the case with contemporary interpretations of Second International theoreticians) or, if it retained Marxism's original spirit, was *in principle* impossible to carry out. After initial unsuccessful efforts at such a systematization, Labriola quickly came to the conclusion that the metaphysical framework necessary to hold it together—the secularized Hegelian philosophy of history—could not be retained. And in his attempt to think through the problems that resulted, he anticipated the whole subsequent trajectory of Western Marxism from Lukács to Adorno.

Labriola's Legacy

Notwithstanding Labriola's close contacts and intense correspondence with German socialists, with the single exception of a very poor review by Konrad Schmidt,[208] his work was all but ignored in Germany.[209] But this was not true in Russia, where the general backwardness of the country made Labriola's concern with adapting Marxist theory to Italian socioeconomic conditions all the more relevant. Plekhanov gave his work a sympathetic review,[210] and both Lenin and Trotsky read the first two essays in the widely circulated French edition and were positively influenced by them. In a letter of 23 December 1897, Lenin wrote his sister Anna, urging her to trans-

---

208. This review, which was published in *Vorwärts*, 24 April 1897, greatly annoyed Labriola, as can be seen from the two letters he wrote to Kautsky, 25 June and 29 August 1897. Labriola, "Lettere a E. Bernstein", pp. 307. 313.

209. In this respect, it is indicative that whereas French, English, Russian, Spanish, etc., translations of Labriola's works have been available for over seventy years, only recently (1968) has a German translation of his work appeared.

210. Plekhanov, *Questions du Marxisme*

late into Russian at least part of the second essay,[211] a task that had already been undertaken by someone else, since a Russian translation of that second essay appeared in 1898.[212] Trotsky fondly recalls in his *Autobiography* how he read the same essays while in prison in Odessa, although he disparages Labriola's "brilliant dilettantism"—an evaluation that dismayed Gramsci, according to whom such a ridiculous evaluation "cannot be understood . . . other than as an unconscious reflex of the pseudo-scientific pedantry of the German intellectual group which had so much influence in Russia."[213]

In spite of the wide circulation of his essays, as Gerratana points out, "in Italy as well as on the international scale, the diffusion of Labriola's work remained only at the surface, and it did not translate into a real influence."[214] At best, his work was received as that of one of the most erudite *systematizers* of Marxism—this despite the fact that the subtle but crucial theoretical result of his work was precisely that no systematization of Marxism was possible without falling back into a type of covert idealism that Marxism had left behind. Without a philosophy of history sustained by an implicit collective consciousness, no systematization is possible that can retain a revolutionary thrust. If a *forced* systematization were carried out, as in the case of the Second International, it could be achieved only by trying to pass the Hegelian *Geist* as matter, identifying the given as the already realized concrete totality. But in this case, critical consciousness can only extend the hypostatized determinations of the given—the predicament of all opportunism and revisionism.

Few of those readers perceptive enough to discern a tension in Labriola's four essays have regarded this tension as the gradual surfacing of a fundamental problem of Marxist theory. Instead, they have more conveniently chosen to freeze this tension between two fixed positions projected back onto Labriola from the experiences of later

211. This letter is reprinted in *Rinascita* X, 3 (March 1954), 184.

212. For a detailed account of this, see Gerratana, *Storia del Marxismo*, pp. 148 ff.

213. Gramsci, *Quaderni del Carcere*, II, 1507.

214. Gerratana, *Storia del Marxismo*, p. 149. As Tronti also puts it, "Those few who in Italy read Marx actually read Labriola's account, and ironically enough, like Marx, rarely has Labriola been understood in terms of what he really wrote." Mario Tronti, "Tra Materialismo Dialettico e Filosofia delle Prassi: Gramsci e Labriola," in

Marxist deformations. Tronti, for example, writes:

> Within Labriola's thought there is a fundamentally weak point, which he
> shares with a whole traditional trend of interpretations of Marxism. . . .
> We are referring to that radical rupture, that break between *"two parts"* of
> Marxism, which is like an opening through which will pass all those who
> will want to "liquidate" Marxism. It is the distinction between an interpre-
> tation of history and a general conception of the world and of life, as if they
> were two separate and superimposed things. . . . It is what will become
> within orthodoxy and in the Marxist *Vulgate* the distinction between histor-
> ical materialism and dialectical materialism.[215]

It takes quite an imagination to translate Labriola's tormented reflec-
tions in *Socialism and Philosophy* or in the fourth unfinished essay
titled "From One Century to the Next"—which are attempts to
correctly formulate problems that emerged in the two earlier essays—
into a philosophical systematization such as "dialectical materialism"!

Although Labriola left no disciples either able or willing to continue his work, his thought did shape the Italian Marxist tradition
along lines that made it qualitatively different from its counterparts in
German social democracy or orthodox Marxism-Leninism. The continuity, however, was disrupted by the fact that Italian socialism
before World War I became a typical—if somewhat more internally
diversified—branch of the Second International, with all the positivist
trappings and reformist politics that this entailed. The tradition of
Labriola's Marxism was indirectly kept alive by his most illustrious
student, Croce, who at the same time deradicalized it within a generally liberal outlook. Gramsci's Marxism was essentially a reradical-
ization of Croce. According to the previously discussed Korsch-
Labriola explanation for the *theoretical* decline of Marxism—which
was also shared by Gramsci—in order to pick up the thread of the
Spaventa-Labriola tradition and resume the elaboration of the philos-

La Città Futura (Milan, 1959), p. 147.

215. Tronti, "Materialismo Dialettico," p. 151. A similar interpretation can be
seen prefigured in Ernest Untermann's postscript to the English translation of *Socialism
and Philosophy* ("Antonio Labriola and Joseph Dietzgen," pp. 222–260). The only
difference, however, is that Untermann sees the split as desirable and, to the extent that
he does not feel that Labriola had sufficiently elaborated "dialectical materialism," he
brought in Dietzgen to "complete" Labriola!

ophy of praxis, it is necessary to jump more than a full decade to Gramsci's critique of Italian socialism.

Further difficulties arise, however, when one considers that the Gramscian heritage has been appropriated by the Italian Communist Party and instrumentalized in a way that makes its reconstruction much more difficult than otherwise. Consequently, any attempt to articulate and evaluate Gramsci's outlook entails keeping a constant watch on Togliatti and the party that he led for so long.

III

From Philosophy to Politics

"The Best Tactician of the International Communist Movement"

On the occasion of the fiftieth anniversary of the formation of the Italian Communist Party (PCI), Lukács described Togliatti's political role in these terms.[1] This comradely praise, fully in line with Marxist-Leninist values emphasizing the political realization of theoretical truths established by Marx and Lenin, also unwittingly repeated what had been the most persistent and discrediting criticism of Togliatti from the time he returned to Italian public life at the end of World War II to his death in 1964. Such a characterization of Togliatti had been used to designate, at best, a man of somewhat limited vision, at worst, a conniving politician understood "in an openly disparaging way, according to a petty bourgeois commonsense . . . tradition of politics considered as the jungle of violence and cleverness, of treachery and power."[2] Lukács's description thus captures, even more than he originally intended, the tragedy and ambiguity of Togliatti's life, as well as the distinctive feature of a party that Togliatti more than anyone else helped to mold. According to accounts within and without the party, Gramsci's theoretical genius has cast such a long shadow as to effectively occlude the decisive impact of such key political figures as Amedeo Bordiga, Umberto Terracini, and Angelo Tasca, so that their decisive impact on party history is all but ignored. After

1. In *L'Unità*, 24 January 1971. Elsewhere, Lukács described Togliatti as an admirable tactician but not "a modern Lenin." See Theo. Pinkus, ed., *Gespräche mit Georg Lukács* (Hamburg, 1967), p. 71. One can only wonder what "a modern Lenin" would look like—especially in Italy!

2. Giuseppe Vacca, *Saggio su Togliatti* (Bari, 1974), p. 462.

Gramsci's early imprisonment and, consequently, his removal from day-to-day political decisions, it fell to Togliatti to accommodate the "philosophy of praxis" to Stalinist realities and translate it into an operational, long-range strategy. Any attempt to locate the roots of the PCI's "historical compromise," or to sketch the political background that makes present-day Italian communism so different from other brands, must begin with an examination of the political predicament of those dark years of exile in the 1920s and 1930s, when Togliatti consistently sought both to retain the Italian party's autonomy and to stay in the international wing of Stalin's deadly bureaucratic apparatus.

The PCI's need to chart an independent course and, at the same time, operate within the mandates of the international communist movement (i.e., the immediate requirements of Russian foreign policy) is only one of many political ambiguities extending from the party's beginning in 1921 to the present. Yet, the most striking feature in this long succession of ambiguities is an underlying, uninterrupted continuity in keeping a Gramscian vision long after its general neo-Hegelian philosophical framework had been displaced by an Enlightenment positivistic philosophy of history and its politics irremediably compromised. A variation of this can be seen in official party accounts that, according to Salvadori, have presented "the party's path . . . as a process of right decisions, after the elimination of Bordighism and of Tasca's Right opportunism."[3] Even today, after more than a third of a century of debates concerning the matter, the official party position remains basically unchanged. Vacca, for instance, still defends this continuity in terms of "the *pertinence* with which [the PCI] has reelaborated and reconsidered the theme of the transition during the last half-century."[4] The particularity of the Italian road to socialism is seen as "supported by a general theory of the revolutionary process and of the transition to socialism,"[5] not as an alternative but as "a specification and articulation of the worldwide revolutionary pro-

3. Massimo L. Salvadori, "L'Attuale Storiografia del Partito Comunista (1921–1923)," in his *Gramsci e il Problema Storico della Democrazia* (Turin, 1970), p. 156.

4. Vacca, *Saggio su Togliatti*, p. 15.

5. Ibid., p. 399.

cess."[6] Even more critical commentators such as Berti essentially accept this account of a triumphant, irresistible march: "Notwithstanding all the errors . . . it has been possible to construct a politics which has allowed not a single party, but all of the progressive forces of Italian society to advance incessantly."[7] The real reasons for the continuity, however, are to be found elsewhere: in the PCI's attempts to realize a Spaventa-Labriola version of the bourgeois revolution (including both *political* and *social* emancipation), which the weak Italian bourgeoisie was unable fully to carry out, and in the PCI's attempts to complete the interrupted process of national unification.[8]

What makes *Italian* Marxism radically different in theory from Marxism-Leninism and in practice from both traditional social democracy and the bureaucratic collectivism of the Soviet bloc and China is its retention of a Gramscian vision, which, while contradicting official Marxist-Leninist ideology, provides an ethical and subjectivistic dimension superior to the discredited materialism of "really existing socialism." Having fully internalized the rejection of Marxism as a philosophy of history, following Labriola and Croce, Gramsci could never impose a plan from above, confident of its propriety because of

6. Ibid., p. 400. This, of course, is a further application of that doctrine of the concrete universal so dear to both Gramsci and Togliatti, which reappears at almost every crucial political turn. According to Vacca, what reconciles a worldwide revolutionary perspective and the seemingly revisionist practice entailed by the "Italian road to socialism" is Togliatti's "new conception of history," which vindicates the primacy of politics and successfully integrates social theory and social practice: "As a unified theory of history able to ground and enlighten the worldwide process of transition from capitalism to socialism, it develops with the advancing of such a historical transcendence and takes the form of an integral science of politics." Ibid., p. 477. Presumably, Togliatti's articulation of this science of politics was what guided him through the various seemingly irreconcilable positions that he came to defend throughout his career. This communist variation of the doctrine of papal infallibility at the level of essence successfully reconciles all decisions that may seem contradictory and politically dubious at the level of appearance. With Vacca, this "science of politics" becomes a retrospective legitimating tool that, in principle, does not allow even the most minute error of judgment. In an all too familiar Stalinist fashion, failures are invariably located not in the political decisions themselves but in their execution. Thus, it turns out that it is always the lower echelons of the party, rather than its leaders, who are responsible for setbacks and defeats.

7. Giuseppe Berti, "Appunti e Ricordi (1919–1926)," *Annali Feltrinelli* VIII (1966), 185.

8. Although the PCI jealously guards its internationalist revolutionary credentials,

its having been deduced from some fictitious Marxist "science." At best, Gramsci's Marxism could seek a cultural hegemony only within an autonomous public sphere that would subsequently elaborate its own goals. From the very beginning, Italian Marxism could interpret the transition to socialism only as economic modernization and political democratization, putting aside all questions as to what form the resulting society eventually would take.

Having begun as a splinter out of the Socialist party in the midst of the fascist drive for state power, matured during the height of Stalinism, and come into its own politically during the cold war, the PCI has had to conceal its real identity even from itself. Ambiguity became its normal *modus vivendi*. After World War II, an unyielding adherence to its occasionally revolutionary rhetoric would have hindered its claim to represent a mass-based democratic Left, and full acknowledgment of its politically modernizing functions and lack of any qualitatively different political alternatives to the liberal state would have alienated its base in the working class. Pending the achievement of a popular majority of full participation in the government, this ambiguity has allowed the party to play its parliamentary role and, at the same time, to pay lip service to vague revolutionary ideals. Precisely because of this, however, the party has also condemned itself to the status of a perpetual oppositional minority seeking to achieve its parliamentary goal through a contradictory ideological posture that comes more and more to contradict its practice—especially when it participates in the government not as the opposition but as part of the active governing coalition. Its electoral and parliamentary successes tend to result in a general alienation of its base because

---

it also makes claims to this national heritage. Thus, Togliatti's own account of this continuity of vision, "whether referring to the value of the historical Right [in the late nineteenth century]—the only nucleus of the revolutionary bourgeoisie prematurely defeated in its intentions and in its contradictory efforts toward national regeneration—or to the rapid exhaustion and overturning of the idealistic rebirth at the beginning of the century, or, lastly, to the progressive value of early Italian Hegelianism," has a great deal of validity. Vacca, *Saggio su Togliatti*, p. 471. That this was a constant theme in Togliatti's perspective can be seen from the fact that it appears in the *Ordine Nuovo* writings in the early 1920s, is repeated in the 1950s, and resurfaces again in a review written a few months before his death in 1964. See his "Rileggendo l'*Ordine Nuovo*," in Palmiro Togliatti, *Antonio Gramsci* (Rome, 1972), pp. 206–216.

of failure to bring about any of the major qualitative changes promised by the official ideology. Consequently, whenever the party comes close to turning into the hegemonic political force that it wants to become, it also generates disillusionment within the ranks, resulting in future setbacks at the polls and the proliferation of various ultra-left splinter groups.

The situation at the international level is just as bad. Seeking to loosen its ties with Russia stemming from the cold war alignments, the Italian Communist Party has repudiated most of the social, economic, and political characteristics of the bureaucratic collectivism predominant in the Eastern bloc. But it has not yet been able to negotiate a working reconciliation with the United States, which is slowly attempting to redefine its pre-Vietnam imperialist strategy in favor of a new economic and cultural mode of international domination—and which is thus very cautious in altering too abruptly any stable, established alliances. Nor has the PCI made any headway in its overtures to Western European social democracy, which is itself fragmented and embroiled in internal conflicts and traditional rivalries.

Such a complex political predicament does not readily lead the Italian Communist Party to undertake a totally unprejudiced confrontation of its own history. A confrontation of this type would yield no immediate political benefits, and would risk inflaming internal oppositional forces that have been smoldering for years. In 1956, the party did apparently make an honest attempt to come to terms with its own past.[9] But now and for the immediate future, any resolution of its fundamental ambiguity is out of the question. This explains why

9. It would be too much to expect the PCI to have remained pure and honest throughout the Stalinist period. Among other things, that would have meant organizational death. Thus, early attempts at historical reconstruction fell fully into line with predominant Moscow positions. The very editorship of Gramsci's prison writings was assigned after World War II to Felice Platone, who, not by accident, has been described as "the honorary commander of ideological firing squads." Giorgio Bocca, *Palmiro Togliatti* (Bari, 1977), II, 421. As might be expected, the operation was not untypical of the Stalinist standard procedure. A comparison of the unedited text of Gramsci's letters published in 1965 with the originally edited version has led Sechi to remark: "What the fascist jailors did not dare to do has been done by *Felice Platone* and his authoritative 'supervisor' [Togliatti]." Without ever informing the reader (and thus creating a presumption of authenticity concerning texts so unfaithfully transcribed), there has been a systematic omission of all the passages in the letters where Gramsci

internal debates are wide open but generally inconclusive, and why the political profile remains as blurred as ever.[10]

The international conditions for a clear-cut resolution of these issues do not exist nor are they likely to develop soon. Internal politics in Italy, as with every small dependent country, remain a function of broader international political configurations tied to the shifting dynamic of major power blocs. Understanding the workings at this level provides a good insight into the reasons behind many of the ambiguities that lie strewn in the path of the party's history. But just as important to understanding this history is an acquaintance with the formation of Togliatti's philosophical, social, and political perspective from the time he became politicized with Gramsci in Turin shortly before World War I to the years between 1926 and 1964, when after accepting first Bukharinism and then Stalinism, he slowly and systematically laid the foundations of what came to be known as the historical compromise, Eurocommunism, and other unorthodox political projects.

---

refers to or discusses Bordiga, Trotsky, and, more indirectly, Luxemburg and the Left opposition.'' Salvatore Sechi, ''Spunti Critici sulle *Lettere del Carcere* di Gramsci,'' *Quaderni Piacentini* VI, 9 (January 1967), 100–127. Thus, any reference to Stalin's enemies was omitted, along with a comparison between the fascist and the Soviet government. Gramsci's critique of Engels disappears, and even the list of books that Gramsci requested from his relatives was pruned of all those works banned by Stalinist censors. A similar fate befell the history of the party's early years, as well as the evaluation of the role of various central figures such as Tasca and Bordiga, who had subsequently broken with the PCI. A maneuver of this type, however, could have been successful only in Russia or in other similarly totalitarian societies. In a still relatively open society such as postwar Italy, it was immediately exposed for the fraud it was, eventually resulting in the slow publication of most of the relevant documents and gradual reevaluations of crucial events. For an excellent account of the PCI's way of dealing with history, see Luigi Cortese, ''Introduzione'' to Angelo Tasca, *I Primi Dieci Anni del PCI* (Bari, 1971), pp. 7–76. This situation has changed considerably. Thus, the recent critical edition of Gramsci's *Prison Notebooks* (1975) could hardly have been put together any better and has become a paragon of scholarly excellence.

10. Although recent reconstructions of the party's past or of Togliatti's biography have reached a very high level of scholarship, the general political line has not significantly changed. Rather, if anything, it has been further entrenched. Paolo Spriano's three-volume *Storia del Partito Comunista Italiano* (Turin, 1967–1970), as well as Vacca's *Saggio su Togliatti* and Ernesto Ragionieri's *Palmiro Togliatti* (Rome, 1976), all reiterate the continuity thesis from *Ordine Nuovo* to the present. Reading these accounts, one would never suspect that, far from being what Cortese has called the PCI's self-evaluation of history as a ''triumphant rectilinear march'' (''Introdu-

Between Croce and Lenin

Although much mention has been made of the parallels in their lives, it is impossible to approach Gramsci's and Togliatti's work without underscoring the remarkable similarities in their biographies. Their formative years resulted in a political outlook that located them within a peculiarly *Italian* cultural tradition, and unmistakably conditioned their reception of what they initially considered to be Leninism.[11] Both shared a Sardinian background[12] and attended the University of Turin on identical scholarships.[13] Togliatti graduated in law and economics in 1915; Gramsci, for various reasons, dropped out of the faculty of letters after April 1915.[14] Both reached adulthood just before the outbreak of World War I (in 1914 Togliatti was twenty-one and Gramsci twenty-three), and their initial contacts with Marxism and socialist politics were guarded (Gramsci was primarily a Sardinian

zione," p. 13), the history of the party is one of defeats, compromises, and forced adjustments. A continuity of aims remains at the level of philosophical orientation and of concrete political practice contradicting explicit ideological tenets. Yet, the ideological smoke screen necessitated to protect the Gramscian vision and the social-democratic practice, first during the Stalinist period and, afterward, when a Frankensteinian pro-Stalin and pro-USSR political base had been created and had to be at least ideologically appeased, has resulted in major political problems that cannot readily be swept under the rug.

11. This is not to say, with Althusser or Hobsbawm, that the tradition was thereby "provincial." See Eric J. Hobsbawm, "The Great Gramsci," *New York Review of Books*, 4 April 1974, pp. 39 ff., and his "Dall'Italia all'Europa," *Rinascita*, 25 July 1975, pp. 15 ff. As Garin has shown, through Croce's teachings Gramsci and Togliatti entered their political careers at the acme of European culture of the time. Eugenio Garin, "Gramsci e Croce," in his *Intellettuali Italiani dell XX Secolo* (Rome, 1974), pp. 343–360.

12. Although Togliatti was born in Genoa in a Piedmontese family, after 1908 he spent some time in Sardinia, where his father had been transferred. Bocca, *Palmiro Togliatti*, I, 4; and Ragionieri, *Palmiro Togliatti*, p. 4.

13. In the same qualifying exams, Gramsci placed ninth and Togliatti second—a detail that Togliatti was often proud to recall for his comrades. Marcella Ferrara and Maurizio Ferrara, *Conversando con Togliatti* (Rome, 1953), p. 3. See also Alastair Davidson, *Antonio Gramsci: Towards an Intellectual Biography* (London, 1977), p. 58 and Giuseppe Fiori, *Antonio Gramsci: Life of a Revolutionary*, trans. Tom Nairn (London, 1970), p. 71.

14. Whatever may have been the reasons for Gramsci's dropping out—presumably related to the suspension of his scholarship in November 1914—they had nothing to do with the quality of his work. More likely, they were connected with his always frail health and with political dissension within the local socialist party as a result of his

nationalist and Togliatti remained generally apolitical). This initial tentativeness is not difficult to understand: during the prewar years, the Socialist party was mired in a deadening version of positivistic Marxism, which had little appeal for bright young intellectuals.[15] It could not begin to compete with official culture dominated at that time by Croce, for whom Marxism as a respectable theory had died at the beginning of the century, along with his friend and teacher Antonio Labriola.[16]

Politically, the situation was even worse. The Socialist party's right wing saw Italian state interventionism in the economy to stimulate the still weak capitalist infrastructure as the road to socialism (Bonomi). This reduced the party from an autonomous political organization to a defender of state capitalism against private interests. The paralyzing political consequences of this position were, paradoxically, shared by the internal Left-opposition. Thus, according to

---

"interventionist" article published in October 1914. Tasca (*I Primi Dicci Anni*, p. 98) writes: "With the end of the war I had one degree, Togliatti two, and Gramsci could have had ten had he bothered to collect them." That Gramsci's decision to leave the university was because of his becoming engaged in political journalism is argued convincingly by Giancarlo Bergami, *Il Giovane Gramsci e il Marxismo (1911–1918)* (Milan, 1977), pp. 78–79.

15. That Gramsci and Togliatti had little patience with the positivism of socialist leaders can be seen readily through a couple of citations. In 1917, Gramsci described Claudio Treves's "theoristic reformism" as "a toy of positivistic fatalism whose determinants are social energies abstracted from man and from will, incomprehensible and absurd: an arid mysticism with no outburst of suffering passion. This bookish vision of life saw unity and effects, but did not see multiplicity and man, whose unity is synthesis." To which he contraposed his voluntarism: "*The tenacious will of man* has been substituted for the *natural law* and for the pseudo-scientists' *fatal course of events.*" Originally published in *La Città Futura*, 11 February 1917; now in Paul Piccone and Pedro Cavalcanti, eds., *History, Philosophy and Culture in the Young Gramsci* (St. Louis, 1975), pp. 41–42. Two years later Togliatti was even more severe in his judgment: "Bless positivism, which used to send its neophytes around in mental asylums to measure the crania of delinquents and did not make out of every 'promising youth' a preacher of the moral renovation of the world." Palmiro Togliatti, "Parassiti della Cultura," originally in *Ordine Nuovo*, 15 May 1919: now in Palmiro Togliatti, *Opere*, ed. Ernesto Ragionieri (Rome, 1967), I, 29. It is not altogether insignificant that the positivists Togliatti had in mind—Enrico Ferri, Cesare Lombroso, Achille Loria, etc.—were also leading figures in Italian socialism.

16. Benedetto Croce, "Come Naque e come Morí il Marxismo Teorico in Italia (1895–1900)," in his *Materialismo Storico ed Economia Marxistica* (Bari, 1973), pp. 293–294.

Arturo Labriola's critique, because of this predicament, "authentic Marxists will be able to do nothing but keep alive the flame of revolutionary critique, waiting for the day when the old antagonism between worker and owner would reappear in a new, definite, and decisive form between the worker and the state."[17] Bissolati went even further and practically wrote off the party as a dead branch destined to be displaced by new shoots from the vigorous trunk of the labor movement.[18] Thus, the party's leadership ended up falling almost by default into the hands of a demagogue such as Mussolini, who, in a fashion reminiscent of Stalin, preached the political subordination of the labor movement to the party and the centralization of all power in a charismatic leader able to mobilize the masses in a state of permanent revolutionary commitment.[19] And Mussolini's ideas were not too far removed from those of prestigious figures such as Sorel, or even Michels and Mosca, who were both teaching at the time at the University of Turin.[20]

17. Gaetano Arfé, *Storia del Socialismo Italiano (1892–1926)* (Turin, 1965), p. 12.

18. Ibid., p. 139.

19. Mussolini, however, never regarded the voluntarism of the active minority as a tactical necessity but as a permanent state of affairs. Furthermore, the revolution was seen almost entirely as an act of faith in a context that was violently anti-intellectual. Mussolini's position could not, from the very beginning, have a secure future in the Socialist party. Renzo de Felice, *Mussolini il Rivoluzionario (1883–1920)* (Rome, 1970), pp. 110–123, where he argues that Mussolini's position cannot be considered socialist at all. For a discussion of the young Mussolini's version of Marxism as an internally coherent system of beliefs, see A. James Gregor, *Young Mussolini and the Intellectual Origins of Fascism* (Berkeley, Los Angeles, London, 1979), pp. 53 ff.

20. It is unlikely that Gramsci and Togliatti were unaware of their works at that time. Leonardo Paggi *Antonio Gramsci e il Moderno Principe* (Rome, 1970), pp. 121 ff. That Mosca and Michels had a profound impact not only on young Italian socialists but also on internationally prominent figures can be seen from G. Zinoviev's book, *Der Krieg und die Krise der Sozialismus* (Vienna, 1924), written while in close collaboration with Lenin during the war, where the author uses Michels's account to refute Trotsky's charges of bureaucratization of the Russian party in 1924. Paggi, *Antonio Gramsci*, p. 147. Of course, to the extent that both Michels and Mosca deal with political parties and "the political class," Gramsci confronted their ideas in his later years. Thus, in a letter of 30 January 1928, he ridicules Michels's book on contemporary France as "a fraud . . . guilty of the utmost hypocrisy for the purpose of academic advancement." Antonio Gramsci *Letters from Prison*, trans. Lynne Lawner (London, 1973), pp. 117–118. In the *Prison Notebooks*, the criticism is even harsher. Michels is deemed a terrible scholar (Antonio Gramsci, *Quaderni del Carcere*, ed. Valentino

During the two years of Mussolini's leadership, the Socialist party attracted all sorts of adventurers and social outcasts, most of whom were to fill the ranks and files of fascism a few years later. But it also caught the fancy of young intellectuals such as Gramsci and Togliatti,[21] who joined the party around that time[22] and remained "Mussolinian" well into 1915.[23] The whole group of young intellectuals in Turin, who in 1919 founded *L'Ordine Nuovo* and subsequently constituted one of the pillars of the newly formed Communist party, had been so enthusiastic about the left wing of the Socialist party that when a special election was called in 1914 to fill the term of a representative who had died, it first proposed Gaetano Salvemini as its candidate and, when he could not run, Mussolini. The effort failed because the rest of the socialists preferred a local worker, but the incident does give some idea of the political climate predominant in the circles that Gramsci and Togliatti frequented.[24]

Gerratana (Turin, 1975), p. 237): "imprecise and wishy-washy" (p. 1203), "superficial" and "infantile" (p. 233), etc. Mosca does not fare any better. His book *Elements of Political Science* was branded as "rough and insipid" (p. 1155), or, at best, "an enormous mess of a sociological and positivistic character" (p. 956).

21. Contrary to much subsequent rewriting of the history of the period, Mussolini did enjoy a great deal of popularity among young Socialist party members. Bocca reports that, when Mussolini would come to speak in Turin, the hall would quickly "fill with youth who recognized in him the fighting, hard socialist who had successfully chased from the party bourgeois types such as Bissolati and Bonomi, and who wrote in a clear, moving way." Bocca, *Palmiro Togliatti*, p. 23. See also Davidson, *Antonio Gramsci*, p. 67. As Gozzini puts it, "Even more than the uneducated masses, Mussolini's demagoguery affected certain nuclei of young socialist intellectuals who wanted the renewal of socialism." Giovanni Gozzini, "La Federazione Giovanile Socialista tra Bordiga e Mussolini (1912–1914)," *Storia Contemporanea* XI, 1 (February 1980), 103.

22. Gramsci entered the Socialist party toward the end of 1913, but, given the disastrous state of socialist politics, he did not immediately become very active. Davidson, *Antonio Gramsci*, pp. 63–65. Togliatti claims to have joined the party in 1914; others deny it. Since a fire destroyed the archives of the Turin section of the Socialist party on 18 December 1922, there is no way to verify either account. At any rate, it is clear that although not too active, both Gramsci and Togliatti "were in 1914 part of a small group of socialist intellectuals, . . . Togliatti in the shadow of Gramsci." Bocca, *Palmiro Togliatti*, pp. 18–19.

23. Tasca reports that, as late as 1917, Togliatti still held Mussolinian positions and defended the need for a *pax Britannica* for Europe as a result of the war. Tasca, *I Primi Dieci Anni*, p. 96; and Berti, "Appunti e Ricordi," p. 13n.

24. Tasca, *I Primi Dieci Anni*, pp. 91–92; and Antonio Gramsci, "The Southern

This enthusiasm for Mussolini was not an accident but was rather typical of their position at the time. It surfaced again when Mussolini broke with the socialist position of neutrality with respect to Italy's involvement in the war. Although Togliatti vigorously denied it in his reconstruction of party history, both he and Gramsci came close to leaving the Socialist party of that time in support of Mussolini when he broke with the party position.[25] Far from being "hesitant,"[26] Gramsci's support of Mussolini extended to the point that he sought to contribute to Mussolini's new mouthpiece, *Il Popolo d'Italia*, which was launched after his loss of the editorship of the socialist paper *Avanti!*[27] It was at that time that Gramsci, in full agreement with Togliatti,[28] wrote his well-known article defending Mussolini against Tasca's critique.[29]

Already in this early article, Gramsci articulated a style that has characterized most of the history of the Italian Communist Party down to Togliatti's post–World War II theses concerning polycentrism and his efforts to gain for his party some measure of independence from Moscow. It is a variation of the old Hegelian doctrine of the concrete universal, which, in Tasca's words, electrifies Gramsci's vision as "the idea of freedom realizable by the will."[30] The totality does not exist above and beyond the particulars that constitute it, but obtains its primacy precisely through them. By itself, the totality is an empty theoretical abstraction that receives its life and meaning only through the concrete activities seeking to realize it.[31] Thus, Gramsci saw the

Question," in his *The Modern Prince and Other Writings*, trans. Louis Marks (New York, 1957), pp. 32–33.

25. Palmiro Togliatti, *La Formazione del Gruppo Dirigente del Partito Comunista Italiano* (Rome, 1971), pp. 13–14.

26. This is how John Cammett has described it. See his *Antonio Gramsci, and the Origins of Italian Communism* (Stanford, Calif., 1967), p. 37.

27. Bocca, *Palmiro Togliatti*, p. 24. See also Berti, "Appunti e Ricordi," pp. 14, 42–43.

28. Ferrara and Ferrara, *Conversando con Togliatti*, p. 36; Davidson, *Antonio Gramsci*, p. 67; and Fiori, *Antonio Gramsci*, p. 97.

29. Antonio Gramsci, "Active and Operative Neutrality," *Il Grido del Popolo*, 31 October 1914; now in Piccone and Cavalcanti, *History, Philosophy and Culture*, pp. 116–120.

30. Tasca, *I Primi Dieci Anni*, p. 103.

31. The political articulation of this basic Hegelian doctrine was not restricted to

validity of the goals of the Second International not as absolute but strictly as a function of *how* these goals were realized in particular situations. For Gramsci, whenever the letter contradicts the spirit, it is the former that must yield: life is always more important than any of its abstract expressions. Against the Socialist party's principled but abstract stand of "absolute neutrality" toward the war, Mussolini had called for what Gramsci took to be a reconsideration of such a position in order to intensify political conflicts and eventually wrest control of the state from the incompetent and discredited bourgeoisie. Mussolini's position vindicated the particularity of the Italian situation against the abstract universality (the "doctrinaire formalism") of the remaining party leadership. Gramsci sought instead to transcend both the abstract universality of the party leadership and the equally

---

Gramsci and Togliatti, but became the trademark of all major Hegelian Marxists at that time. Thus, in Lukács, it became a highly sophisticated means of justifying Stalinism. This, however, does not mean that it follows—as Jay has inferred—that "the very use of totality as an expressive category, combined with the idea of 'imputed class consciousness,' is a license for tyranny." Martin Jay, "The Concept of Totality in Lukács and Adorno," in Shlomo Avineri, ed., *Varieties of Marxism* (The Hague, 1977), p. 156. It becomes that, unwittingly, in Lukács only because he systematically dismisses the *living* precategorical dimension to the point of relegating it to the level of a reactionary repository of irrationalism. As a result, the domination of the concept is unchecked, and all particularity ends up dissolved by the teleology of embodied reason—in this case, the party, and subsequently Lenin and Stalin. Paul Piccone, "Dialectic and Materialism in Lukács," *Telos*, No. 11 (Spring 1972), pp. 105–133. That this is merely a Lukácsian idiosyncrasy, rather than a necessary consequence of all varieties of Hegelian Marxism, can be seen by the way Korsch and, even more, Togliatti and Gramsci were able to deal with the same problems differently. To the extent that Korsch always emphasized the historically specific character of knowledge as mediation, he tended to evaluate theory from the viewpoint of a political praxis considered epistemologically primary rather than the other way around, as in Lukács. This is why he had to break with Marxism. Paul Piccone, "Korsch in Spain," *New German Critique* VI (Fall 1976), 153 ff. Since Korsch also had a notion of theory as formal constructs pretty well fixed once and for all, as Oskar Negt has shown in his "The Problem of Constitution in Korsch," *Telos*, no. 26 (Winter 1975–76), pp. 120–142, his Marxism could not be reconstituted and had to be either kept or scrapped as a whole. In Togliatti, and even more so in Gramsci, theory is not only regarded instrumentally, as in Korsch, but it is also considered informal and open-ended, so that its malleability allows for constant reconstitution in the light of changing historical conditions, and its spirit is salvaged at the preconceptual level to provide the criteria whereby the reconstitution takes place. This is why Gramsci and Togliatti side with Korsch on epistemological matters, and substantially follow Lukács's choices at the political level.

abstract particularity of Mussolini's still confused position,[32] in favor of a reasoned reconciliation that would have "taken what there could have been of vitality in Mussolini's position." The closing sentence of the article emphasized what was Gramsci's main target: the party's "comfortable position of absolute necessity," resulting in a paralyzing predicament of "naive Buddhist contemplation."

Thus, no matter how rash his "interventionist" position may appear in retrospect, it was not out of character or generally inconsistent with Gramsci's political philosophy. The key passage reiterates what subsequently became a familiar theme in Gramsci, i.e., the idea that "revolutionaries . . . conceive of history as the creation of their own spirit, made by an uninterrupted series of lacerations of other active or passive forces." Inasmuch as the main critique of the reformists by the left wing of the Socialist party (Arturo Labriola, Salvemini, Mussolini), with whom Gramsci sympathized, focused on the passivity of the reformists' program, it comes as no surprise that Gramsci cautiously sided with Mussolini against the reformers, who in Gramsci's words, "passively expect events to create for them the opportune moment, while the adversaries actively create their own hours and prepare their platform for the class struggle."[33]

Far from being an *orthodox* Marxist at that time, Gramsci was, by his own admission, "rather Crocean," and his main concern was to universalize the Crocean program by raising the masses to the highest levels hitherto achieved by culture.[34] He was violently opposed to the

32. That he regarded Mussolini's position as *abstractly* particular can be seen by the fact that he urged Tasca to distinguish between "Mussolini, the man from Romagna [the impulsive individual] and what was due to Mussolini as an *Italian* socialist." Gramsci, "Active and Operative Neutrality," pp. 118–119.

33. Ibid., p. 118. See also Davidson, *Antonio Gramsci*, p. 68, where, however, the same passage is slightly mistranslated and underemphasized.

34. Gramsci, *Quaderni del Carcere*, II, 1233. For a fuller discussion of Gramsci's Croceanism, see Maurice Finocchiaro, "Gramsci's Crocean Marxism," *Telos*, no. 41 (Fall 1979), pp. 41–56. See also Garin, "Croce," pp. 354 ff; and Davidson, *Gramsci e Antonio Gramsci*, pp. 94 ff. Writing from a perspective that can best be described as an uneasy blend of Althusserianism and *ouvrierisme*, Davidson concludes that Gramsci escaped "the ideological encrustations of his past"—i.e., Croce's philosophy—by adding "to the ideological praxis of his journalism the practical praxis of working among the workers" (pp. 81–82). Allegedly, Gramsci read Marx's "Theses on Feuerbach" in 1915 (p. 104) and, through "ceaseless contact with the workers and in

fatalism, mechanism, and evolutionism typical of the Marxism of the Second International:

> Man is above all spirit, i.e., a creation of history and not of nature. Otherwise, it would be impossible to explain why, to the extent that there have always been exploiters and exploited, and producers and selfish consumers of wealth, socialism has not yet been achieved. It is only because humanity has gradually become aware of its own value and has acquired the right to live independently of the schemes and rights of historically previously established minorities. And this consciousness has been formed not under the ugly goad of physiological necessities, but through intelligent reflection, first on the part of a few and then by a whole class, reflecting on the reasons for certain conditions and on how best to convert them from causes of servitude into symbols of rebellion and social reconstruction. What this means is that every revolution has been preceded by an intense critical effort of cultural penetration, of the infusion of ideas through groups of men who were initially unresponsive and thought only of resolving day by day, hour by hour, their own political and social problems, without creating links of solidarity with others who found themselves under the same conditions.[35]

It is not difficult to trace in this passage, written early in 1916, the outline of Gramsci's "absolute historicism" and general philosophical perspective. Such an approach tended to discourage an automatic reception of the predominant versions of Marxism. For Gramsci, if the Marx fashionable at the time did not fit with such a program of cultural emancipation, so much the worse for Marx:

> We are not amazed by the fact that Marx introduced positivist elements into his work. It can be explained: Marx was not a professional philosopher and he, too, dozed off every so often. What is certain, however, is that the

---

the mutual exchange of education" (p. 118)—especially during the council period—succeeded finally in going beyond Croce's elitism (p. 156). The problem with Davidson's "inventive praxis" is that it cannot account for Gramsci's constant return to Croce in the *Prison Notebooks* and the more important fact that, at every step, what distinguished Gramsci's position from that of other Marxists throughout the period is precisely his unflagging adherence to a version of Croce's neo-Hegelianism. Many young intellectuals have and will become involved with workers' lives and problems, but they do not all thereby become Gramscis.

35. Piccone and Cavalcanti, *History, Philosophy and Culture*, p. 21. The article "Socialism and Culture" originally appeared in *Il Grido del Popolo*, 29 January 1916.

essence of his doctrine is indebted to philosophical idealism and that in the further development of this philosophy the proletarian and socialist movements join and historically support the ideal trend.[36]

The crucial feature of Marxism is its German idealist core, which is also what is to be developed politically. In a manner diametrically opposed to recent efforts by French and English Marxists to salvage the "scientific" economic core of Marxism at the expense of its philosophical shell, Gramsci saw the philosophical element as the core to be saved and the scientistic component as the historically obsolete and irrelevant shell.[37] It is not surprising that *Capital* never rated very highly with Gramsci. If, as in the Russian bourgeois reading, *Capital* entailed a step-by-step succession of historical stages from feudalism to capitalism and only then to socialism, then *Capital* would have to be junked. What was important to save, once again, was the spirit and not the letter of Marxism. In his famous article in which he described the Bolshevik Revolution as "the revolution against *Capital*," he argued that

> in Russia Marx's *Capital* was the book of the bourgeoisie more than of the proletariat. It was the critical demonstration of the fatal necessity that in Russia a bourgeoisie had to be formed, that an era of capitalism had to begin, and that a Western-type civilization had to be installed before the proletariat might be even able to think about insurrection, class vindication, and revolution.

When and if historical materialism becomes a political obstacle, then it should be put aside. His admiration of the Bolsheviks was precisely the result of what he saw as their placing active men above wooden economic laws.

36. Ibid. p. 18. Originally published in *Il Grido del Popolo*, 19 October 1918.
37. In addition to the long-since defunct but once fashionable Althusserian interpretation of Marxism in France, a similar derivative brand of Marxism still thrives in England in journals such as *Economy and Society* and *New Left Review*—although the latter tends to emphasize the primacy of politics. Perry Anderson, *Considerations on Western Marxism* (London, 1976). Earlier in the century, discredited philosophical fads used to leave the continent for the greener pastures of the United States, where they would survive for another couple of decades. The trip must have been too taxing: nowadays such fads seem to drift to the closer and much more receptive British shores in their old age.

[Although] the Bolsheviks deny some of *Capital*'s claims . . . they live the Marxist thought that never dies, which is the continuation of Italian and German idealistic thought, which in Marx was contaminated with positivist and naturalist encrustations. And this thought always sees men—not brute economic facts—as the supreme factor in history.[38]

Aside from the fact that Gramsci's "Bolsheviks" had as much in common with their Italian counterparts as pizza has with borsch, this account is indicative of both his philosophical vision as well as his ignorance of what was going on in Russia.

When the war broke out, Gramsci, whose physical disability exempted him from military service, was called to fill gaps in the socialist press created by the draft. He rapidly developed his skills as a political journalist and rose to a position of influence within the Socialist party. He matured politically also. Togliatti initially was rejected for military service, too, because of his nearsightedness. Yet, he had been affected so much by Mussolini's views that he volunteered for Red Cross duty and was eventually inducted. When in December 1918 he was finally discharged, his political conciousness was decidedly behind that of Gramsci, on whom he relied for guidance over the next couple of years.[39] During this period Togliatti made up

38. Piccone and Cavalcanti, *History, Philosophy and Culture*, p. 123. Originally published in the Milan edition of *Avanti!*, 24 November 1917, and in *Il Grido del Popolo*, 5 January 1918.

39. During the war Togliatti had written a couple of articles for Gramsci's newspaper *Il Grido del Popolo* while he was on leave because of illness. Published toward the end of 1917, these articles dealt with economic issues Togliatti had studied at the university. Particularly relevant is his article "The Two Italies" (now in Togliatti, *Opere*, I, 6—9), where he argues that Italian custom regulations, far from accelerating the still unfinished process of national unification, tended instead to reverse it. The Italian protectionist policies "re-created, at the expense of the Southern provinces, the conditions of old colonial arrangements whereby our country exploited the colonies by denying them the freedom to sell and to buy. Having excluded from the market foreign industrial products, the South was forced to accept the high prices of manufactured goods and tools made in Italy. But commodities are exchanged for other commodities, and the foreign traders who no longer sold their industrial products stopped buying Southern agricultural products, so that, locked into the limited national market, their prices declined." Although conceived in a free-trade framework, this account has remained a cornerstone of interpretations of the relative worsening of the southern Italian economy down to the present. It reappears in Gramsci's unfinished "Southern Question."

for lost time, abandoning his support of free trade and appropriating all of Gramsci's political and philosophical positions.[40] This must not have been too difficult for someone who, as a student, had undertaken to translate more than 150 pages of Hegel's *Phenomenology*,[41] and who, even more than Gramsci, never hid his Hegelian background. This was apparent in 1925, when the International called on the various Communist parties to emulate the Bolsheviks by synthesizing with Leninism what was the best Marxism of their national traditions. Togliatti responded, at the same time indirectly rebuffing Bukharin's denunciation of the rebirth of "old Hegelianism" and of "voluntaristic" idealism within the Italian Communist Party.[42] Togliatti writes: "We came to [Marxism] through the same path followed by Karl Marx, i.e., departing from German idealistic philosophy, from Hegel." The reason for this was that the Marxism predominant at the time was a positivistic travesty:

"The normal path for reaching Marxism among us was that of the so-called scientific positivism, in its most heterogeneous forms, from Auguste Comte's metaphysics to . . . Enrico Ferri's criminology. As a result, there was a curious degeneration of historical materialism into a metaphysical doctrine announcing a social future altogether pre-established in its forms and absolutely and fatally certain as a future. . . . And this fatalism was called faith. And the faith had its preachers: and while the sermon and the waiting for the word bestowed and maintained in the movement a character of a high messianic level, the basest political merchandise was traded in

40. Ragionieri, *Palmiro Togliatti*, pp. 17–22; and Bocca, *Palmiro Togliatti*, pp. 25–28.

41. Cf. Ferrara and Ferrara, *Conversando con Togliatti*, p. 29. Although there is only Togliatti's testimony to support this claim, it is neither unlikely nor out of character. After all, even as late as 1957, when he was up to his neck in the political turmoil caused by Khrushchev's revelations concerning Stalin and the ensuing anti-Stalinism, Togliatti himself translated—or had translated—in *Rinascita*, the party's main political organ (XIV [1957], 34–35), Hegel's short essay, "Wer denkt abstrakt?" which emphasized that particular phenomena should be seen within the context of the totality in order to be properly appreciated. In fact, in discussing how to make sense out of, for example, an assassin, Hegel had written that it would have been abstract "to see in the assassin nothing other than this abstraction, that he is an assassin, and with this sole quality annihilate all the remaining human qualities." It is as if Hegel himself had written what was to become a standard communist apology for Stalin a century and a half earlier! Ragionieri, *Palmiro Togliatti*, pp. 39–41.

42. Ragionieri, *Palmiro Togliatti*, pp. 186–189.

contraband, behind the broad flag of Marxism and of the proletarian revolution. Passivity, the lack of a critical spirit, and rhetoric became the characteristics of the political organization of the Italian proletariat.[43]

This article, appropriately titled "Our Ideology," has been described as the philosophical foundation of Togliatti's entire subsequent "political thought and, in all probability, also the key to understanding the political struggles of the next 40 years." In fact, it was more of a philosophical testament, since the vindication of the Hegelian heritage and of voluntarism were joined to a call for party unity, which, only a year later, forced Togliatti to buckle under Bukharin's and Stalin's brand of Marxism-Leninism and thus accept a crude Enlightenment ideology completely at odds with "the philosophy of praxis"—as can be seen from Gramsci's violent rejection of Bukharin's philosophical platitudes in the *Prison Notebooks*. Far from being a new theoretical departure, Togliatti's "Our Ideology" merely summarizes an outlook that he had shared with Gramsci from the very beginning of *L'Ordine Nuovo* in 1919. Already at that time his critique of positivism and of the passive attitude it encouraged had been uncompromising. The project of cultural universalization that had been the socialists' trademark was attacked precisely because of its *contemplative* reception by the masses: it was counterproductive. Emancipation would take place only if the people actively relate to it as subjects by creating and re-creating that culture, thus really making it their own. Otherwise, it would be merely a matter of substituting one set of idols for another:

> We criticize and fight the concept of culture as a complex of notions and information. It is believed that the people are elevated by increasing the number of *things* that they have by communicating to them, as absolute truth, the result of scientific research. In this fashion scientific truths take the same place in the mind of the worker and of the peasant previously occupied by other absolute truths such as those of faith.

The emphasis is clearly on active subjectivity. What is important is the *process*, not the *product*. The recurring Hegelian doctrine of the

---

43. Togliatti, *Opere*, I, 648–649. Originally published in *L'Unità*, 23 September 1925.

concrete universal is what informs Togliatti's critique. Cultural emancipation can be attained only if the part actively appropriates and thereby becomes integrated into the whole and, at the same time, retains its character as an autonomous part:

> A scientist who formulates a hypothesis such as that of evolution is aware of this value which is in the mental labor of men and generations that have allowed him to reach that point, so that research and the formulation of the result is a genuine raising of his individual consciousness, a progress of man over himself, and has an intrinsic moral and spiritual importance. Take this result and feed it in the form of pills to someone else, and all the value is lost.[44]

The task is not to substitute science for old myths and religion, but to create a new humanity aware of itself as subject and creator. The task of socialism is to introduce all into *active* life:

> Science [must] take the place of the lost religious faith, and we want to raise workers to the modern conception, which is neither religious nor scientific, but is a conception of life, of history, of institutions, and of human beliefs as creations of men's free activity.[45]

It is the same argument that, in the *Prison Notebooks*, reappears as the Gramscian theory of intellectuals.[46]

Togliatti's relation to Gentile and Croce, the two pillars of twentieth-century Italian idealism, was as close, if not closer, than Gramsci's. In 1919, Togliatti acknowledged Croce as "the major educator of our generation in Italy" and as one whom "few can match in intelligence and in concrete historical evaluation of men and

---

44. Ragionieri, *Palmiro Togliatti*, p. 37.

45. Palmiro Togliatti, "Scienza e Socialismo," originally published in *Ordine Nuovo*, 19 July 1919; now in Togliatti, *Opere*, I. 47–48.

46. Thus, in the *Prison Notebooks*, trans. Quintin Hoare and Geoffrey Nowell-Smith (London, 1971), p. 9, Gramsci argues that "all men are intellectuals . . . but not all men have in society the function of intellectuals." In other words, to the extent that living necessitates thinking, all men deal with ideas, but, because of prevailing social relations, only some men function as intellectuals within a division of labor that relegates the majority of intellectuals to passivity and to an alienated existence. Socialism and communism in Gramsci's thought were always seen as allowing the destruction of these inhibiting social conditions so as to enable everyone to become fully and actively human.

events.''[47] Far from attacking Croce and Gentile for their idealism, he criticizes them from a perspective that regarded Marx as the culmination of Hegel:

> It has been German romantic philosophy that has been closed, in Hegel, with the assertion that history is the progress of freedom, and that the progress of freedom is the progress of consciousness. Karl Marx drew this truth from the cold and calm Olympus of philosophy and gave it new life by immersing it in the warm and moving wave of doctrines and beliefs in a social renewal.[48]

Both Croce and Gentile, however, seemed unable to descend from their philosophical Olympus and could not, as Ragionieri writes, ''comprehend the importance of the revolutionary antithesis as a moment necessary for historical development.''[49] At a time when Togliatti and many of his radical contemporaries thought revolution to be imminent, he criticized Croce's disenchantment with Marxism as being the result of a ''loss of subjective faith''—a faith upheld by socialists who were ''the heirs and continuators of the best human traditions.''[50] In 1919 the revolutionary rupture in socioeconomic realities was defended in terms of a cultural continuity that bourgeois society had already broken. Later, it was not this cultural continuity that was given up and brought into line with a socialist socioeconomic break; rather, it was the other way around, with socialism becoming increasingly the road to modernization for societies caught between

47. Palmiro Togliatti, ''Pagine sulla Guerra di Benedetto Croce,'' originally published in *Ordine Nuovo*, 7 June 1919; now in Togliatti, *Opere*, I, 39–40. That this evaluation of Croce's role was not altered too much afterward can be seen from another passage, written by Togliatti almost forty-five years later, shortly before his death, when, although overemphasizing the difference between *Ordine Nuovo* and Croce for political reasons, he again acknowledges the deep Crocean influence: ''It cannot be denied that, at least, he [Croce] awakened many from their slumber! For us in *Ordine Nuovo* the cultural renewal carried out by Crocean idealism had meant, first of all, the definitive liberation from every metaphysical and mechanistic encrustation of whatever origin and brand and, therefore, the acquisition of a great faith in the development of men's consciousness and will, and of ourselves as part of a great historical renovating class movement.'' Togliatti, *Antonio Gramsci*, p. 209.

48. Palmiro Togliatti, ''Per Chiudere una Polemica,'' originally published in *Ordine Nuovo*, 2 August 1919; now in Togliatti, *Opere*, I, 52.

49. Ragionieri, *Palmiro Togliatti*, p. 28.

50. Togliatti, ''Pagine sulla Guerra,'' pp. 41–42.

the economic domination of the multinationals and the political dead-weight of the bureaucratic apparatus.

Of course, the path to polycentrism and "the Italian road to socialism" took decades. Togliatti's youthful revolutionary enthusiasm was subdued after 1926, following the failure of various European revolutionary efforts and the coming of fascism, not to mention his forced exile in Russia and the impossibility of mounting even token opposition to Stalin. As with Lukács, who lived through a similar shock and made substantially the same political choice to remain within the communist movement during the darkest hours of the 1930s, Togliatti never abandoned the Hegelian framework. What was recycled within a contradictory framework and in much more positive terms than before was that Enlightenment tradition so readily maligned and dismissed as obsolete at a time when communism seemed just around the corner from post—World War I capitalist ruins. But capitalism became stabilized or, as in Italy and Germany, was replaced by regimes that, to safeguard existing socioeconomic relations, did not hesitate to discard whatever gains the unfinished bourgeois revolution had started. Both Togliatti and Lukács had gradually to redefine the role of the communist movement *away from* any sharp revolutionary break ushering in an unspecified but qualitatively new order, and increasingly *toward* defending and universalizing precisely those bourgeois values capitalism could no longer uphold—a feature that had been an inextricable, if not always sufficiently emphasized, part of their outlook from the very beginning of their political careers. Lukács ended up rewriting nineteenth- and twentieth-century intellectual history as a struggle between the growing irrationalism of bourgeois culture and the rationalist tradition carried out by the communist movement.[51] Togliatti, in contrast, redefined the communist goal as the completion of the bourgeois revolution through parliamentary means, which, in the Italian context, could only mean further economic rationalization, social modernization, and political integration within the existing power relations.

51. Georg Lukács, *Die Zerstörung der Vernunft* (Berlin, 1954). For a fuller evaluation of Lukács's work along these lines, see Marco Macciò, "On the Later Lukács," *Telos*, no. 11 (Spring 1972), pp. 135—141; and Ferenc Feher et al., "Note on Lukács' *Ontology*," *Telos*, no. 29 (Fall 1976), pp. 160—181.

The revolutionary Croceanism that Gramsci and Togliatti shared made their encounter with Lenin, their participation in the workers' councils, and their subsequent founding of the Communist party fraught with scores of ambiguities that have been made all the more impenetrable by retrospective and politically motivated interpretations. Fascism, Stalinism, and World War II made the clarification and further elaboration of fundamental questions secondary (for all, except Gramsci, who pursued these questions in the *Prison Notebooks*), and ambiguities, far from being eliminated, were perpetuated as a means of survival in a volatile political context where principled stands could readily translate into death sentences under the shifting winds of Stalinist policies. The cold war simply extended that state of affairs, even when, after 1956, adherence to Stalinism began to entail grave political consequences.

Deprovincialization through the Workers' Councils

It is simply wrong to regard Gramsci and Togliatti as provincial in their overall theoretical vision or their political work. In 1919, however, they did seek to realize their project of national cultural renovation primarily in terms of the particular industrial situation in Turin.[52] Consequently, when the success of the council strategy became a matter of its political universalization, the deadweight of a much more backward Italy rapidly condemned the whole project to the same failure that parallel council experiments met in Bavaria and Hungary at roughly the same time and for similar reasons. The interpretation of this failure as a result of the inadequacy of the existing Socialist party, the subsequent formation of the PCI as a truly revolutionary alternative, and the full adherence to what Togliatti and Gramsci considered

52. As early as 1920, Amedeo Bordiga pointed out these limitations in their positions in a series of articles published in *Il Soviet* between 1 January and 22 February 1920; they now appear in Antonio Gramsci, *Selections from Political Writings (1910–1920)*, trans. John Matthews (London, 1977), pp. 214–233. See also Gwen A. Williams, *Proletarian Order: Antonio Gramsci, Factory Councils and the Origins of Communism in Italy (1911–1921)* (London, 1975), pp. 175–184, where Bordiga's position is elevated to that of a "Marxist science," and Gramsci's views are downgraded to those of an idealist dilettante. For a more balanced account, see Martin Clark, *Antonio Gramsci and the Revolution That Failed* (New Haven, Conn., and New York, 1977), pp. 74–95.

to be Leninism at the time signaled not only the attainment of a political maturation propelling them into the broader national and international context but also the beginning of all those ambiguities associated with the reception of Leninism. Yet, even in the council experience, the first of a long series of failures, their approach was idiosyncratic and fully in accordance with their vision of Marxism as a twentieth-century version of "the Protestant Reformation plus the French Revolution."[53]

This formula was more than just a felicitous metaphor. It captured almost perfectly the character of the social milieu within which Gramsci and Togliatti moved toward their first major political test during the workers' councils period. This can be seen through the vivid description of their group provided by Bocca:

> They have gone their own way [separate from the sections of the old Socialist party] . . . to form a different section, without those old "drunkards" practicing puritanical rules: prohibition against kissing in the circle, struggle against "love for sale," virginity advised until marriage, the duty to always be honest with comrades—to the point that young Massola stands up during a meeting to ask "comrades Luigi Longo and Teresa Noce what they were doing the previous evening in the garden." And an electoral commission excludes from the list a comrade "because he has married a rich woman."[54]

It did not take much to project this puritanism onto the workers' councils. At a time of considerable labor unrest resulting from the austerity measures in the difficult postwar period, a young and vigorous labor force confronting what was wrongly perceived as a corrupt and inept industrial leadership could easily be identified as the social agency capable of renovating both the labor movement and society as a whole.

Gramsci recklessly projected his elegant philosophical scheme onto the Turin labor struggles without any realistic evaluation of the nature of predominant power relations. As Adler and others have shown, the Turin working class was forced into struggle not only by postwar austerity but, more importantly, by the industrialists' reorganization

53. Gramsci, *Prison Notebooks*, p. 395.
54. Bocca, *Palmiro Togliatti*, pp. 31–32.

of the productive process.[55] Far from being merely a parasitic and passive order that became "irresponsible and therefore more autocratic, merciless, and arbitrary because of the separation, during the imperialist phase of capitalism, of ownership and management,"[56] the Turin industrialists were at that time probably among the world's most innovative and dynamic. Under the leadership of Giovanni Agnelli and Gino Olivetti, they had, on their own initiative, reconstituted the productive process in a way paralleling the innovations cautiously introduced by Henry Ford and Frederick W. Taylor in the United States a few years earlier, and which were to become universalized after the Great Depression.[57] Those *commissioni interne* that later turned into the workers' councils were "neither transformative nor prefigurative—they were essentially *defensive* and *competitive*, they were intrinsically products of capitalism and as such never fundamentally challenged the logic of the whole."[58] They never had a chance to carry out the revolutionary task ascribed to them.

As a Crocean, Gramsci tended to overemphasize philosophy and culture at the expense of science and technology. This disparaging attitude toward the "practical" resulted, strangely enough, in

55. Franklin Adler, "Factory Councils, Gramsci and the Industrialists," *Telos*, no. 31 (Spring 1977), pp. 67–90.

56. Antonio Gramsci, "The Factory Council," originally published in *Ordine Nuovo*, 12 June 1920; now in Gramsci, *Political Writings*, p. 262.

57. Gramsci, of course, occasionally recognized the high quality of Italian industrial leadership. For example, he writes: "The capitalist Agnelli is a committed believer in perpetual peace [The League of Nations]. . . . A great idea has conquered his consciousness. Can a man of action, a doer, a creator, a man of Agnelli's stature, let great ideas get moldy in the attic of consciousness? Giovanni Agnelli's consciousness is a block of rock without interests or cracks: faith means action, universal concept means concrete historical act. Agnelli is a modern man, he is a militant of democratic ideology, he wants people's freedom, the recognition of nationalities baptized and christened through plebiscitary self-decision. He wants in a concrete way. Therefore, as a faithful militant of the ideal, he generates, in the sphere of action of his individual will, the necessary and sufficient conditions so that the true becomes fact, so that the ideal turns into an efficient historical institution." Antonio Gramsci, "Un Soviet Locale," originally published in *Avanti!*, Piedmont Edition, 5 February 1919; now in Giansiro Ferrata and Niccolò Gallo, eds., *2000 Pagine di Gramsci* (Milan, 1971), I, 357. Since, however, he saw Agnelli completely engaged in that project of capitalist reconstruction, which he deemed impossible to carry out in the face of growing working-class insurgence, the stature of the opponent was automatically diminished.

58. Adler, "Factory Councils," p. 72.

Gramsci's falling victim to that same productivist perspective so widely accepted within the European Left, from Lenin to Korsch to all the lesser luminaries of social democracy.[59] Gramsci's productivism, however, had roots quite different from those of orthodox Marxism, which ascribed ontological primacy to the base. Gramsci simply assumed this base as derivative and relatively unproblematic. This approach immunized him from the predominant scientistic pretenses—he relegated science to the level of superstructure and ideology,[60] and he described it as a "higher witchcraft" when too much is expected from it[61]—but it caused him to pay little or no attention to the possible uses of science and technology in production to deactivate and control whatever revolutionary aspirations the working class may entertain. Gramsci was not as concerned with objective constraining conditions as he was with the *subjective* dimension—demonstrated by the fact that he saw in those subjective struggles the emergence of the collective workers' will: "For the first time in history it happened that a proletariat undertook a struggle for control over production without *having been driven* into action by hunger and unemployment [emphasis added]."[62]

The importance of the economic sphere for Gramsci was entirely a function of its conditioning—but not determining—role in the formation of consciousness. He saw the rise of "collective man" in relation to the development of the economic base ("large factories, Taylorization, rationalization, etc."), which in turn was seen almost as a natural result of capitalist growth. While in the past the collectivity was cemented by extraneous factors such as the "hero" or a representative individual, "modern collectivism is essentially formed from the bottom up, on the basis of the position occupied by the collectivity in the world of production." A particular agency, i.e., the party, is still

59. For an account of Lenin's productivism, see Frederic J. Fleron and Lou Jean Fleron, "Administration Theory as Repressive Political Theory: The Communist Experience," *Telos*, no. 12 (Summer 1972), pp. 63–92; and François George, "Forgetting Lenin," *Telos*, no. 18 (Winter 1973–74), pp. 53–88.
60. Gramsci, *Quaderni del Carcere*, II, 1457.
61. Ibid., p. 1459.
62. Antonio Gramsci, "Il Movimento Torinese dei Consigli di Fabbrica," in Ferrata and Gallo, *2000 Pagine di Gramsci*, I, 566. The English translation in Gramsci, *Political Writings*, p. 310, is unsatisfactory.

ascribed a totalizing function, but only a transitory one that "can disappear without causing the collective cement to disintegrate and the construction to fall."[63] Unlike Sartre, who used the Bolshevik Revolution as an example of the inexorable unfolding of groups from an initial seriality through totalization and back again into seriality, Gramsci considered the constitution of individuality resulting from the revolutionary process to be an irreversible development preventing any subsequent disintegration.[64] For Gramsci, the fully individualized ego is not the starting point of sociopolitical revolution, but the result. Consequently, while "collective and individual life must be organized around the optimization of the productive apparatus," the economic achievements of this project created the conditions for freedom:

> The development of the economic forces on new bases and the gradual instauration of the new structure will resolve the contradictions which will not be lacking and, having created a new "conformism" from below, will allow new possibilities for self-discipline, i.e., Freedom, even on the individual level.[65]

This analysis is the basis for Gramsci's vision of the party in which the leadership and the masses are not sharply differentiated but are part of a "close tie between the great masses, the party, the ruling group, and the whole complex, well articulated, . . . [moving] as a "collective man."[66]

The workers' councils always remained part of Gramsci's general political strategy, even after the defeats of the 1920s led him to put considerably more emphasis on the party organization.[67] Having misinterpreted the industrialists' strengths as weaknesses, and lacking a realistic understanding of the depoliticizing and privatizing potential

63. Gramsci, *Quaderni del Carcere*, II, 862.

64. Jean-Paul Sartre, *Critique of Dialectical Reason*, trans. Alan Sheridan-Smith (London, 1976), pp. 661 ff.

65. Gramsci, *Quaderni del Carcere*, II, 863.

66. Ibid., p. 1430.

67. Thus, not only do positive references to the workers' councils as organizational expressions of the "collective worker" resurface in the *Prison Notebooks* (Gramsci, *Quaderni del Carcere*, II, 1137–1138), but even during the darkest hours of fascist oppression—in 1926, immediately prior to his arrest—Gramsci sought to recycle them, against Tasca's and the Comintern's general opposition, as agitation committees. Spriano, *Storia del Partito Comunista*, II, 22.

of the new technological developments in the factory, Gramsci never came to grips with the intrinsic shortcomings of his interpretation of the workers' council experience. His inability to provide an adequate analysis of their failures constitutes one of his major limitations. In a report to the Comintern sent in July 1920, he argues that

the movement encountered determined resistance from the trade-union officials and from the leadership of the Socialist Party . . . so it did not succeed in establishing itself outside of Turin. . . . The whole machinery of the trade unions was set in motion to prevent the working masses in other parts of Italy from following the Turin lead.[68]

Later, in a letter of 28 January 1924, he shifts responsibility for the failure onto himself and his friends:

Essentially, we are now paying for the serious errors we made in 1919–20. For fear of being thought power-hungry careerists, we did not try to create a definite faction that could have been organized throughout Italy. We did not want to give the Turin factory concils an autonomous directing group that might have greatly influenced the whole country because we were afraid of a split in the unions and a premature expulsion from the Socialist Party.[69]

Even in the *Prison Notebooks*, he still regarded technology as *neutral* and, therefore, as creating the conditions for generating that "collective worker" whose revolutionary role had been spelled out by Marx in the twelfth chapter of the first volume of *Capital*.[70]

Gramsci developed a penetrating analysis of how, in the United States, prohibition and sexual repression had been successfully employed to discipline the working class,[71] but he never fully realized the profoundly counterrevolutionary character of Fordism and of the culture industry, how they checkmated any revolutionary possibility in the traditional Marxist sense. He insisted on seeing "Americanism" as not qualitatively different from the old "Europeanism."[72] His analysis of cultural hegemony touched on the prob-

68. See Gramsci, *Political Writings*, pp. 318–319.
69. Togliatti, *La Formazione del Gruppo*, p. 183.
70. Gramsci, *Quaderni del Carcere*, II, 1138.
71. Gramsci, *Prison Notebooks*, pp. 293–306.
72. Ibid, p. 318.

lem but remained enmeshed within the logic of traditional party politics at a time when social life was being rapidly depoliticized and more effective mechanisms of political domination were being introduced with such new, sophisticated means as the culture industry and the assembly line. The resulting intensified alienation ruled out the direct connection postulated by orthodox Marxism between being and thought, without which objective interests cannot be translated into class consciousness, which in turn can be politically organized by parties understood in the classical sense of institutions representing objective class interests. In this new historical context, parties lose their class character and turn into substitute bureaucratic structures seeking to take over and direct the state apparatus, which, because of its increasingly massive machinery, becomes less and less susceptible to sharp political steerings. This is precisely how the PCI has come to see itself with its return to legality after World War II. Years earlier, in the *Prison Notebooks*, Gramsci began to tackle these Weberian accounts.[73] Yet, he did not manage to develop their crucial political implications beyond an elaboration of the revolutionary party as, at best, a political pedagogical agency. This explains why he remained grudgingly committed to the party and to the International long after he had become aware of their almost total internal degeneration.

At any rate, the workers' councils had little meaning outside of Turin[74] and, in the broader context, represented a labor aristoc-

---

73. Although it was not found among the books that Gramsci had in prison, in the *Notebooks* there are three positive references to Weber's work on parliament and government in Germany (which had been translated into Italian in 1919 as *Max Weber, Parlamento e Governe nel Nuovo Ordinamenta della Germania, Critica Politica della Burocrazie e della Vita dei Partiti*, trans. Eurico Ruta [Bari, 1919]). Unlike his evaluation of Michels, Mosca, and most other contemporary sociologists and political scientists as charlatans and pompous windbags, Gramsci had nothing but the highest regard for Weber, of whom, in addition to the previously mentioned book, he had read at least parts of *The Protestant Ethic and the Spirit of Capitalism* (which had been serialized in an Italian journal in 1932), and knew about *Wirtschaft und Gesellschaft*. Gramsci, however, merely used Weber's account of the role of political parties in Germany (*Quaderni del Carcere*, I, 230; III, 1527) and the analysis of Calvinism to elaborate the possibility of popularizing Marxism in the same way that revolutionary religious ideas had been popularized in the past (II, 1389–1390).

74. Franco De Felici, *I Comunisti a Torino* (Rome, 1974), pp. 16 ff.

racy's last stand in the effort to protect professional options associated with a rapidly disappearing craftsmanship under the onslaught
of the new production processes requiring only unskilled workers.[75]
What Gramsci and the rest of the *Ordine Nuovo* group saw as the
beginning of a new socialist era was really only the end of the
industrial conditions for it. Far from constituting capitalism's last
gasp, fascism turned out to be primarily an authoritarian version of
the New Deal meant to stabilize and regulate capitalism. Within
this restructuring process, it was necessary to checkmate any political obstacles. Thus, traditional labor organizations—including
Communist parties—were either destroyed outright (fascism and
Nazism) or relegated to the role of internal regulatory mechanisms
as modernizing and rationalizing agencies (Stalinism and the New
Deal).

With hindsight, it is easy to see shortcomings in the councils that
were not so readily apparent at the time they were being organized.
Then, most of the young socialists who were shortly to break with the
Socialist party and form the PCI shared, in various degrees, Gramsci's
enthusiasm for the councils. What distinguished Gramsci's interpretation of them from both Tasca's and Bordiga's more cautious accounts
was his "provincialism" and moralism. The more realistic and experienced Tasca—who had been one of Gramsci's political mentors[76]—

75. Enzo Rutigliano, "Gramsci and Capitalist Rationalization," *Telos*, no. 31
(Spring 1977), pp. 91–99. Other commentators have adduced different interpretations
for the councils' failure. Thus, Cammett places blame on the *Ordine Nuovo* group's
internal dissension (*Antonio Gramsci*, p. 108); Clark sees it as a function of the
strength of the industrialists' reaction, failure by the *Ordine Nuovo* group to impose
discipline, and the potential of the councils to be readily integrated within existing
social relations (*Gramsci and Revolution*, pp. 210–211). For an excellent account of
how the workers' councils, "which originated as a wedge for revolution, ended up
heralding a new approach to industrial relations" over most of Europe, see Charles S.
Maier, *Recasting Bourgeois Europe: Stabilization in France, Germany and Italy after
World War I* (Princeton, N. J., 1975), pp. 150 ff.

76. Fiori, *Antonio Gramsci*, pp. 79–80, where he reports that in May 1912, Tasca
had presented Gramsci with a French edition of *War and Peace* bearing the following
dedication: "To my fellow student of today, and my fellow combatant (I hope) of
tomorrow." Tasca had already become involved in socialist politics as early as 1909.
Tasca, *I Primi Dieci Anni*, pp. 84–85. See also Davidson, *Antonio Gramsci*,
pp. 73–75.

was from the very beginning skeptical of the exclusive role that Gramsci ascribed to the councils in the revolutionary struggle:

> It was absurd that the factory councils could have developed and conquered political power by expressing it through their very structure, fighting at the same time against the bourgeoisie, the state, the Socialist Party, the labor organizations and the unions.[77]

Bordiga's objections were more than just tactical; they involved basic principles. More Leninist than Lenin himself, Bordiga did not see how the councils could possibly transcend a narrow economistic perspective without the help of a truly revolutionary party free from the socialists' reformist shackles. Completely the opposite of Gramsci, for whom subjective and cultural considerations were always primary, Bordiga boasted of never having read a page of either Croce or Gentile,[78] and he held a mechanistic view of revolution: "The revolution does not occur as a result of the education, culture, or technical capacity of the proletariat, but as a result of the inner crises of the system of capitalist production."[79] Since the proletariat lacked the expertise and knowledge to transform economic crises into political confrontations and carry them through to victory, what was needed most of all was the political leadership of a party with "a superior knowledge of the conditions of the class struggle and the proletariat's emancipation than the proletariat itself."[80] Thus, he argued that "the problem of forging a genuine communist party in Italy is much more important than the problem of creating Soviets."[81]

Throughout this period Gramsci stood out as the theoretician of the workers' councils and as the intellectual power behind *Ordine Nuovo*, but Togliatti was not far behind. With Tasca, Terracini, and Gramsci,

---

77. Tasca, *I Primi Dieci Anni*, p. 101. Tasca's original critical articles were published in *Ordine Nuovo* between 12 June and 3 July 1920. They are now in Gramsci, *Political Writings*, pp. 269–290.

78. Andreina De Clementi, *Amadeo Bordiga* (Turin, 1971), pp. 12 ff.

79. Amadeo Bordiga, "Towards the Establishment of Workers' Councils in Italy," in Gramsci, *Political Writings*, p. 223.

80. Ibid., p. 231.

81. Ibid., p. 232. In the same series of articles, Bordiga also distinguished between factory councils and soviets, and considered emphasis on the former rather than the latter another political error.

he was one of the four founders and main contributors to the journal, and when in May 1919 Gramsci decided suddenly to redirect *Ordine Nuovo*'s focus from "a vague passion for a vague proletarian culture" toward a political commitment to the workers' councils,[82] Togliatti went along, rapidly shifting his emphasis from earlier cultural themes to more concrete political problems. Using Gramsci's language, Togliatti saw the activity of the workers' councils as "a training for the producers in the exercise of power . . . both in the strictly economic as well as in the political field."[83] Even if initially the struggling faction will be only a minority, "the goals of this struggle can be readily reached, . . . and the workers' organization within the factory will end up by engaging all, as the true expression of the will, the true organic form of proletarian power."[84] The Gramscian trademark permeates all of Togliatti's writings during this time: the factory as the revolutionary alcove, self-management as the road to qualitative social change, and the rise of the will of the collective workers as the ultimate goal. Very little is devoted to technical considerations or future forms of social and political organization, not only because at that time the whole *Ordine Nuovo* group felt itself to be part of an irresistible worldwide insurrection led by the new International, but also because—and this is what is really crucial—the real goal was the constitution and genuine universalization of a new individuality, beyond the obsolete institutional limitations imposed by capitalism.[85]

When the workers' council experiment finally ended in defeat in April 1920, it seemed natural to blame its failure on the Socialist party, which many thought failed to coordinate a broader national effort in support of the Turin insurrection. By this time, Togliatti had reached full political maturity and began to develop his own position

82. Antonio Gramsci, "On the *Ordine Nuovo* Programme," originally published in *Ordine Nuovo*, 14 August 1920; now in Gramsci, *Political Writings*, p. 291.

83. Palmiro Togliatti, "I Consigli di Fabbrica," originally published in *Ordine Nuovo*, 25 October 1919; now in Togliatti, *Opere*, I, 77.

84. Ibid., p. 78.

85. On 1 November 1919, Togliatti writes: "The class struggle follows everywhere the same rhythm, and the same problems appear in all countries to all the workers who have reached a certain level of economic and political development. . . . The International is a living reality also, rather primarily, in the field of experiences (better yet: 'experiments') of the proletariat." Ibid., p. 83.

on many of the complex issues facing the *Ordine Nuovo* group. After Gramsci's polemic with Tasca on the status of the councils as part of a broad revolutionary strategy, Gramsci began to shift toward Bordiga's positions in the summer of 1920. Togliatti and Terracini, however, sided with Tasca in seeking a way to push the Socialist party in a more revolutionary direction and, at the same time, to within established working-class organizations. This early minor disagreement prefigured those features of Gramsci's and Togliatti's politics that were to reappear time and again in the future and that had significant consequences for the PCI during some of its most difficult years. Where Gramsci emphasized principles and goals, Togliatti tended to ascribe a privileged position to organization and institutions.

Gramsci's drift toward Bordiga's position—abstentionism from parliamentary politics—was strongly conditioned by the failure of the Hungarian revolution and the interpretation of this event provided by the International. According to the predominant interpretation held by people as different as Karl Radek and Béla Kun, the causes of the Hungarian defeat were not so much the result of bad timing or lack of preparation by the party as they were to the fusion of the communists with the social democrats after the former took power.[86] At a time when the Red Army was marching toward Warsaw and revolution seemed imminent elsewhere, the break with the Socialist party may have appeared as the only way to stay in step with the political rhythm set by the international situation—although it did not take political genius to realize, with Paul Levi and Clara Zetkin, who were in Italy at the time, that during a reactionary fascist offensive and while the Italian Left was in shambles, it was crazy for an extreme Left minority to split from the socialists.[87] To the extent, however, that Gramsci's whole conception remained highly moralistic and rooted in the primacy of the workers' councils as the nucleus of the new revolutionary organization, a fresh start was needed.[88] In doing so, he found himself

86. Paggi, *Antonio Gramsci*, pp. 316–320.

87. For a detailed discussion of this, see Berti, "Appunti e Ricordi," p. 91 f.

88. Davidson, *Antonio Gramsci*, pp. 156 ff. As already indicated, however, Davidson's account is vitiated by the mistaken assumption that to become a Marxist in 1920 meant, for Gramsci, moving beyond all of his earlier "idealist" and Crocean positions. Marxism had never been nor will it ever be a unitary coherent world view. At

very close to Bordiga, with whom, because of deep theoretical differences, all but a *tactical* alliance was out of the question.[89] Gramsci found himself isolated and remained so for the next couple of years.[90] Only later, on the main issue of fascism, did he find the support he needed for his positions to succeed Bordiga as the leader of the party.

Togliatti's decision in 1920 to side with Tasca against Gramsci had no major political consequences, nor did it last long. It did, however, reveal fundamental traits in their respective political profiles. Gramsci remained uncompromising in his emphasis on the councils as the new catalytic institutions that would generate the collective consciousness needed to ensure that the projected revolution would do more than re-create the alienating existing state of affairs. Togliatti, meanwhile, placed more weight on organizational structures and chose the tactical compromise of deemphasizing basic theoretical differences pending the development of a more favorable sociopolitical context. As Ragionieri puts it:

> Gramsci, with his striking ability already at that time to penetrate the general awareness of a universal historical situation even at the level of a section of the party, [appeared] ultimately profoundly trusting in the historical revolutionary and critical powers, while Togliatti [was] more prudent and realistic, basically concerned with the continuity of a historical line, but at the same time worried about confronting the obstacles that its realization encounters in its path; Gramsci [was] interested in the creation

best, its various brands have always been constellations of various otherwise discrete and unrelated positions, held together by one or more underlying unifying principles, such as the primacy of economics; in Gramsci's case, it was the primacy of culture and politics, in the process of the creation of a public sphere of critical individuals. This individuality is the result of their newly achieved social position as active producers in a context characterized by political as well as socioeconomic democracy. Thus, contrary to Davidson, there is no necessary contradiction between Gramsci's Marxist politics and the Crocean philosophy that he never abandoned.

89. As Paggi has pointed out (*Antonio Gramsci*, pp. 335–336), Gramsci's tactical alliance with Bordiga *after* 1920 was dictated by two main considerations: (1) the need to prevent an influential and well-known right-wing faction that had broken with the Socialist party from taking over the new Communist party; and (2) the need to prevent a return to the old conception of politics.

90. In his recollections, Berti describes the great amount of animosity that remained against Gramsci within the left-wing socialists, who came to form the Italian Communist Party in 1921, for his earlier interventionist and Mussolinian positions. See Berti, "Appunti e Ricordi," p. 34.

of new institutions primarily as expressions of a moment in permanent creation, while Togliatti [was] more inclined to recognize the importance of historically asserted and realized institutions.[91]

Where Gramsci did not hesitate to pay the price of political isolation rather than compromise his basic positions, Togliatti stressed the primacy of organization.[92]

Unforeseen events, such as the failed attempt to occupy the factories in September 1920, pushed these issues into the background and precipitated the formation of the PCI in January 1921. By that time, both Gramsci and Togliatti had integrated their moralism into a broad political strategy, which, in framing problems within a national and international context, also transcended the limits of their vision of the previous two years. Unable to count on the Socialist party to rejuvenate itself from within and thus function as the revolutionary agency they considered necessary to bring the Soviet experience to Italy, they began to look to a new Communist party as an alternative. As Berti puts it: "The fall of the myth of the councils, along with the acrimony of the struggle against . . . the whole tradition of Italian socialism, ended up by throwing a man like Gramsci and the whole *Ordine Nuovo* group into [the arms of Bordighism]."[93] At this point, especially in Togliatti,

> the focus of attention has clearly shifted. While in the writings of the 1919–1920 period the center of inspiration was the subjective moment— whether in the reflection concerning cultural currents or in the theorization of the fundamental class-contrast coming to the fore in the councils movement—now it shifts onto facts and things, deals with social classes and public authorities, looks at daily events and not just at history.[94]

This new breadth of vision was immediately called on to make sense out of the new political quandaries brought about by the formation of

91. Ragionieri, *Palmiro Togliatti*, p. 57.

92. As Salvadori puts it ("L'Attuale Storiografia," p. 177): "After the break with the Socialist party, what remained for Togliatti as a supreme political *value* was the organization as a self-legitimating world; for Gramsci, organization remained always an instrument for the realization of ends against which the very nature of the organization had to be measured."

93. Berti, "Appunti e Ricordi," p. 58.

94. Ragionieri, *Palmiro Togliatti*, p. 70.

the Italian Communist Party and its always problematic relation with the Comintern, in a period characterized by the rise of fascism and the Left's inability to deal with it.

Bolshevization

Owing primarily to Grasmci's and Togliatti's insistence on imposing their philosophical project on a situation torn by other social dynamics, the strategy followed during the councils period was based on a whole series of misunderstandings concerning the real configuration of political forces and, consequently, objective possibilities. With the foundation of the Communist party and the coming of fascism, it became necessary to generalize that philosophical vision on a national scale, but, far from being rectified, previous political and tactical mistakes were compounded, resulting in a strategy that, if anything, facilitated the rise of fascism and the fall of the Left.[95] For reasons having nothing to do with agreement on principles but largely dictated by political exigencies, Togliatti and Gramsci joined Bordiga and accepted his leadership in the Communist party's early years. With the creation of a new party committed to provide the broad organizational framework necessary for coordinating local political efforts on a national scale, the failure of the councils because of lack of national support would not be repeated. That Bordiga's vision was rather different from Togliatti's and Gramsci's seemed, at that point, of only secondary importance. Since, however, the Comintern reversed its position concerning revolutionary possibilities in the West shortly after the creation of the party, the entire PCI leadership, still autonomous and "un-Bolshevized," suddenly found itself at loggerheads with Moscow.

The PCI had been formed at a time when the International's official policy was still based on the resolutions reached in the Second Congress of the Comintern, held in the summer of 1920. These resolutions embraced the idea that the Russian Revolution was destined to spread like wildfire throughout the world:

95. Thus, Cammett writes: "The particular schism that occurred at Livorno was disastrous. Thanks to that Congress—and to Mussolini—the Italian Left was eliminated from political life for the next 22 years." *Antonio Gramsci*, p. 153.

The world proletariat confronts decisive struggles: the epoch in which we live is the epoch of civil war. The decisive hour is coming. Almost in all countries with an important labor movement the working class faces a series of harsh struggles with arms at hand.[96]

But after the failure of the "März Aktion" in Germany and other setbacks, the Third Congress of the Comintern, meeting in July 1921, replaced this offensive strategy with a defensive one, corresponding to Russia's efforts to stabilize diplomatic relations, prevent total economic collapse by means of the New Economic Policy (NEP), and consolidate revolutionary gains.[97] A united-front policy was launched, which threatened the very being of the still relatively weak PCI, whose *raison d'être* was precisely the now-discarded thesis that revolution was imminent and it was necessary to create a revolutionary organization to lead it. Otherwise, there was no reason to split from the much stronger Socialist party, which, internally revitalized, would have been far better able to carry out a defensive struggle— even to the point of perhaps preventing or at the very least retarding the rise of fascism. With the possible exception of Tasca and a few people on the Right,[98] the whole PCI leadership stood fast on the Second Congress positions and refused to fall in line with the new Third Congress turn, as became standard practice after fascism and Stalinism had destroyed every possibility of an independent organization.

From the very beginning, the Comintern had been wittingly or unwittingly a tool of Russian foreign policy—even when Lenin himself believed that its function was to precipitate world revolution. After the Red Army had finally defeated the White Army, Lenin wrote *Left-Wing Communism* in April–May 1920, both to internationalize the Bolshevik party's hegemony in the communist movement, and to initiate an international strategy designed to discourage military inter-

96. Quoted in Arthur Rosenberg, *Storia del Bolscevismo* (Florence, 1969), p. 179.

97. According to Rosenberg, "In the summer of 1921, Russia had retreated unto itself; it was accommodating itself to an existence for which the expansion of the revolution was unnecessary, and Lenin no longer believed in the immediate success of workers' revolutions in Europe." Ibid., p. 181.

98. Tasca, *I Primi Dieci Anni*, pp. 131–135; and Spriano, *Storia del Partito Comunista*, I, 125–126.

vention against the Soviet Union by strengthening parliamentary road-blocks to it within the various hostile countries involved. As the revolutionary wave seemed to be gaining momentum, it became advisable to go on the offensive also in the international political arena. Communist parties were hastily founded all over the world to participate in this revolutionary offensive. The Italian Communist Party was born at the crest of this wave of international insurrectionary enthusiasm. When this international offensive strategy stalled as a result of Russian military setbacks in Poland, insurrectionary failures in Germany, and near total economic collapse at home, the Russian government began to retrench, launched NEP, sought to reestablish diplomatic relations with bourgeois governments, and encouraged united-front strategies everywhere. Since at that time (1922) the infrastructure of the PCI had not yet been scattered by fascist terror, it was still possible to chart an independent course consistent with the founding principles. It remained strategically committed to its original positions (those of the Second Congress) and resisted every attempt to back off from an offensive stance and assume a defensive posture. This also explains why the well-known ''Rome theses''—the resolutions of the Second National Party Congress—were at odds with the new winds blowing from Moscow. As the Comintern representative at that congress was to claim in a report of 26 March 1922, the International's positions were endorsed only by the minority right-wing factions led by Tasca and Antonio Graziadei.[99]

Although the Comintern's policies later became notorious for zig-zagging between Left and Right—and thus creating indescribable confusion in the various national Communist parties attempting to stay in step—the orientation of the Italian Communist Party changed slowly and with great difficulty:

> Not only was the PCI born on an extreme Left platform, but even when its direction changed, in 1923–24, the new leadership immediately indicated that the Left platform was to be modified, but not substantially rejected. It

99. Quoted in Spriano, *Storia del Partito Comunista*, I, 188. According to Spriano, this report is presumably included in Humbert-Droz's still unpublished work, *L'Internazionale Communiste et la Formation de la Direction du Parti Communiste Italien.*

100. Berti, ''Appunti e Ricordi,'' p. 26.

can be found again, almost intact, in the center's theses of May 1924 (which were written by Togliatti); it can be found also, much deemphasized but not altogether changed, in the Lyon theses (1926)—which were primarily the work of Gramsci—and only in the years 1927–28 (during the joint leadership of the Tasca-Togliatti-Grieco group) there seems to be a distancing away from this platform.[100]

Even at the individual level, the shift away from the original Left orientation turned out to be extremely problematic. As Berti recalls,

> It was a slow, gradual, and difficult process which did not happen at once. . . . For some of the pro-Bordiga leadership [it] began in 1925 and was over by 1926, for others it began in 1925 but was concluded only much later, as can be seen by the reappearance of extremist positions of considerable weight in the party in the years 1927–28. For others, it was never concluded.[101]

In more than one way, the shift successfully reshaped the party's very nature. Although Stalinist "administrative measures" were clearly never imported to Italy, in 1925 the Gramsci-Togliatti takeover of the party was hardly an example of democracy in action. Galli may be exaggerating in claiming that

> the victory of the Gramsci-Togliatti group [was] obtained with the same technique [used by the Stalinist apparatus], thus not by defeating the adversary after a serene and high-level ideological and political debate, but by overcoming him through the distortion of his thought, the most gratuitous accusations, disciplinary provisions, and through the manipulation of assemblies.[102]

But the fact remains that the party's precarious predicament in a context of growing fascist terror certainly facilitated "the administrative road" in changing leadership.

More importantly, however, in the long run the shift had profound theoretical consequences. For people such as Togliatti it meant the rejection of the messianism that, immediately after World War I, had projected a social revolution as a *qualitative* break with the past, in favor of a gradualistic, linear Enlightenment philosophy of history,

101. Ibid., p. 162.
102. Giorgio Galli, *Storia del Partito Comunista Italiano* (Milan, 1958), p. 112.

where socialism is defined as the sociopolitical rationalization of capitalism through the enfranchisement of the working class, and in favor of a recycling of the previously discarded Second International world view. As Vacca puts it:

> The new conception of history thus allows the individuation of a *continuous* historical process, which directly connects past and present, whose dominant characters are a function of the progressive emergence of the working class as the subject of history.[103]

The problem with this approach is that it no longer offers anything new or revolutionary. It is, rather, a capitulation to that very bourgeois vision so disdainfully dismissed during the pre-Bolshevization period.

The restoration of this Enlightenment view of history meant scrapping Gramsci's eschatological philosophy in order to salvage his politics. Revolution is still a matter of the emancipation of the masses, but no longer does this come about through the creation of a "new humanity" and a qualitatively different society, but through political democratization and a more equitable economic distribution. Realpolitik took its toll, and the dream faded into the far future. Whether communism will ever be possible in the utopian form in which it was originally projected—as a society of new subjects—will be something to think about *after* the more pressing political tasks have been fulfilled. Thus, the *concretization* of the Italian Communist Party's politics within the double bind of fascism and Stalinism also meant an *impoverishment* of its ideology and a twilight of the utopian, quasi-religious spirit that originally animated it. The prophets gave way to the bureaucrats, who came to use the prophets as mere tools for efficient administration.

The break with the party's leftist founding fathers—an ambiguous coalition of the Bordiga and the *Ordine Nuovo* groups—meant considerably more than *tactical* shifts in order to bring the party in line with the Comintern's requirements. Eventually it meant a major strategic rethinking of the very meaning of communism. It was a tormented process made all the more difficult by intensifying fascist terror and the deadly struggle for leadership of the Bolshevik party

103. Vacca, *Saggio su Togliatti*, p. 476.

after Lenin's death. And the fact that Bordiga was the head of the party made the shift even more difficult. Unshakable from his fixed orthodox positions, Bordiga had never really accepted the Comintern's break with the theses of the Second Congress—which, after all, had been the basis of the original split with the Socialist party that led to the PCI's formation. His adamant opposition to the Comintern's united-front strategy launched after the Third Congress almost resulted in Togliatti leaving the party altogether after having been brusquely rebuked by Bordiga for seeking to accommodate the Comintern's directives.

Togliatti's position was understandable. The break with the Socialist party had been predicated primarily on its refusal to accept the Second Congress's twenty-one conditions and to expel the reformist wing. Early in October 1922, the Socialists did both, and, especially in view of the Comintern's pressure to have communists and socialists combine forces to meet the fascist challenge, it seemed that a reunification not only made a lot of sense but also was inevitable. Yet, Togliatti's mere hint of the desirability of such a reunification in a short article[104] brought on Bordiga's wrath and resulted in Togliatti's exclusion from the Italian delegation to the Comintern's Fourth Congress.[105] This, along with the intensification of fascist terror shortly thereafter, led Togliatti to drop out of political life for the next few months. He resurfaced in March 1923[106] at his comrades' exhortations, and fell back in step with the predominant Bordighian line.[107] Despite this, a split was becoming increasingly likely—especially after Bordiga's arrest, which left a vacuum in the party's leadership.

At that point, the Comintern saw an opportunity to give the party a

104. Palmiro Togliatti, "Dopo la Scissione," originally published in *Ordine Nuovo*, 5 October 1922; now in Togliatti, *Opere*, I, 418–419.

105. Berti, "Appunti e Ricordi," p. 124.

106. Bocca, *Palmiro Togliatti*, pp. 78–81. For a more apologetic but unconvincing account, see Ragionieri, *Palmiro Togliatti*, pp. 30–92.

107. Thus, in a report to the Comintern of 13 May 1923, Togliatti still balked at the idea of a united front with the Socialists: "The truth is that the Socialists do not at all want to have contacts with us, but prefer to have simple . . . platonic relations with the Communist International, so much so since they know very well that the unfolding of these relations serve their aim of regaining a virginity in front of the masses, and to discredit in practice the International and its Italian section." Togliatti, *Opere*, I, 749.

right-wing turn by appointing to its executive committee Tasca and others of a political persuasion more palatable to its own. But even then, Togliatti and Terracini continued to buck the Comintern, insisting that it was not enough simply to pay lip service to a united-front strategy and that it was high time to move toward implementing such a strategy by joining forces with the Socialists against the fascist offensive. Tasca describes a typical meeting:

> Terracini proposes that it is necessary to prejudicially accept the International's decision, and subsequently undertake a factional struggle aimed at deriving the most possible utility for our group. He wants to conserve "positions such as to secure us the domination of the party and of the political situation." Togliatti is even more firm in sabotaging the International's new policy: he can resign himself to accept it for the moment, with the condition "that an open polemic with the International and with the party's minority is immediately begun, through a series of declarations of principles and polemics that must not only be transmitted to the International, but diffused among the masses." If this takes place, he will agree to remain within the party's leadership, otherwise not.[108]

While the PCI stubbornly held its own against the Comintern, Gramsci, who was in Moscow at the time, came under heavy pressure to move away from the Bordighian positions of the Italian party and at least partially implement the Comintern directives. According to Berti,

> Trotsky recalled for Serrati how he had been part, during the second half of 1922, of the Italian Commission together with Zinoviev and Bukharin, and how much difficulty the Commission had encountered in the discussions with Gramsci: "We had to press him a lot," he claimed, "to convince him to take a position of struggle against Bordiga, and I don't know whether we have succeeded."[109]

Gramsci eventually came to realize that, in the face of growing fascist terror, the party's isolation, and the increasing role of the Comintern in determining the PCI's internal affairs, it was necessary to compromise, especially since he also saw that the right-wing minority within the party was about to take over under the Comintern's auspices.

108. Tasca, *I Primi Dieci Anni*, pp. 134–135.
109. Berti, "Appunti e Ricordi," p. 33.

Already in January 1923, Graziadei, probably the most right-wing member of the party's minority, had openly criticized the PCI's majority in the Leipzig Congress of the German Communist Party, and his criticism had been exactly the same as that put forth by the Comintern's executive committee. Gramsci immediately saw the implications and was understandably appalled, since he still considered the party's right wing as "social democrats in disguise," against whom the party was originally formed: "Because of the fact that, in view of the changed tactic of the Comintern's orientation, they can appear as the most orthodox and faithful followers of the International's line, should they take over the party?"[110] The only solution was to accept the unavoidable compromise. By sacrificing Bordiga, the party could be saved from a takeover by the right wing. Otherwise, Gramsci wrote Togliatti, "the opposition [i.e., Tasca and company] will actually come to represent the Party and we will be cut out, we will suffer a political defeat—maybe an irremediable one."[111]

When Bordiga, from his jail cell in March 1923, drafted a manifesto meant to precipitate an open break with the Comintern, Gramsci refused to go along.[112] After gradually and laboriously convincing reluctant members of the party leadership—Togliatti among the most reluctant[113]—to form a "centrist" faction opposed to Tasca on the Right and Bordiga on the Left, Gramsci took over the party with the endorsement and the financial support of the Comintern.[114] Gramsci assumed leadership precisely at a time when the national and international situation was inexorably pushing the party underground, abroad, and toward increasing dependence on the Comintern. Within the space of a few years, it was reduced to nothing but a tool of the

110. Spriano, *Storia del Partito Comunista*, p. 247.

111. Quoted in Togliatti, *La Formazione del Gruppo*, p. 64. See also Berti, "Appunti e Ricordi," p. 153.

112. This document has been published by Stefano Merli in his "Nuova Documentazione sulla 'Svolta' nella Direzione del PCI nel 1923–24," *Rivista Storica del Socialismo* (September–December 1964), pp. 515–521.

113. As late as 1924, Gramsci still complained, in a letter to Alfonso Leonetti, about Togliatti's hesitations. Togliatti, *La Formazione del Gruppo*, p. 183.

114. How difficult such a takeover turned out to be can be seen by the fact that as late as May 1924, at the Como Party Congress, the Bordiga wing still retained the majority. See Spriano, *Storia del Partito Comunista*, pp. 359 ff.

Stalinist apparatus.

In becoming allied with Bordiga, whose concept of the party stressed discipline, political purity, and a formalistic but principled approach to problems, Gramsci and Togliatti accepted his leadership primarily because it seemed to guarantee a sharp break with past politics and the difficult beginning of that reorganization they regarded as essential to implement a truly revolutionary strategy. But, as later became evident, when tensions between the "center" and the Left factions reached the breaking point, there were fundamental differences from the outset in their respective philosophical outlooks, politics, and conceptions of the party.

Bordiga was essentially a traditional Marxist who regarded the Third International as "a return to that Marxist orthodoxy which the Second International, during the last decade, had abandoned, with the exception of a Left minority to which he belonged."[115] No one could have been more opposed to Gramsci, whose "absolute historicism" requires theory to be constantly reconstituted to mediate historically modified living experience. Bordiga held a mechanical conception of a party organized around those who had theoretically sound political positions. Thus, although for Bordiga the party was an *organ* of the working class, it remained separate and above the ranks of the proletariat. Gramsci and Togliatti, in contrast, saw the party as an integral part of that class and inextricably tied to its historically contingent dynamics. As Togliatti was to point out, Bordiga's intransigence was grounded in a fatalistic philosophy of history alien to the party's center faction, which emphasized the will, even if a collective one.[116] This

115. Berti, "Appunti e Ricordi," p. 12.

116. In 1926, Togliatti attacked Bordiga's account of the party for its emphasis on consciousness and will within a context otherwise seen in mechanical and deterministic terms. Thus, Bordiga's party was one "whose organization, nature, and function are, in the ultimate analysis, determined by an idealistic, abstract, aprioristic process, on the one hand, while on the other the proletarian masses are moved by purely mechanical laws, in virtue of the fatal march of things." This sharp contraposition of unchanging theoretical principles, on the one hand, and a fatalistic philosophy of history, on the other, according to Togliatti, froze Bordiga's tactics and prevented him from dealing effectively with changing historical conditions. Palmiro Togliatti, "Le Fondazioni Ideologiche del Bordighismo," originally published simultaneously in *L'Internationale Communist*, April 1926, and in *Die Kommunistische Internationale* VII, 3 (1926), 224–232; now in Togliatti, *Opere*, II, 18–27. That Bordiga's was one of the

allowed Gramsci and Togliatti the kind of political flexibility that Bordiga later showed he lacked, and it was Bordiga's shortage of flexibility that prevented him from revising those positions that in the particular historical situation of 1920 had happened to coincide with those of the International.

In brief, for Bordiga the politically autonomous party would grow along with the unavoidable intensification of the capitalist crisis, thus creating simultaneously both the subjective as well as the objective conditions necessary for the qualitative revolutionary leap.[117] For Gramsci and Togliatti, the party was meant primarily to oversee and coordinate efforts "from below"—efforts that would eventually push to the fore new political subjects, the producers, able to challenge what was seen as a rapidly disintegrating social order.[118] In other words, Bordiga expected the *objective* effects of the intensifying economic crisis to lead the masses into the arms of the already fully organized party, but Gramsci and Togliatti were concerned primarily with the subjective development of the new revolutionary agents. Nonetheless, their strategies happened to coincide in their hatred of the reformism and internal corruption of the Socialist party, as well as in the recognition of the need for a truly revolutionary organization. Both of these factors also placed them against the main thrust of the Comintern's policies after the Third Congress. The continuing emphasis on discipline, principles, and organization—precisely the areas in

---

predominant, if not *the* predominant, Leninist conception of the party (Antonio Carlo, "Lenin on the Party," *Telos*, no. 17 [Fall 1973] pp. 2–40), and that it described accurately how most Communist parties were to function in this century, does not alter the fact that Gramsci's and Togliatti's version had substantially different theoretical roots and entailed different tactical consequences.

117. De Clementi, *Amadeo Bordiga*, pp. 154 ff. See also Berti, "Appunti e Ricordi," p. 19: "For Bordiga the party was a union of orthodox Marxists able to point out to the working class the road to liberation. Only they could have been able to formulate a truly revolutionary program, strategy, or tactic: sooner or later the masses will recognize, in that program and in that party, their table of salvation and their guide, and will follow it."

118. Giorgio Bonomi, *Partito e Rivoluzione in Gramsci* (Milan, 1973), pp. 115–152. Obsessed with attempting to show a sharp Althusserian *coupure* between the Crocean and the Leninist phases in Gramsci, Davidson (*Antonio Gramsci*, pp. 156 ff.) fails to appreciate the theoretical continuity in Gramsci's various positions concerning the party during the early 1920s.

which the Socialists had so miserably failed—made their alliance acceptable.

Within their joint strategy, the main target became the internal right-wing minority, seen as the agency that might defuse—as in the past—objective revolutionary possibilities.[119] This way of posing the problem blinded them to the dangers of fascism, which was dismissed as a ripple in the normal functioning of the liberal state or as a preliminary sharpening of social contradictions prior to the final confrontation between the two struggling camps. Typical of such a cavalier attitude was Terracini's report in *International Correspondence*, where he writes of the advent of fascism as follows:

> It is a matter of a somewhat lively ministerial crisis. No other definition is better suited for the events that have taken place in Italy between 27 October and 1 November. *Coup d'etat*? Revolution? We reject the use of such terms for these circumstances. May the Italian proletarians finally understand that the conservative classes, who have made use of the white terror, and the democratic state, which places itself at their service, are in the same way their mortal enemies.[120]

When Lenin, on his deathbed, asked Bordiga about the fascist takeover, Bordiga replied that it was more a matter of a ridiculous and noisy event than a politically significant development.[121] Togliatti even saw something positive in this turn of events:

> What is dead, therefore, is not the revolution, but revolutionary opportunism. We do not mean thereby that the reaction has been welcome and salutary. This was fatal since social democracy and social revolutionary opportunism unavoidably lead to counter-revolution, of which they are the vanguard. From the subjective viewpoint, the defeat of social-democratic opportunism thus represents a revolutionary progress.[122]

119. Tasca, *I Primi Dieci Anni*, p. 123. During this period it was not rare to find the Christian Popular party, the fascists, and the social democrats bunched together under the general designation of counterrevolutionaries in the communist press. Palmiro Togliatti, "Destra e Sinistra," *Ordine Nuovo*, 27 July 1922; now in Togliatti, *Opere*, I, 392–394. Thirty years later, Togliatti still freely admitted that what they feared most at that time was "to become confused with the rightist group led by Tasca." Ferrara and Ferrara, *Conversando con Togliatti*, p. 103.

120. Tasca, *I Primi Dieci Anni*, p. 122.

121. Quoted in Berti, "Appunti e Ricordi," p. 100.

122. Palmiro Togliatti, "Disfatta della Rivoluzione?" *Il Lavorate*, 9 December

Although Communist strategy at that time was politically disastrous in that it kept the Left fragmented, thus facilitating the fascist takeover, it was not in any way counter to what both Gramsci and Togliatti, or even Bordiga, understood as Marxist theory. Fascism was a new phenomenon. It was all too easy to interpret it as the bourgeoisie's last violent attempt to retain a social and political hegemony, which was in the process of being historically displaced. The orthodox, unilinear Marxist philosophy of history could account neither for a bourgeois stabilization after the beginning of the proletarian offensive, nor for a new, qualitatively different, and stable authoritarian order. This was Bordiga's position. His schematic way of framing political issues had the advantage of clarity and rigor, but it also forced complex situations into simple and foreign categories that destroyed their historical meaning. Thus, he could see the fascist party only as "the organ of bourgeois direction of the state during the period of the decline of imperialism."[123] Clearly, if such was the case, and if a communist order was seen as the only possible lasting outcome of the political conflicts of the time, then any coalition with either socialist or centrist forces to defeat fascism would have appeared as an unwarranted political tactic threatening the integrity of the still relatively weak Communist party and slowing down the revolutionary tempo.

Although Gramsci and Togliatti came at that time to roughly similar political conclusions, they did so for entirely different reasons. Unlike Bordiga, an engineer proud of his ignorance of the Italian neo-Hegelian cultural tradition and convinced of the absolute truth of a mechanical version of Marxism, Gramsci and Togliatti had already rejected that Marxist philosophy of history that Croce had so vehemently attacked at the beginning of the century. Their acceptance of the intransigent Bordighian line of 1921–1922 was based on considerations quite apart from philosophical ones, including the shared but unwarranted belief that Italian capitalism was on its last leg and that, even if not guaranteed by any "historical necessity," only a communist reconstruction could come to terms with the predicament facing

1922; now in Togliatti, *Opere*, I, 448.
   123. Ragionieri, *Palmiro Togliatti*, p. 110.

Italian society. Consistent with their earlier voluntarism, they continued to interpret the revolutionary break as a creative effort rather than as an unavoidable transition guaranteed by a transcendental metaphysical scheme, as believed by Bordiga. This helps explain why they immediately sought to change the PCI from an elite revolutionary group to a mass party when they took over the leadership role.[124] While Bordiga remained *ideologically* committed to a Marxism-Leninism of the most vulgar Stalinist brand even while engaged in a political struggle with Moscow,[125] Gramsci and Togliatti sought to recycle Labriola against Bukharin and other lesser Comintern luminaries.[126]

As in the past, however, their vastly superior philosophical and cultural perspective did not prevent them from making political mistakes at least as serious as those of Bordiga. Their analysis of fascism, for example, was woefully inadequate. What was new in fascism, i.e., its authoritarian transitional character as a political catalyst facilitating the transition of a weak and under-developed entrepreneurial capitalism into a new type of organized capitalism, escaped them until it was too late to do anything about it. In 1923, Togliatti still emphasized the continuity of fascism with "the program of 'typically Italian' governments during the last 30 years, . . . the program of transformism," whereby the opposition is systematically integrated within a corrupt political elite that leaves predominant relations of domination unchanged.[127] Although fascist illegality was seen as a new departure,

---

124. Palmiro Togliatti, "Il Problema del Reclutamento," originally published in *Stato Operaio* II, 12 (17 April 1924); now in Togliatti, *Opere*, I, 552–555.

125. It is not surprising, therefore, that it was Bordiga who first published in his own journal an Italian translation of Stalin's "Problems of Leninism," *Prometeo* V, VI (May, June–July 1924).

126. For an excellent account of the growing rift after 1924 between Gramsci and the Comintern's version of Marxism-Leninism, see Leonardo Paggi, "Gramsci's General Theory of Marxism," *Telos*, no. 33 (Fall 1977), pp. 27–70. It is no accident that Labriola's letters to Engels were published in the communist journal *Stato Operaio* shortly after Gramsci's imprisonment in 1926. It was part of an effort, cut short by the intensification of the fascist terror as well as the growing influence of the Comintern, to contrapose a *different* Marxist tradition to what was perceived as a mistaken theoretical return by the Comintern to some of the long-since discredited theses of the Marxism of the Second International.

127. Palmiro Togliatti, "Ieri Dicevamo," *Lo Stato Operaio*, 16 August 1923; now

it was written off as merely another expression of the seriousness of the crisis. Early in 1924, the task was still not seen in terms of forming political coalitions in the defense of "bourgeois freedoms," but to force the only solution possible:

> The goal of proletarian opposition must be . . . to unveil the real meaning of the fascist dictatorship to show that its instauration has opened for the Italian proletariat a period of continuous struggle that cannot be closed with a return to constitutional legality, but only with a complete reversal of the present situation.

Worse yet: "Every opposition to fascism that remains on the terrain of the vindication of constitutional liberties has, as a result, not the weakening, but the strengthening of fascism in power."[128] But Bordiga was just as bad as Gramsci and Togliatti in this case: "The fascists want to destroy the parliamentary shack? We will be very happy about it!"[129]

Communist strategy thus facilitated the institutional stabilization of fascism and, what's more, eventually resulted in the ultimate disintegration of the Left as an effective political entity. The immediate result was to make the party's continued existence contingent on the Comintern's wishes. Gramsci came to acknowledge grudgingly this new predicament and, with Togliatti, began to move the party toward less intransigent positions. As might be expected, they were accused of opportunism by Bordiga, but their turn was in fact principled and consistent with their general orientation.[130] With the rise of fascism

---

in Togliatti, *Opere*, I, 502.

128. Report to the Comintern's executive committee, 19 January 1924, quoted in Ragionieri, *Palmiro Togliatti*, pp. 126–127. In May of the same year, social democracy is still seen "not as the right-wing of the labor movement, but as the left-wing of the reactionary bourgeoisie" (Palmiro Togliatti, "Le Elezioni Tedesche," *L'Unità*, 11 May 1924; now in Togliatti, *Opere*, p. 565), and the "anti-fascist factions of the Italian bourgeoisie" are considered as already working "in the interest of tomorrow's 'bourgeois order' " (Palmiro Togliatti, "Un Dilemma per i Socialisti," *L'Unità*, 1 August 1924; now in Palmiro Togliatti, *Opere*, p. 573). Thus, the task is not "to fight only against fascism, but against all bourgeois elements that are practically allied with fascism." Palmiro Togliatti, "I Socialisti e la Nostra Proposta," *L'Unità*, 26 October 1924; now in Togliatti, *Opere*, I, 358 ff.

129. Amadeo Bordiga, "Casa Vuole il Fascismo," *Ordine Nuovo*, 26 July 1922. Quoted in Bocca, *Palmiro Togliatti*, p. 67.

130. Spriano, *Storia del Partito Comunista*, I, 358 ff.

and in the effort to become integrated within a broader international communist movement, Gramsci and Togliatti had come to interpret national events from an international perspective. It is only natural that the role of the Comintern would become significantly larger—especially in view of the growing fragility of the party in Italy. Pushing them in this direction was a statute passed at the Second Congress of the Comintern, which stipulated that its deliberations were obligatory for the particular national parties. Although it was not until the Sixth Congress in 1928 that the various national Communist parties were redefined as mere sections of the International, it was quite clear from the very beginning that membership did not merely involve participation in a federation of relatively autonomous national parties.[131] In fact, Togliatti himself in 1924 explicitly defined the International, for the first time, as "the worldwide Party" and warned against decentralizing tendencies:

> It is necessary to pitilessly fight as liquidationist every tendency seeking to diminish the centralization of the International either in the name of the adhering Party's autonomy or on the basis of the recognition of the particular conditions in the various countries, and to substitute for it a federalistic criterion.[132]

Given the success of the Bolshevik Revolution, it is easy to see how the Russian party could dominate the International at a time when world revolution was still on the agenda and the various national parties were still trying to define themselves.

But Russian policy was itself crucially affected by fascism and the general international stabilization of capitalism. Thus, precisely at a time when the PCI was coming to depend on the Comintern for both political direction and financial support, the Comintern was being redefined in terms of the new perspective of "socialism in one country." This eventually came to mean simply that the party and its members either accepted Stalinism lock, stock, and barrel, thus com-

131. For an elaborate discussion of this, see Berti, "Appunti e Ricordi," part 5, "L'Internazionale Comunista e il Movimento Operaio Italiano negli Anni 1919–1924," pp. 71–101.

132. Palmiro Togliatti, "Schema di Tesi sulla Tattica e sulla Situazione Interna del PCI Presentato dalla Maggioranza del C. C. del Partito," originally published in *Lo Stato Operaio*, 15 May 1924; now in *Annali Feltrinelli* VIII (1966), 187.

promising nearly everything for a vague faith in the future international emancipatory potential of Russian socialism, or else faced banishment from the International. Bolshevization eventually came to that. One by one, Tasca, Bordiga, and everyone unwilling to accept all that Stalinism entailed were dropped by the wayside. In jail, Gramsci was spared the humiliation of a formal expulsion, even though his objections to the social-fascism line did lead to his isolation from the party as well as from the rest of the communist political prisoners.[133] Togliatti chose to bite the bullet and, in order to save the party, pay the necessary price. For the next twenty years, then, the PCI's development can be understood only in terms of the politics of survival. Far from leaving the general philosophical and cultural framework unaffected, these two decades in the Comintern's political purgatory left an indelible mark on the party. It was during this period that Togliatti matured into the political figure who, after becoming a Marxist-Leninist with a lingering Gramscian vision, was to lead the PCI through the cold war and lay the foundations for the "historical compromise" and the politics of reconciliation that were put into effect after his death.

From Gramsci to Bukharin

The Italian Communist Party found itself forced to mature in a period characterized by the worldwide defeat of the Left and the stabilization of both fascism and Stalinism. Given its diminished strength on the national level, it looked more and more to the Soviet Union for help.[134] Bordiga was able to define the party's early profile only so long as real revolutionary options remained a possibility—

133. For a number of accounts of Gramsci's everyday life in prison and his relations with other political prisoners, see Mimma Paulesu Quercioli, ed., *Gramsci Vivo nelle Testimonienze dei suoi Contemporanei* (Milan, 1977).

134. Already in 1924, the requirements of Soviet foreign policy were considered far more important than the various national strategies. Thus, during the major crisis of the fascist regime immediately after the Giacomo Matteotti assassination, Mussolini sought to defuse the Left by diplomatically recognizing the Soviet Union, which not only accepted this recognition jubilantly but went so far as to propose through its ambassador in Rome a political and military treaty. For a vivid recollection of these embarrassing events from one intimately involved with the International, see Jules Humbert-Droz, *De Lenine a Staline: Dix Ans au Service de L'Internationale Communiste (1921–1931)* (Neufchatel, 1971), pp. 248 ff.

however remote. The Matteotti assassination in June 1924, and the ensuing stabilization of the fascist regime after the opposition's failure to topple it, meant the eventual elimination of all remaining possibilities of legal political activity and the end of the vision that, after World War I, had projected an almost automatic shift to socialism resulting from intensified capitalist crises. A defensive stance became the only viable option.

Bordiga's hostility toward any kind of united front with the Socialists became increasingly counterproductive. His inability to redefine his strategy within a drastically changed context isolated him and eventually sealed his political fate. Internationally, the stabilization of capitalism and the final defeat of the Left in Germany precipitated the general retreat characterized by Stalinism's doctrine of "socialism in one country," built on the ruins of Trotsky's unwavering "permanent revolution." Within such a context, it was almost natural for Bordiga's positions to become associated with those of Trotsky—and with similar results in the party in which internal opposition was becoming unacceptable.[135] Yet, as Galli puts it,

> There was no connection whatsoever between Bordiga and Trotsky, and their positions, already conflicting when the problem of the united front was originally raised, converged on the basis of the defense of freedom and discussion and criticism within the parties and the International.[136]

Unintimidated by the new Stalinist leadership in the Comintern, Bordiga did not hesitate to defend Trotsky openly and immediately met considerable resistance within both the Italian party and the International.[137] Since Bolshevization meant the redefinition of individual national parties as integral parts of the International, it also entailed internal discipline and total subjugation to Moscow. So long

135. Gramsci himself made this analogy in a meeting of the central committee on 6 February 1925, and, in a letter of 15 February 1925, Togliatti informed the Comintern's secretary of the existence of "a current sympathetic to Trotsky and Trotskyism, probably organized by Bordiga himself." Quoted in Spriano, *Storia del Partito Comunista*, I, p. 442. This letter is not to be found in Togliatti's *Opere*.

136. Galli, *Storia del Partito*, p. 106.

137. Thus, Bordiga's article "La Questione di Trotsky" was originally written 8 February 1925, but was not published until 4 July of that year because the party's executive committee stalled its publication. Spriano, *Storia del Partito Comunista*, pp. 442–443.

as the situation in Russia remained fluid, this policy of centralization did not cause extensive friction, but it rapidly deteriorated with the involution of the Russian party at a time when fascist terror had left the Italian communist movement and its leadership in total disarray. The problems developing in Russia since Lenin's death were becoming more and more evident. Yet, given their particular intellectual orientation, Bordiga, Gramsci, and Togliatti confronted this development at different times and in different ways. Without detracting from Bordiga's personal courage and integrity, it was only natural that he be the first to point out that Russia's new emperor had no clothes. In this case, Bordiga's political shortcomings turned into a virtue. Obviously, it is much easier to reach political judgments when one has clear-cut criteria derived from a fairly well-fixed theoretical framework than it is for "absolute historicists," whose criteria are themselves inextricably a function of those changing conditions under scrutiny. But Gramsci, too, finally came to see through the Russian situation. By this time, however, he was in a fascist jail and had no voice in party matters. His views were safely swept under the rug, and the party itself was forced to turn its full attention to a major repressive wave unleashed by the fascist regime—the same wave that had resulted in Gramsci's arrest. In exile in Moscow, Togliatti's concern with the party's very existence within an increasingly Kafkaesque international situation led him to accept Stalinism as the only alternative to his party's disintegration. But the choice entailed a political mortgage that turned out to be extremely difficult to pay off—even after Stalin's death.

From the first few years of the Bolshevik Revolution, Bordiga had interpreted the Russian events differently from Gramsci, for whom the similarity of the socioeconomic situation in the two countries made possible the transposition of what he thought was the Soviet experience to Italy with only minor modifications.[138] Although Bordiga fully supported Lenin and the Bolsheviks, he had no illusions about Russia's backwardness and the political implications of this:

---

138. Thus, in "Workers and Peasants," originally published in *Ordine Nuovo*, 2 August 1919 (now in Gramsci, *Political Writings*, p. 85), Gramsci writes that "historical conditions in Italy were not and are not very different from those in Russia." As late as fall 1926, he still saw the differences in quantitative terms only:

The historical conditions within which the Russian revolution has developed do not resemble the conditions within which the proletarian revolution will develop in the democratic countries of Western Europe and America. . . . The tactical experience of the Russian revolution cannot be integrally transposed to other countries.[139]

This view had little bearing so long as the proletariat's imminent rise to power was taken as all but accomplished. But it grew in significance with the Stalinist turn to "socialism in one country" and the ensuing power struggle with Trotsky and the Left opposition, who insisted on permanent world revolution as the only way to save the integrity of socialism in Russia. Bordiga did not accept for a minute the subordination of the Comintern to the Russian party—as Stalin personally sought to impress on him.[140] He reaffirmed his old thesis of the radical

---

"All the problems inherent in the hegemony of the proletariat will present themselves to us in a form certainly more complex and acute than in Russia, because the density of the rural population in Italy is enormously greater, our peasants have a very rich organizational tradition and have always succeeded in making their specific mass weight felt in national political life, because with us the ecclesiastical organizational apparatus has a 2,000-year-old tradition and is specialized in the organization and propaganda among peasants in a way unequaled in other countries." Antonio Gramsci, "La Lettera di Gramsci al Comitato Centrale del Partito Comunista Sovietico nel 1926," in Ferrata and Gallo, *2000 Pagine di Gramsci*, I, 823–824. Only in, for example, the *Prison Notebooks*, p. 238, when, ironically enough, Gramsci polemicizes against Trotsky's allegedly "superficially national and superficially Western" cosmopolitanism, did he fully come around to Bordiga's early position: "In Russia the State was everything, civil society was primordial and gelatinous; in the West, there was a proper relation between State and civil society, and when the State trembled, a sturdy structure of civil society was at once revealed. The State was only an outer ditch, behind which there stood a powerful system of fortresses—and earthworks: more or less numerous from one State to the next, it goes without saying—but this precisely necessitated an accurate reconnaisance of each individual country."

139. Amadeo Bordiga, "Sulla Questione del Parlamentarismo," *Rassegna Comunista*, 15 August 1921; quoted in De Clementi, *Amadeo Bordiga*, p. 126.

140. When in Moscow in February 1926, Bordiga inquired as to why the internal problems of the Russian party should not be dealt with by the International, as would have been the case with the internal problems of every other party, Togliatti arranged a meeting with Stalin during which the latter unhesitatingly pointed out to Bordiga that "the Russian Communist Party's position in the International is such that it is not possible to resolve through procedures the problems dealing with the relations between the same Russian party and the International and the other parties. Of course, the position of the Russian party within the International is a privileged one." See the minutes of that meeting in "Seduta del 22 Febraio 1926 della Delegazione Italiana col Compagno Stalin," *Annali Feltrinelli* VIII (1966), 270.

differences between Russia and the rest of Europe,[141] rejected the centralization of power and the "administrative measures" that were being adopted against even old Bolsheviks as a result of the intense power struggle, and defended the need for internal factions and opposition in his famous speech to the executive committee of the Comintern, which remains the only truly dissenting attack ever delivered within that body.[142] Naturally, in spite of the Italian party's insistence that Bordiga remain in Moscow and work within the Comintern, his presence was no longer welcome. Over the protests of Gramsci and others, he was kept out of any further embarrassing squabbles within the Comintern until his final expulsion from the Italian party in March 1930 for factional activity.[143]

Gramsci's response to the final phase of Bolshevization was milder and slower, but no less to the point. Only his imprisonment prevented the matter from precipitating into an open, dramatic break. During most of 1926 Gramsci had gone along with the Italian party's decision not to intervene in the Russian question, not to redefine the issues of the involution of the Bolshevik Revolution and of Trotsky's opposition as *procedural* questions of discipline and factionalism—a stan-

---

141. Amadeo Bordiga, "Il Poderoso Discorso di Bordiga alla VI Sessione del CE Allargato della IC," *Prometeo*, 15 July – 15 September 1928. Quoted in Bocca, *Palmiro Togliatti*, I, 118: "The Russian party struggled under special conditions, i.e., in a country where the feudal aristocracy had not yet been overcome by the capitalist bourgeoisie. What is necessary for us is to know how to attack a democratic, modern bourgeois country, which has, on the one hand, resources able to corrupt and sidetrack the proletariat and, on the other, defends itself on the terrain of armed struggle with much more efficacy than the czar ever did."

142. In this speech, Bordiga did not mince words: "Lately, within the parties, a sport is practiced which consists in hitting, intervening, break, attack: and in these cases those who are hit are often excellent revolutionaries. I find this sport of terror within the party as having nothing in common with our work. . . . Unity is judged by facts and not by a regime of threats and terror. . . . We absolutely need a more healthy regime in the party; it is absolutely necessary to give the party the possibility to construct its opinion. . . . Factions do not represent the illness; they are nothing but a symptom of the illness, and if you want to cure the illness, you must first discover and understand it. . . ." Quoted in Bocca, *Palmiro Togliatti*, I, 118.

143. Bordiga was not purged earlier because, toward the end of 1926, his house in Naples was sacked by the fascists and he himself was arrested and condemned to three years in prison. He was finally thrown out in 1930 after Berti, himself in jail, reported Bordiga's factional activities among communist prisoners in favor of Trotsky. De Clementi, *Amadeo Bordiga*, pp. 247–248.

dard bureaucratic gambit to avoid confronting the real issues.[144] But the Russian question could not be simply ignored in Italy, where the fascist, anticommunist press did not waste any time in exploiting the matter.[145] "Socialism in one country" was readily identified as a shift away from an international revolutionary perspective, and NEP and the economic stratification it had reintroduced were paraded as evidence that the proletariat was no longer the ruling class, if it ever had been. It mocked Russia's reintroduction of a kind of state capitalism designed to lift that country out of its feudal status[146]—an analysis that was also gaining favor among oppositional Left-communists in Germany and that, strangely enough, Bordiga had warned would be the road leading away from communism and into political impotence.[147] Gramsci saw an ominous shift in the press coverage of Russia. Unlike the vacuous, bombastic style of most previous attacks on Russia, this time the articles were "technically well constructed for propaganda, with a minimum of demagogy and of injurious attitudes," and exhibiting "an evident effort at objectivity."[148]

In addition to all this, Gramsci was worried about some of the same issues that had bothered Bordiga: the poor treatment of old Bolsheviks, whom he still considered his masters and comrades, and an irrevocable, disastrous split in the leadership of the Russian party. In the name of the Italian party, he wrote all this in a letter addressed to the central committee of the Russian Communist Party.[149] Although

144. Spriano, *Storia del Partito Comunista*, II, 45–46.

145. As Grieco puts it in a discussion of the PCI's central committee, 1–3 November 1926: "There was a worldwide campaign against Russia; not on the basis of the usual crude lies constantly denied by those very visitors of the Soviet Union, but in an apparently objective form seeking to make appear inevitable and near the collapse of Bolshevism through the liquidation and dismemberment of the very Bolshevik party and its leadership." *Annali Feltrinelli* VIII (1966), 319.

146. For Gramsci's rebuttals, see "L'URSS verso il Comunismo" and "In che Direzione si Sviluppa l'Unione Sovietica?" in Antonio Gramsci, *Scritti Politici*, ed. Paolo Spriano (Rome, 1967), pp. 686–694.

147. To Korsch, 28 October 1926, originally published in *Il Prometco* 1 October 1928; quoted in Spriano, *Storia del Partito Comunista*, II, 50–51.

148. Antonio Gramsci, "La Lettera di Gramsci," p. 822.

149. This letter by Gramsci, as well as Togliatti's subsequent reply and Gramsci's final rebuttal, can be considered, as Ragionieri writes, "emblematic of the more general positions of the two correspondents in the face of the problems of the historical period, which, for the Soviet Union and the International communist movement, was

he couched his criticisms in the most friendly and diplomatic language possible, the main points were unmistakably clear—so clear, in fact, that Togliatti, to whom it was sent in Moscow, never got around to delivering it. In fairness to Togliatti, it should be noted that when he received the letter, it seemed as if the issues it addressed were already practically resolved.[150] Yet, the major differences between him and Gramsci did surface very clearly. Given the particularly difficult time in which all of this took place, however, the incident remained all but unknown until 1964, when Togliatti, under pressure, made it public.[151] Since Gramsci was arrested shortly after writing the letter (8 November), the whole matter became moot in the face of the more pressing problem of the party's survival under the new fascist repression unleashed after an attempt on Mussolini's life. What is clear is that Gramsci had no intention of condoning the Stalinist "administrative measures" that were becoming popular in Russia, and that he was not inclined to participate in the transforming of the Italian party into what it became in the 1930s: an irrelevant and impotent tool of Stalin's apparatus.

Togliatti's reaction to this same situation is exemplified in what he wrote back to Gramsci explaining why he had not delivered the letter. Closer to the ongoing debates in Moscow than Gramsci, Togliatti realized that "from now on the unity of the old Leninist guard will no longer, or with difficulty, be upheld in a continuous way."[152] Given the disarray of the Italian party—which was to collapse almost totally during the next few months—it seemed useless to oppose Stalin when the opposition not only seemed completely defeated but also was no

---

about to open under Stalin's direction." Ragionieri, *Palmiro Togliatti*, p. 226.

150. Franco Ferri, "Introduzione" to "Il Carteggio Completo tra Gramsci-Togliatti sulla Situazione nel Partito Bolscevico (1926)," *Rinascita* (24 April 1970), 11–19. Manuilski himself, the Comintern's secretary, explained this to Gramsci in a letter of 21 October 1926, published by Ferri along with the Togliatti-Gramsci correspondence.

151. Of course the existence of the letter was well-known long before 1964. Not only had Tasca published a version of it in his *Problemi della Rivoluzione Italiana*, second series, no. 4, (April 1938), but Deutscher reports mention of it in Trotsky's *Bulletin Oppositsi*, ns. 17–18 (1930), and earlier in Rosmer's correspondence with Trotsky. See Isaac Deutscher, *The Prophet Outcast: Trotsky 1929–1940* (New York, 1963), III, 31.

152. To Gramsci, 18 October 1926, *Annali Feltrinelli*, VIII (1966), 317.

longer tolerated. The Italian party had become almost fully dependent on Russian support. Opposition would have meant the end of the Italian party as an organized entity, or at least the end of any continuity with what might have remained of its former self. Togliatti also saw the only role that the party leadership could henceforth play: that of a transmission belt carrying Moscow's mandates to the base. And he made this very clear in his reply to Gramsci: "We must learn to keep our heads in place and to let our comrades at the base do the same. And we must initiate ourselves and the party militants in the knowledge of the Russian problems in order to be able to judge and follow the line of political principles and positions." There was a crisis and the opposition was defeated. The Italian party could not do anything about the course of events. Thus, "the best way to contribute to the overcoming of the crisis is to express our adherence to this line [Stalin's] without posing any limitations."[153] In a paranoid context characterized by a sharp demarcation of positions, any such "limitations" could themselves be considered opposition[154]—as they were by Bukharin, Jules Humbert-Droz, and a few others to whom Togliatti privately showed the letter.

Gramsci rejected Togliatti's arguments since he was not at all ready to sacrifice moral principles to political necessities. In his reply to Togliatti, he accused him of being too abstract and schematic—even to the point of irresponsibility. While it may have been true that the unity of the old Bolshevik leadership may be gone forever, this did not mean that they should remain quiet and refuse to point out the dangers that lay ahead for their Russian comrades: "We would be rather pitiful and irresponsible revolutionaries if we were to let accomplished facts passively take place, by justifying a priori their necessity." He was not supporting the apparatus but, instead, proposing to deal with the opposition in a proper way: "Our letter was *wholly* an indictment against the opposition, not in demagogic terms, but precisely because of this, more serious and affective."[155]

153. Ibid., pp. 317–318.

154. As Berti puts it: "To raise fundamental questions itself was an act of open struggle against certain administrative methods—a political fact of unerasable value." Berti, "Appunti e Ricordi," p. 306

155. Thus, in a letter to Berti, 6 May 1964, Humbert-Droz reported that at the time

What is crucial in this disagreement between Gramsci and Togliatti is not any anticipation of Gramsci's possible break with Moscow over the practical inevitability of Togliatti's tactical acceptance of Stalinism, but the profound theoretical divergence that had developed between Gramsci and Togliatti. Gramsci had remained committed to his vision of a subjectivist and historicist Marxism, for which communism meant the rise of a qualitatively new collective consciousness represented *in nuce*, first, in the revolutionary party, then in the state (understood as the dictatorship of the proletariat), and then in all of society. Togliatti, in contrast, had redefined his theoretical framework in terms of an Enlightenment perspective whose objective historical progress takes primacy over the subjective dimension and the qualitative leap into a new era.[156] In Togliatti the eschatological and messianic dimension was quantified in mundane terms, leaving altogether unaffected the predominant alienation and subhumanity, whose overcoming had been the main target of Gramsci's Hegelian Marxism. This is why, as Ragionieri points out, Gramsci places so much emphasis on retaining the *unity* of the leadership and Togliatti instead emphasizes the primacy of the general political line: "Where for Gramsci the Soviet Union and the Russian Communist Party" carried out a revolutionary task only when they acted as " 'one struggling unity working within the general projection of socialism,' for Togliatti this task . . . 'was carried out first of all through the fact of having taken power, and then to the extent that . . . the proletariat can *construct socialism*, and . . . in Russia *socialism is being constructed.*' "[157]

The subjective dimension is crucial in Gramsci, whether it is manifested as the existence and growth of a new form of political entity, as the modern prince, or as the totalizing collective consciousness, whose very existence already presupposes the ushering in of a

---

in Moscow there was fear that the Italian party would go over to the Trotskyist opposition. See *Annali Feltrinelli* VIII (1966), 302. This, however, is not confirmed in Humbert-Droz's memoirs, where no mention is made of the matter. Humbert-Droz, *De Lenine a Staline*, pp. 274–275.

156. "Il Carteggio Gramsci-Togliatti sulla Situazione nel Partito Bolscevico (1926)," pp. 13–14. This letter had not been made public before 1970 and was believed lost.

157. Ragionieri, *Palmiro Togliatti*, p. 242.

new era.[158] The dissolution of the inner unity of the Russian party, independently of whatever faction would win out, was not "the end of the world."[159] But it did mean the degeneration of the new revolutionary subject from the organic agency needed to usher in communism, to a mechanical political aggregation whose very character already meant a re-creation of and regression to precisely those bourgeois forms that the revolution was to overcome. This is why, throughout 1926, Gramsci always insisted on Bordiga working in Moscow with the Comintern, even though he knew very well how Bordiga had already shown himself to be the square peg unwilling to fit into the round hole.[160] Internal opposition had to be recuperated organically and its negativity reintegrated into an organization that would thereby retain its radically new sociopolitical integrity. Only as an integral unity constantly absorbing internally generated negativity and, at the same time, organically related to the masses could the party continue to perform its historical function. Apart from any other positive political or economic results it may have achieved, this was the *sine qua non conditio* for the party's being the concrete universal that would thereby be revolutionary. Togliatti's letter annoyed Gramsci so much that he wrote back claiming it had "left him with a very painful [*penosissima*] impression." It was a radical departure from what Togliatti himself had written a year earlier against Bordiga and Trotsky concerning factions:

> The factional struggle is incompatible with a party which is "the revolutionary party of the working class; and tends to prevent it from becoming one, since it shifts the problems of its life and development from a terrain within which they can be resolved to a terrain within which they will never receive but an external and formal solution."[161]

But while for the ever-Hegelian Gramsci this meant that internal party

158. Independently, Lukács had postulated something very similar when he wrote that "the objective theory of class consciousness is the theory of its objective possibility." in Georg Lukács, *History and Class Consciousness*, trans. Rodney Livingstone (London, 1971), p. 79.

159. See Gramsci's reply to Togliatti of 26 October 1926, in Ferri, "Introduzione," p. 18.

160. Spriano, *Storia del Partito Comunista*, II, 15–17.

161. Palmiro Togliatti, "Partito e Frazione," *Ordine Nuovo*, 1 March 1925; now

debate should result in an eventual new unity by constantly reintegrating the opposition, for Togliatti, rapidly shifting toward an objectivistic and pragmatic perspective, it came to mean that the retention
of internal unity could be achieved simply through the expulsion of
recalcitrant elements.

Togliatti's shift of emphasis from the primacy of the communist
movement as a concrete universal to the objective correctness of the
party's politics represents in theory what his acceptance of Stalinism
meant in practice: capitulation to the previously rejected bourgeois
view of politics and bourgeois theory of history. Like Lukács, Togliatti ended up redefining the communist movement as the *defender* of
bourgeois values that the bourgeoisie itself could no longer defend—a
position that postponed indefinitely any revolutionary agenda either in
practice or in theory.[162] For Gramsci, Togliatti's objectivistic shift
meant the abandonment of what made communist politics qualitatively different from its liberal and reformist counterpart: the organic
and internal rather than mechanical and external relation between the
leadership and the masses. Togliatti's new emphasis on objective
results at the expense of the subjective constituting process was a
reversal of a long-standing political and ontogenetic approach, and
entailed a break with the core of his theoretical vision.

Togliatti came to accept Bukharin's positions not only in practical
politics but at least partly in theory as well. This can be seen in
Togliatti's political choices, in his lapse into objectivistic positions,
and even in his acceptance of a version of Bukharin's technological
determinism against members of the German Communist Party.[163]
Gramsci's indirect response to Togliatti came later in the form of a
critique of Bukharin in the *Prison Notebooks*. Yet, it could not have
been any louder or clearer. Such a shift meant nothing less than a

in Togliatti, *Opere*, I, 634.

162. Ragionieri realizes this difference between Togliatti's 1925 positions and the
one he took a year later, but considers Togliatti's subsequent position an advance over
the earlier Gramscian one, deemed "susceptible to turn into an ideological wrapping
able to justify more than comprehend" (*Palmiro Togliatti*, p. 234).

163. Thus, with Bukharin, Humbert-Droz, and others, Togliatti argued against
Ernst Thälmann, Karl Schüller, etc., to the effect that only the *consequences* of
capitalist rationalization rather than rationalization itself should be fought. Ragionieri,
Palmiro Togliatti, p. 258.

capitulation to discarded bourgeois forms of thought and an abandonment of the revolutionary project.

The Making of an Oxymoron

Togliatti's capitulation to Bukharin's brand of Marxism-Leninism was not a failure of nerve or a political betrayal of earlier ideals. Given the configuration of political forces in 1926–1927, it was the only way to remain a communist and hope to participate in some concrete political activity with emancipatory potential. With the Italian party exiled to Moscow or in jail in Italy, the struggle within the Russian party was heating up to the point that, in a few years, would lead to the annihilation of the Left opposition. Mussolini's regime and capitalist governments worldwide had regrouped and showed no signs of weakening. In such a situation, acceptance of "socialism in one country" and Stalinism seemed unavoidable. The fate of Bordiga, Tasca, Korsch, and many others who refused to compromise testifies to the politically hopeless predicament of communists at that particular historical junction: either one went along with Stalin, Bukharin, and the majority, or else one retired from active politics—by keeping a low profile or by being physically eliminated, as Trotsky and others were. Efforts to find a third alternative were fruitless. Seen from this angle, Togliatti's eventual "Bolshevization" is not only rationally defensible but almost psychologically inevitable for someone who, from the very beginning of his political life, had placed so much emphasis on organizations and institutions.

Thus, the PCI's break with the Italian Marxist tradition did grudgingly take place, but it was never formally acknowledged. In fact, Gramsci's ultimately unsuccessful but sustained efforts to integrate his Crocean philosophy with Leninist politics were hypostatized to the level of official orthodoxy by automatically resolving, in favor of the Leninist side, any conflicts that would arise between the two. In this sense, Gramsci could be practically sanctified—especially after his death—and, at the same time, reduced to nothing more than the Italian translator and particularizer of the Leninist framework considered universally valid. But this operation could be successful only so long as Gramsci's pre-1926 works remained buried in unavailable party newspapers and journals, and while the stack of his prison notebooks were zealously kept under Togliatti's lock and key. With the eventual publication of almost all of the available documents, the myth of the uninterrupted continuity from Gramsci to the present had to explode, but not until it was too late to rectify the political and organizational consequences of the Italian Communist Party as an ideological oxymoron. Polycentrism, the historical compromise, and eventually Eurocommunism thus became its bastard offspring by extending rather than correcting a problem precipitated by what were initially only external historical circumstances.

Gramsci's own brand of Marxism is qualitatively different from Lenin's or any other version of Marxism-Leninism. It is an almost direct continuation of the Italian tradition of social and political thought, which, from Spaventa to Labriola to Croce, sought to develop a neo-Hegelianism whose goal of human emancipation focused on social individuality and a qualitatively new form of existence. This was and is irreconcilable with any form of economistic, deterministic, or generally objectivistic vision that sees progress as the further extension of the logic of the given by removing such obstacles as private property or bourgeois institutions. The shotgun marriage of the two produced a schizophrenic political organization, which, while presenting itself as a standard version of Marxism-Leninism, seeks to retain Gramscism as a repressed memory resurfacing at every turn and constantly clashing with an orthodoxy completely foreign to it.

Whatever the other shortcomings of Gramsci's thought, none was as monumental as his believe that the project of human emancipation could be realized by means of Leninist politics. In a classic example of the means overwhelming the end, Gramsci's Marxism has been suffocated for over half a century by precisely the mode of political translation that Gramsci thought would realize it.

IV

Gramsci's Marxism versus Lenin's

Toward a Demystification of Gramsci

Almost half a century after his death, Gramsci's work has finally taken its place among the classics of Marxist social thought. His imprisonment from 1926 up to his death, and the advent of fascism and Stalinism, succeeded in suppressing his mature writings until well after the end of World War II.[1] Even then, the Gramscian heritage became so much a part of the theoretical support for the policies of the Italian Communist Party that Perlini is right in claiming that "to deal with Gramsci necessitates first and foremost coming to grips with [that] party."[2] What happened to Gramsci, to a great extent, parallels what happened to Marx after his death when Engels, in further elaborating and popularizing his thought, defused it of most of its relevant features, transformed the dialectic into a positivist manifestation, and generally paved the way for the ideological travesties that were the Marxisms of the Second International.[3] In Togliatti, Gramsci found

---

1. For an accurate account of the exodus of Gramsci's *Prison Notebooks* from his death up to the recently published definitive edition, see Valentino Garratana, "Prefazione" to Antonio Gramsci, *Quaderni del Carcere*, ed. Valentino Gerratana (Turin, 1975), pp. xxix–xxxv. For a generally accurate reconstruction of the history of Gramscian studies, see Alasdair B. Davidson, "The Varying Seasons of Gramscian Studies," *Political Studies* XX, 4 (December 1972), 448–461. For a highly polemical, repetitive, and generally disorganized—yet at times penetrating—analysis, see Tito Perlini, *Gramsci e il Gramscismo* (Milan, 1974), especially pp. 7–35.

2. Perlini, *Gramsci e il Gramscismo*, p. 8.

3. These developments, however, must, to a great extent, be traced back to ambiguities in Marx's own works. Gramsci himself was aware of this early in his life. He writes: "The fact that Marx introduced in his work positivistic elements is not astonishing and is explained by the fact that Marx was not a professional philosopher,

his Engels.[4] Whereas Marx and Engels were two German émigrés in England, Gramsci and Togliatti worked closely together first as students in Turin and then as militants in the Italian Communist Party. In both cases, there was a lifelong friendship resulting in the two survivors, Engels and Togliatti, becoming the heir and leading interpreter of Marx and Gramsci respectively.[5] But both Togliatti and Engels turned out to be much more modest thinkers than their friends, with the unfortunate consequence that it took over half a century to rediscover Marx, and almost as long to evaluate Gramsci's thought properly. The multiplicity of interpretations of Marx also has its counterpart in Gramsci. "Gramsci . . . has become a fountain from which everyone takes whatever water they need," Salvadori notes.

For some, he is the father of a conception of authentic proletarian democracy; for others, he is a strict Stalinist—for still others, he is a social democrat, maybe even of a right-wing variety; there are those who consider

---

and he occasionally dozed off. What is certain, however, is that what is essential in his doctrine is its dependence on philosophical idealism." Antonio Gramsci, *Scritti Giovanili 1914–1916* (Turin, 1958), p. 328. (This article originally appeared on 19 October 1918.) For an excellent discussion of Gramsci's debunking of all positivist and determinist elements in Marxism, see Eugenio Garin, *Intellettuali Italiani del XX Secolo* (Rome, 1974), pp. 352 ff. For an account of the Marxism that Gramsci was reacting to, see Albrecht Wellmer, *Critical Theory of Society*, trans. John Cummings (New York, 1971), chapter 2, "The Latent Positivism in Marx's Philosophy of History," pp. 67 ff; and Andrew Arato, "The Second International: A Re-examination," *Telos*, no. 18 (Winter 1973–74), pp. 2–52.

4. This parallelism was addressed by Lukács a few months before his death, on the occasion of the fiftieth anniversary of the founding of the Italian Communist Party. He writes: "In the theoretical crisis of the twenties, Gramsci was one of the exceptional personalities who sought a way out. Yet, the orientation of the united front of the thirties became a fundamental patrimony of the whole movement through Togliatti's activity—a man who, up to now, has been maybe the greatest tactician of our movement." See Georg Lukács's message in *L'Unità*, 24 January 1971. The same parallelism, of course, had already been drawn between Marx and Engels by Viktor Adler in his eulogy of Engels. For a further elaboration of this, see Ernesto Ragionieri, "Introduzione" to Palmiro Togliatti, *Opere*, III, book 1 (1929–1935), CCXXXII–CCXXXIII.

5. Ernesto Ragionieri reiterates the importance of this parallel without, however, fully developing all of the consequences in his "Prefazione" to Palmiro Togliatti, *Antonio Gramsci* (Rome, 1972), p. xv. Of course, a roughly similar argument could be made for the Lenin-Stalin relation. In fact, Perlini writes: "Gramsci must first of all be . . . separated from the Gramscians and from Togliatti, who has sought to place himself in relation to Gramsci-Socrates as a new Plato, thus introducing a relation

him an orthodox Marxist-Leninist; while in the eyes of others, to conclude, he is an incorrigible idealist who has never understood anything of Marxism—or just about.[6]

Yet, for a number of reasons, the official Italian Communist Party interpretation became the dominant one, setting the pace for all other interpretations.[7] Although the PCI has always been and remains the most open and intellectually dynamic of all Communist parties, its account (or, better, accounts) turn out to be hopelessly one-sided. Thus, notwithstanding an immense literature on the matter, even in Italy the Gramsci debate is far from over.[8]

Togliatti can be held responsible for most of what happened to Gramsci's work in the years just after Gramsci died. He succeeded Gramsci as the head of the Italian Communist Party and proceeded systematically to embalm Gramsci's thought as the main pillar of the party's de facto social-democratic policy and theory. After World War II, official communist ideology was under Stalin's uncontested control, and all of Marxist theory was presented as an uninterrupted development of a single theoretical trend from Marx to the present. To

---

similar to that which Stalin established between himself and the cynically manipulated ghost of Lenin.'' Perlini, *Gramsci e il Gramscismo*, p. 171.

6. Massimo L. Salvadori, *Gramsci e il Problema Storico della Democrazia* (Turin, 1970), p. 164.

7. It is no accident, therefore, that Gramsci's writings are usually prefaced by claims that they ''could not be understood and evaluated in their correct meaning independently of the progress made during the first three decades of this century by the theoretical and practical activity of Lenin and Stalin. Gramsci's Marxism is Marxism-Leninism.'' ''Prefazione'' to Antonio Gramsci, *Il Materialismo Storico e la Filosofia di Benedetto Croce* (Turin, 1966), p. xvi. See also Giansiro Ferrata, ''Prefazione'' to Giansiro Ferrata and Niccolò Gallo, eds., *2000 Pagine de Gramsci* (Milan, 1971), I. 18, where he argues that ''nothing can be understood of Gramsci if an 'internal' personality is separated from the fundamental elements of Marxism-Leninism.''

8. As Garin, the foremost Italian intellectual historian, puts it: ''Unfortunately, the need for clarity and rigor that accompanied the 'discovery' of Gramsci in Italy, soon gave way, on the cultural level, to old habits: verbal syntheses mistaken for real syntheses; love, typically academic, for the thaumaturgic virtues of agreement; and, finally, the restoration of obfuscations whose technical jargon badly conceals the nostalgia for the old 'metaphysical' disputes. [Thus], socialist culture itself has not had the courage to approach the confrontation from autonomous positions and, in a profound inferiority complex, has sought all sorts of agreements.'' As a result, ''Gramsci has increasingly—even if reverently—been left in the dark.'' Garin, *Intellettuali Italiani del XX Secolo*, pp. 341–342.

fit Gramsci into the official party chronology, he therefore had to be subsumed as a follower of Lenin—a Lenin who himself already had been tailored according to the Stalinist model, cleansed of nearly all his revolutionary features, and reduced to the level of a harmless social democrat. What made the party regard this integration of Lenin's, Gramsci's and Stalin's thought as vital was the particular historical situation of postfascist Italy. According to Lentini, the task was "to reconcile the rich Gramscian theoretical heritage, and what there is in his political orientation that is relevant and plausible, with the very different reality of the international communist movement."[9] This was particularly true in 1945, when

> Ercoli [Togliatti's pseudonym] could not present himself to his comrades as the author of a policy lacking roots in the tradition of the Italian Communist Party; nor could he approach other forces, whose alliance he sought as the pure and simple executor of the new phase of Soviet policy. In Gramsci's teachings he readily sought the support of a stronger authority for his policies—an authority rooted in Italian politics and culture, in the history of the party, and in the antifascist struggle.[10]

Initial and unsuccessful opposition to this travesty of theoretical manipulation was mounted by several Crocean intellectuals, who rightly saw Gramsci as one of their own.[11] Still, the instrumentalization of Gramsci as the "Italianizer" of what in the postwar period was general Soviet policy was easily accomplished. A selective reading of his works, the hypostatization of some of his historically contingent policies to the level of the party's basic program, and a prudent silence concerning Gramsci's growing opposition to Stalinist policies provided a politically marketable Gramsci.[12] Thus, Togliatti became the

9. Giacinto Lentini, *Croce e Gramsci* (Palermo, 1967), p. 95n.

10. Luigi Cortese, "Palmiro Togliatti, la 'Svolta di Salerno' e l'Eredità Gramsciana," *Belfagor*, XXX (31 January 1975), 10.

11. For a brief summary of the postwar debate between Crocean and communist intellectuals concerning the Gramscian heritage, see Davidson, "Gramscian Studies," pp. 453–455.

12. According to Cortese, "As it happened in Russia with the relationship between Lenin and Stalin, the [Gramsci-Togliatti] continuity was idealized at the price of a total silence concerning the phases of dissent and clash that took place both before as well as after Gramsci's arrest. . . . The real drama of Gramsci's life in jail, where the torment of loneliness with respect to the party and its political line intensified and multiplied the

main architect of the myth of Gramsci as a brilliant theoretical footnote to Lenin—or rather, to the Stalinist reconstruction of Lenin.
This, it was thought, would provide post—World War II Italian Communist party policies with a legitimating antecedent, and would cover
up major divergences between official Marxism-Leninism and Gramsci's Crocean brand of Marxism.

---

effects of reclusion and of the fascist oppression . . . were placed under the most
absolute censure." "Palmiro Togliatti," pp. 10–11. Since the mid-1960s, with the
publication of Athos Lisa's 1933 report to the party of his account of Gramsci's
opposition to the 1929 Comintern policies of "social fascism" (Lisa was in prison with
Gramsci at the time), with additional corroborating evidence given by other fellow
prisoners, such as Ley and Ceresa, and with Fiore's interview with Gennaro (Gramsci's
brother), it has become clear that Gramsci was not the faithful Stalinist party-man who
has hitherto been depicted in official Communist accounts. Rather, he came increasingly to oppose party policies to the point of becoming almost totally isolated from his
fellow communist prisoners. Athos Lisa, "Discussioni Politiche con Gramsci," *Rinascita*, 12 December 1974; now in Athos Lisa, *Memorie. In Carcere con Gramsci* (Milan,
1973); Giovanni Ley, "Colloqui con Gramsci nel Carcere di Turi," *Rinascita*, 20
February 1965; Alfonso Leonetti, "Il 'Cazzotto nell' Occhio' o 'della Costituente'," in
Note su Gramsci (Urbino, 1970), pp. 191–208; Giuseppe Fiori, *Antonio Gramsci: Life
of a Revolutionary*, trans. Tom Nairn (London, 1970), pp. 252–258; Quintin Hoare
and Geoffrey Nowell-Smith, "Introduction" to Antonio Gramsci, *Prison Notebooks*,
ed. Quintin Hoare and Geoffrey Nowell-Smith (London, 1971), pp. xci ff. Maria
Antonietta Macciocchi, in *Per Gramsci* (Bologna, 1974), has given as close a reconstruction of the events surrounding the break as is possible. In her book, she relates her
misadventures in London in the futile attempt to locate one of the crucial documents
that still remains unpublished (pp. 367–390). According to her, it was the party's
break, even more than fascist brutality, that ultimately killed Gramsci: "When, beyond
the bars of his cell, Gramsci saw yet more bars—those of political suspicion: the
dissent that had arisen between him and the party—it was at this point that he died"
(p. 38). The issue that led to the break between Gramsci and the International was
exactly the same as that which led Lukács, after the "Blum Theses," to give up any
further directly political activity—at least up to 1956. In view of all this, it is surprising
that Davidson ("Gramscian Studies," p. 456n.) uncritically accepts "official"
accounts by Garratana and Ragionieri denying Gramsci's break. For Ragionieri's
argument, see his "Il Dibattito Teorica nel Movimento Operaio Internazionale" in
Pietro Rossi, ed., *Gramsci e la Cultura Contemporanea* (Rome, 1963), I, 134–137.
This argument is based on textual analyses of the parts of the *Notebooks* that Gramsci
was writing when the question of the 1929 Comintern reached him. According to this
interpretation, Gramsci accepted the thesis that the 1929 economic crash was a prelude
to a major political crisis—hence, he followed in principle the Cominterin's disastrous
policy of splitting the Left and thus helping to bring about, among other things, Nazism
in Germany. A close examination of the texts cited by Ragionieri, however, does not
support his conclusions. In these texts Gramsci analyzes the 1929 crisis as the failure of
certain countertendencies within a capitalism that had been in crisis for more than half a

Historically, the Italian extraparliamentary Left opposed to the party has accepted the party's dubious appropriation of Gramsci and has constantly attacked Gramsci as a non-Leninist, non-Marxist, and social democrat.[13] According to Merli, originally one of the leading extraparliamentary leftist anti-Gramscians,[14] Gramsci ends up forfeiting the very idea of a "revolutionary break" in favor of a "revolution in two stages," or a "revolution without a revolution," by posing the "war of position" as the first stage of a strategy allegedly leading to the eventual "war of maneuver," which, unfortunately, never comes. Consequently, the evolutionary approach, which would have the party take power gradually and through electoral means, is seen as a direct continuation of Gramsci's "revolution without a revolution," and both are rejected as social democratic. Aside from abstractly

---

century: "The crisis is nothing other than the quantitative intensification of certain elements, neither new nor original, but especially the intensification of certain phenomena, while others have been inoperative or have altogether disappeared. In sum, the development of capitalism has been a 'continuous crisis' . . . i.e., a very rapid movement of elements which balance and check each other out." Gramsci, *Quaderni, del Carcere*, III, 1756–1757. In another text cited by Ragionieri, Gramsci seeks to interpret the 1929 crisis in terms of a shortage of savings, which have been devoured by new, unproductive, and parasitic groups in the post–World War I period. *Quaderni, del Carcere*, II, 792–793. Fortunately, Gramsci did not pursue further such a weak and conservative thesis. At any rate, none of the alleged evidence adduced by Ragionieri indicates any adherence or even affinity with the Comintern line, and everything is fully in accordance with Gramsci's position as reported by Lisa, Ley, and Gennaro Gramsci. While it is clear that Gramsci did remain a Marxist throughout, it is not true that this implies in the least acceptance of the predominant Comintern line.

13. It is impossible as well as unnecessary to enumerate here all the various interpretations of Gramsci—something, at any rate, already done fairly well by the cited works of Davidson and Perlini. Special mention, however, should be made of Giuseppe Tamburrano's *Antonio Gramsci, La Vita, Il Pensiero, L'Azione* (Bari, 1963). It is an openly social-democratic interpretation of Gramsci, and, although violently rejected by party intellectuals, it has had a major influence in redirecting Gramscian studies in the 1960s. Thus, Tamburrano and the extraparliamentary Left roughly agree, although giving radically opposed evaluations of Gramsci's political relevance.

14. See, among others, Stefano Merli, "I Nostri Conti con la Teoria della 'Rivoluzione senza Rivoluzione,' " *Giovane Critica* XVII (1967); Andreina De Clementi, "La Politica del Partito Comunista d'Italia nel 1921–22 e il Rapporto Bordiga-Gramsci," *Rivista Storica del Socialismo* XXVIII (1966); and Giacomo Marramao, "Per una Critica dell'Ideologia di Gramsci," *Quaderni Piacentini* XI, 46 (March 1972). Marramao, however, has moved away from his earlier crypto-Althusserian position; for a self-criticism, see his "Ideologia e Rapporti Sociali," *Rinascita*, 25 July 1975, pp. 23–25.

condemning Gramsci for posing the *only* viable alternative in a very limited sociohistorical context, this appraisal of Gramsci uncritically assumes as its theoretical measure a Leninist model that, even in its unadulterated original version, is immensely inferior to Gramsci's and that on closer examination, turns out to be a mere extension of predominant bourgeois ideology.

This comedy of errors surrounding Gramsci interpretations is continued in the Trotskyists' positive evaluation and appropriation of Gramsci.[15] At first sight this seems unlikely. Given the Trotskyists' close political affinities to and their tragic fate within the official communist movement, it would seem that the Italian Trotskyists would side with Bordiga against Gramsci. Bordiga, after all, "saw certain essential things before Trotsky and was more coherent than the latter in drawing the due conclusions."[16] But Bordiga had been branded very early as "sectarian" and "extremist" by Trotsky himself at a time when he still harbored hopes of gaining hegemony within the Russian party. Even after the true character of Stalinism had become all too clear, Trotsky remained openly opposed to Bordighian-type factionalism in order to salvage the appearance of a unified party. Italian Trotskyists take great pains to separate Gramsci from Togliatti, starting from an open disagreement between the two concerning Stalin's administrative handling of Trotsky and the Left opposition before Gramsci's arrest in 1926.[17] Without venturing here into the particular merits of this anti-Stalinist interpretation of Gramsci, it should be pointed out that Italian Trotskyists have rendered an invaluable service in helping to clarify several crucial historical points.[18] Yet, on the whole, their account remains unconvincing in light of Gramsci's evaluation of Trotsky and the fact that, when all is said and

15. This Trotskyist interpretation of Gramsci had already been outlined in the mid-1950s by Livio Maitan's *Attualità di Gramsci e Politica Comunista* (Milan, 1955). Of particular significance, within this literature, is Silverio Corvisieri, *Trotsky e il Comunismo Italiano* (Rome, 1969).

16. Perlini, *Gramsci e il Gramscismo*, p. 189.

17. Crucial in this respect is the previously cited correspondence between Gramsci and Togliatti. See Franco Ferri, "Introduzione" to "Il Carteggio Completo tra Gramsci-Togliatti sulla Situazione nel Partito Bolscevico (1926)," *Rinascita* XXVII, 17 (24 April 1970).

18. For an almost exhaustive account of these problems, see Perlini, who devotes

done, Trotsky's theoretical outlook is a carbon copy of Lenin's, with some additional defects of its own thrown in for good measure.[19]

Given the breadth and variety of interpretations of Gramsci, it is not clear what constitutes the theoretical legacy he bequeathed and what it means in today's world, whose problems are vastly different from the ones Gramsci addressed. The historical regrounding of theoretical frameworks in contexts other than those that gave birth to them poses a difficult question that taxed to the limit the theoretical arsenal not just of Gramsci but of all his Hegelian Marxist contemporaries, a difficulty that applies, as well, to their endeavor to apprehend Marx, Lenin, and the Second International. As already indicated, the reduction of the wealth of Gramsci's social thought to only a few of its minor elements is almost identical to the fate of Marx's works in the late nineteenth century. Facilitating this development in both cases was the fact that both thinkers followed roughly the same pattern of intellectual development—from initially explicit idealist perspectives to specific and historically determinate positions. Since the original framework was never abandoned but only increasingly relegated to a no longer visible background, what came down as their heritage was precisely those specific and historically determinate positions rendered obsolete by historical developments that were themselves partly precipitated by the attempt to realize the political implications of these positions. This is why the reduction of Marx's thought to its bare economic components resulted in a systematic impoverishment of Marxism within the Second International and led even Lenin to dig out Hegel's *Logic* in order to make sense out of *Capital*, through the reintegration of its faded philosophical background without which Marx's economics are meaningless.[20]

Unfortunately, this story has no happy ending. Reintegrating the forgotten theoretical framework with its severed moments is not sufficient for all to be well and for theory and practice to live together happily ever after. History takes its toll. Korsch notes this: "All attempts to re-establish the Marxist doctrine as a whole in its original

---

two full chapters to them. *Gramsci e il Gramscismo*, pp. 22–35, 103–144.

19. See John Molyneux, *Leon Trotsky's Theory of Revolution* (New York, 1981).

20. V. I. Lenin, *Collected Works* (Moscow, 1965), XXXVIII, 180 ff.

function as a theory of the working class' social revolution are reactionary utopias.''[21] Pending the dubious achievement of the Hegelian Absolute, all theoretical constructions must be relegated to one-sidedness and can receive their validation only as historically grounded mediations that cannot be extrapolated beyond the context from which they arose.[22] Taking this reasoning a step further, all *theoretical* claims to absolute knowledge turn out to be epistemological frauds that, as Castoriadis points out, have had as their sole aim in the twentieth century the justification of bureaucratic domination.[23] This is why the more philosophical elements of Marx's work become the most salvageable. The economic analyses in *Capital* and *Theories of Surplus Value* remain inextricably bound to the competitive market conditions of nineteenth-century capitalism, but the *1844 Manuscripts* and the *Grundrisse*—as well as the not strictly economic parts of *Capital*—can still provide a philosophy applicable to present conditions. Marxism survives as faith because as Adorno put it, it was not (and we should add, *it could not have been*) realized.[24]

The fate of Gramsci's thought is similar. As with Marx, the early

21. Karl Korsch, "Ten Theses on Marxism Today (1950)," *Telos*, no. 26 (Winter 1975–76), p. 40.

22. This is why Lukács's Marxism in *History and Class Consciousness* ultimately failed: the rediscovery of the Hegelian foundations of Marxism was mechanically reintegrated with the sociohistorical analyses of *Capital*, which had long since ceased to be valid over half a century after their formulation. As a result, Lukács's main categories were utterly abstract and lacking any objective historical referent, thus precipitating the whole theory into an idealistic vacuum that could be concretized only via a forced reconciliation with the given—which explains Lukács's otherwise incomprehensible coming to terms with Stalinism. Paul Piccone, "Dialectic and Materialism in Lukács," *Telos*, no. 11 (Spring 1972), pp. 105–134.

23. Cornelius Castoriadis, *L'Institution Imaginaire de la Société* (Paris, 1975), pp. 82 ff. Among other things, this explains why perspectives presupposing an Absolute Knowledge standpoint, as found, for example, in Richard Winfield's "The Logic of Marx's *Capital*," *Telos*, no. 27 (Spring 1976), pp. 111–139, readily generate neo-Stalinist positions. The precision of the philological reconstruction hides the epistemological Achilles' heel: the viewpoint of an already achieved Absolute explicitly denied by almost the entire Marxist tradition is implicitly presupposed, thus casting doubt on the whole enterprise and, at the same time, reproducing its totalitarian character in every particular expression of the theory. By generally ignoring economics, Gramsci's absolute historicism successfully avoids both this epistemological cul-de-sac as well as its disastrous political implications.

24. Theodor W. Adorno, *Negative Dialektik* (Frankfurt, 1966), p. 13.

works are openly Hegelian (Crocean)—a feature that is deemphasized in what he wrote as a party official but that reappears full-blown in the *Prison Notebooks*.[25] Also, as in Marx, what has been embalmed as official Gramscian thought consists of ideological falsifications for the most part, as well as those historically determinate notions of Gramsci's that are least likely to survive the test of time. Togliatti undertook this construction of the "official Gramsci" in a series of extremely influential essays written for the most part between the end of World War II and shortly before his death in 1964.[26] It is useful to examine Togliatti's portrait of Gramsci not simply to refute it but because it provides a guide to some of Gramsci's key notions. Their distance from those of both Lenin and the various brands of Marxism-Leninism indicates their potential relevance for the political outlook of the Italian Communist Party today and, more generally, for a radical social theory of late capitalism irreducible to the neo-Gramscism that Perlini justifiably calls "an insidious ideology of the adversary camouflaged as revolutionary theory."[27]

Marxist Methodology

In any theory, basic notions receive their meanings in relation to the theory's logical structure and to the roles assigned to other notions in that theory. Thus, similar claims may have substantially different functions and meanings in different theories. Since Lenin and Gramsci have different theories of Marxism, it follows that although they may be using similar phrases, they may not mean the same thing. Togliatti,

25. Gramsci, *Prison Notebooks*, p. 404: Marxism "is a reformulation and development of Hegelianism."

26. Most of these essays are now collected in Togliatti, *Antonio Gramsci*; fourteen more obscure but related articles have recently been republished by Cortese, "Palmiro Togliatti," pp. 17–44. Davidson, "Gramscian Studies," shows convincingly how, chronologically, Togliatti's views were sharpened in the face of growing criticism, eventually almost explicitly to acknowledge that very little of Lenin's theories remain in Gramsci. For Davidson's own views on the relationship between Lenin and Gramsci, see his "Gramsci and Lenin 1917–1922," *Socialist Register* (1974), pp. 125–250. where he argues that "Gramsci's ideas were not dependent on those of Lenin and . . . in fundamental respects their views were different." In fact, he continues, "this movement *away* and *beyond* Leninism is what allows Gramsci to give a much clearer theoretical formulation of his own practice than Lenin did."

27. Perlini, *Gramsci e il Gramscismo*, p. 194.

for example, is correct in claiming that "to do politics [for Gramsci] means to act in such a way as to transform the world. Hence politics contains everyone's real philosophy along with the substance of history."[28] But it does not follow that for Gramsci the truth of his political thought is reducible to "the method which is Marxist and Leninist," as Marxist-Leninists understand it.[29] Although Togliatti did not bother to document these claims, it is not difficult to provide an army of quotations to support them.[30] Lenin and Gramsci, however, do not mean the same thing by "method."

The question of Marxist methodology, in fact, is one of the most confused within the present state of theoretical discussion. Lenin and the official Communist version puts methodology in a *formal* domain accessible only to the "leaders of the working class" and applicable to the political struggle leading to the overthrow of capitalist relations.[31] But for Gramsci such an objectification of method leads Marxism to "become an ideology in the worst sense of the word, that is to say, a dogmatic system of eternal and absolute truths."[32] Although within Marxism-Leninism the specific content of theory is considered variable as a function of changing historical circumstances, the method whereby this variable content is properly dealt with is itself reified to the metaphysical level of absolute truth. That this method becomes the sole possession of the revolutionary technicians of the party, and thus considerably widens the gap between those who know and those who do not—the very gap that the revolution was meant to bridge—makes

28. Togliatti, *Antonio Gramsci*, p. 136.

29. Ibid., p. 138.

30. Thus, as early as 1918, immediately following the assassination attempt on Lenin, Gramsci wrote an article entitled "Lenin's Work" (14 September, 1918—now in Pedro Cavalcanti and Paul Piccone, eds., *History, Philosophy and Culture in the Young Gramsci* [St. Louis, 1975], pp. 134–139), praising Lenin for "applying the method devised by Marx"; and in the *Prison Notebooks*, Gramsci repeatedly makes it clear that the task of "elaborating . . . the concept of philosophy of praxis as historical methodology" is central for revolutionary Marxists.

31. This formal and objectivistic interpretation of Marxist methodology is widespread even among some North American Marxists. Martin Nicolaus, "Foreword" to Karl Marx, *Grundrisse* (London, 1973). For a detailed critique of Nicolaus's objectivistic metaphysics, see Paul Piccone, "Reading the *Grundrisse*: Beyond Orthodox Marxism," *Theory and Society* II, 2 (1975), 235–259.

32. Gramsci, *Prison Notebooks*, p. 395.

methodology into the opposite of what Gramsci sought.[33]

For Gramsci, the Marxian method is fundamentally subjective and informal (i.e., irreducible to a series of steps or procedures). He regards Marxism as the most recent synthesis of the Western tradition, presupposing the "Renaissance and the Reformation, German idealism and the French Revolution, Calvinism and English classical economics, secular liberalism and this historicism which is at the root of the whole modern conception of life."[34] For this reason, Marxism's goal is the same as the goal sought by this tradition: that same free social individual described by Marx in the *Grundrisse* and prefigured even earlier in the citizen of the Greek *polis* or in the *soul* of Christianity.[35] Only with the advent of communism, however, is it possible to finally realize this goal by abolishing the last expression of the class divisions that kept most of mankind from becoming human beings in the fullest sense, and that degraded the various expressions of this Western tradition to "manifestations of the intimate contradictions by which society is lacerated."[36] Gramsci saw Marxism as an "absolute historicism" that synthesized Marxism with the predominant Western tradition and worked out the practical means to destroy the last and most advanced forms of internal social divisions and thus achieve mankind's emancipation.[37] Since both the historical content and the very tradition that is to be fulfilled are constantly under development, no *formal* method to mediate between the two can be given once and for all—which explains why *praxis* is the central Marxist category: it is the creative activity that reconstitutes the past and allows a forging of political tools in the present that will bring about a qualitatively different future.

This is why Gramsci hailed the Bolshevik Revolution as "the

---

33. For an account of how, starting with Lenin, official Soviet communism reproduces all of the bourgeois mechanisms that the revolution was to have eliminated, see François George, "Forgetting Lenin," *Telos*, no. 18 (Winter 1973–74), pp. 53–88; and Frederick J. Fleron and Lou Jean Fleron, "Administrative Theory as Repressive Political Theory: The Communist Experience," *Telos*, no. 12 (Summer 1972), pp. 63–92.

34. Gramsci, *Prison Notebooks*, p. 395.

35. Marx, *Grundrisse*, p. 705.

36. Gramsci, *Prison Notebooks*, p. 404.

37. Ibid., p. 465.

revolution against *Capital*."

> In Russia, [*Capital*] was the critical demonstration of the fatal necessity
> whereby a bourgeoisie had to come into being, a capitalist era had to begin
> along with a civilization of the Western type, before the proletariat could
> even consider its class vindications, its revolution.

For this reason, it had to be put aside. In the official social-democratic
interpretation, *Capital* had been seen as a blueprint for the necessary
stages of historical development. This objectivistic interpretation was
politically stifling:

> Events have exploded the critical schemes within which the history of
> Russia would have had to develop according to the canons of historical
> materialism. . . . The Bolsheviks are not "Marxists," [but] they live the
> Marxist thought that never dies, . . . which always posits man, and not
> brute economic facts, as the supreme factor in history.[38]

Thus, in 1918, Gramsci already had seen the obsolescence of the
historically specific features of classical Marxism (as seen by the
Second International) and what made it still valid: the primacy of
human activity over and above its theoretical objectifications, the
ability of "Marxist thought" to elaborate concretely the revolutionary
tradition without becoming trapped in any of its historically specific
moments. This is why Gramsci's Marxian method boils down to
sociohistorically grounded political activity faithful to an emancipatory teleology but not reducible to any preconstituted set of procedures. As Salvadori puts it, "The actively organizing element within
Gramsci's work was not the scientific and philological reconstruction
of Marx's and Engels's thought [as in the case, we could add, of
Lukács], but rather the concrete requirements of political praxis."[39]
In Togliatti's interpretation, however, Gramsci's originality ends up
reduced to his mere adherence to party politics dictated by the needs of
the world communist movement—something too reminiscent of
Togliatti's own political role.[40]

38. Gramsci, "The Revolution against Capital" (24 November 1917); now in
Piccone and Cavalcanti, *History, Philosophy and Culture*, pp. 123–126.

39. Salvadori, *Gramsci e il Problema*, p. 111.

40. What makes Togliatti's claim all the more credible was Gramsci's constant
stress on discipline, which, in 1924, had led him to oppose Trotsky even though he was

This also explains Gramsci's description of his own views as Leninist. The Lenin that Gramsci knew and admired was quite different from both the historical Lenin and the sanctified version embalmed in Red Square. As he wrote in prison, his Lenin is to Marx as St. Paul is to Christ: "They represent two phases: science and action, which are homogeneous and heterogeneous at the same time," yet are both "necessary to the same degree."[41] Gramsci knew Lenin as the man of action who had carried out a major revolution. Information about Russia, Lenin, and the Bolshevik Revolution around the 1920s was very inadequate,[42] and by 1968 even leading party intellectuals, such as Ragionieri, could not escape the conclusion that Gramsci's Leninism of 1920 was a far sight different from theirs.[43] Gramsci, for instance, did not know most of Lenin's works written before 1922. What has since become the foundation of Marxism-Leninism was simply not available to him (and Lenin himself had managed to junk most of the crude ideas contained in these works). Togliatti acknowledges that Lenin was practically unknown in Italy prior to 1917, when some of his works began to filter in through French and American journals such as Max Eastman's *Liberator*. Even after 1918, when Lenin's name exploded on the world scene with the Bolshevik Revolution, the works that were translated into Italian (and other languages, for that matter) were primarily those "devoted to the immediate struggle of those years, against social chauvinism and centrism, for the foundation and organization of the communist International."[44] With the possible exception of the pamphlets *Imperialism* and *State and Revolution*—written between the two main phases of the Russian

---

theoretically in agreement with him. Salvadori, *Gramsci e il Problema*, pp. 27–29; and Hoare and Nowell-Smith, "Introduction" to the *Prison Notebooks*, who correctly point out how Gramsci's perception of the Russian events of the time was conditioned by a similar situation in his own party brought about by Bordiga's opposition.

41. Gramsci, *Prison Notebooks*, p. 382.

42. See Alberto Caracciolo, "A Proposito di Gramsci, la Russia e il Movimento Bolscevico," in *Studi Gramsciani* (Rome, 1969), pp. 95–104.

43. Ragionieri, "Il Dibattito Teorica."

44. Togliatti, *Antonio Gramsci*, pp. 139–140. Through more careful research, Davidson has established convincingly that the Lenin Gramsci knew was closer to Daniel De Leon than to the historical Lenin. The first anthology of Lenin's writings was put together by Alfonso Leonetti in 1920 and contains precisely the material that Togliatti refers to. Davidson, "Gramsci and Lenin," pp. 130–131.

Revolution—all the works involved are precisely those that present Lenin as the dedicated political leader who, never losing sight of the final goal, was nonetheless able constantly to reorient strategy according to the requirements of changing social conditions. What passed for Leninism in the early post—World War I years thus was not the same Leninism that Stalin and Marxism-Leninism codified in the post—World War II period.[45]

Given this fact, Togliatti's claim that Gramsci is little more than a footnote—albeit a brilliant one—to the Leninist heritage appears highly suspect. It is instructive to examine closely Togliatti's *full* evidence. According to Togliatti, "There are in Lenin at least three main chapters which determine the whole development of his action and thought: a doctrine of imperialism as the highest phase of capitalism; a doctrine of revolution and therefore of the State; and a doctrine of the Party."[46] The acceptance and development of these chapters is, for Togliatti, "the decisive factor in Gramsci's whole evolution as a thinker and as a political man of action." But a second look reveals that, far from constituting fundamental pillars of Lenin's thought, these three chapters are three main tenets of Marxism-Leninism. The structure of Lenin's thought is much more ambiguous and complex than Togliatti indicates, and the relationship between Lenin and Gramsci is radically different.

The Theory of Imperialism

More than sixty years after it was originally developed, Lenin's theory of imperialism appears today decidedly obsolete. It projected that "the export of capital influences greatly accelerates the development of capitalism in those countries in which it is exported," and it may tend "to arrest development in the capitalist exporting countries."[47] Thus, imperialism was to help the economic growth of the Third World—something that contradicts all of the historical events of the twentieth century. As Emmanuel points out, there does not seem to have been any significant export of capital from Britain between 1870

45. Davidson, "Gramsci and Lenin," p. 139.
46. Togliatti, *Antonio Gramsci*, p. 161.
47. V. I. Lenin, *Imperialism, the Highest Stage of Capitalism* (Moscow, n.d.), p. 107.

and 1914—the period that Lenin studies—and he quotes John Maynard Keynes to the effect that there had not been "any net export of capital since . . . 1580, when Queen Elizabeth invested Drake's treasure in the Levant Company and later used the profits to found the West India Company!"[48] Carlo shows the whole theory to have been self-contradictory from the very beginning since, in another part of the same pamphlet, Lenin

> emphasizes the growing importance of foreign-produced income for metropolitan capitalism: thus, from 1865 to 1898 such income grows ninefold, while English wealth on the whole only doubles, and serves to maintain the unproductive consumption of a significant mass of rentiers (around a million) or to corrupt labor aristocracies or, finally, to finance extravagant horse races.[49]

The examples could be multiplied. The point, however, is that Lenin's *Imperialism* was from the very beginning "a marginal work which never had any scientific pretensions, . . . and far from being a general theory of imperialism, it was only an empirical analysis conditioned by a particular historical situation."[50] Purely in terms of Lenin's intellectual biography, *Imperialism* must be regarded—contrary to Togliatti's claims—primarily as a political tract rather than a scientific treatise. Its success owes more to "the personality of the author and to the practical results obtained by his political action than to the book's actual content."[51] In the context within which it was written, it was a polemic against social-democratic theories that projected the eternal development of capitalism (and the possibility of the increasing betterment of the workers' lot within it through trade unionism) in the same way that Luxemburg, in a similar mechanistic and economistic vein, saw socialism as the inevitable result of the eventual collapse of capitalism because of its unresolvable internal contradictions. In either case, what was not taken into account was

48. Arghiri Emmanuel, "Colonialism and Imperialism," *New Left Review*, no. 73 (May–June 1972), p. 52.

49. Antonio Carlo, "Towards a Redefinition of Imperialism," *Telos*, no. 20 (Summer 1974), p. 109.

50. Emmanuel, "Colonialism and Imperialism," p. 36.

51. Lelio Basso, "La Teoria dell'Imperialismo di Lenin," *Annali Feltrinelli* XV (1973), 713.

precisely what Samir Amin, and Lukács before him,[52] sees as the lasting contribution of Lenin's pamphlet: "the objective ties between the monopolies and revisionism" in a world context typified by new contradictions as well as by a new type of working class.[53] The political thrust of *Imperialism* consists in identifying the struggle against revisionism in the advanced capitalist countries as the primary task in a new economic world order where the heaviest burden of exploitation had already been shifted to the Third World (thus generating new revolutionary possibilities there). What separated Lenin from the rest of the social democrats—and even from Rosa Luxemburg— was his voluntarism and his constant emphasis on the Bolshevik party's organization. The pamphlet *Imperialism* must therefore be seen as essentially another powerful blast meant to demolish any fatalistic account of imperialism and affirm the centrality of the conscious subjective moment, i.e., the party (even if it tended to take on fetishistic forms). But even this "political" reading of *Imperialism* does not bring Lenin much closer to Gramsci. Lenin still presents what is ultimately an *economistic* explanation of reformist ideology, whereas Gramsci's account is throughout focused on the *cultural* dimension.

In official Communist historiography, Lenin's views on imperialism have been reintegrated into a linear theory of history according to which there are *necessary* stages of social development, and imperialism is once again seen as the final phase of capitalism inevitably brought about by the logic of the system—exactly along the mechanis-

52. According to Lukács, "Lenin's superiority—and this is an unparalleled theoretical achievement—consists in *his concrete articulation of the economic theory of imperialism with every political problem of the present epoch.*" Georg Lukács, *Lenin, A Study on the Unity of His Thought* (London, 1970), p. 41.

53. Samir Amin, "La Crisi dell'Imperialismo Contemporaneo," *Terzo Mondo* III, 27 (January–March 1975), 3–16. Pushing this line of reasoning to its extreme logical consequences, Emmanuel concludes that the exploitation of the Third World ends up benefiting the workers of advanced industrial societies who, in participating in the new worldwide exploitation, no longer have socialism as their objective goal. Unlike in Lenin, where a labor aristocracy remains as a privileged minority of workers in advanced societies, with Emmanuel it is almost the whole working class that becomes a labor aristocracy vis-à-vis the majority of the workers in the Third World. See Arghiri Emmanuel, *Unequal Exchange*, trans. Brian Pearce (New York, 1972).

tic lines of social democracy.[54] It is important to keep in mind this process of social-democratic involution of official Communist philosophy of history. Without reference to this, it is impossible to understand the party's integration of Gramsci's views on questions of economic development—as, e.g., worked out in his famous "The Southern Question." In fact, seen from the party's perspective, the problem of southern Italian underdevelopment becomes one of modernizing its semifeudal social structure. Thus, contrary to what Gramsci himself says in the unfinished manuscript on the subject, written just prior to his arrest in 1926, the PCI, in "Leninizing" his account, came very close to reducing it to the "ideology of the lead ball," according to which the underdeveloped Italian South is seen as an economic drag on the remaining industrialized and economically dynamic North. But this ideology of the lead ball is precisely what Gramsci fought as *bourgeois* ideology, and he tried to show how the workers in Turin had already rejected it in 1914 when they offered to have Salvemini, a leading southern advocate (*meridionalista*), run as their own candidate.[55]

Neither Lenin's own account of imperialism nor the official Communist assimilation of it has, therefore, much to do with the Gram-

---

54. Amin calls this phenomenon "the second revisionism" and locates it from the 1930s on. It is typified by the work of Bukharin, Varga, and Mendelsohn. Amin, "La Crisi," pp. 10–11.

55. Antonio Gramsci, *Il Risorgimento* (Turin, 1977), pp. 79–81. See also Antonio Gramsci, *La Questione Meridionale* (Rome, 1970), pp. 135–136. Although the authors of the "Introduzione" to this latter volume, Franco De Felice and Valentino Parlato, point out how Gramsci's account was far from being dualistic or reducible to the above dimensions, it is clear that the debate has tended to focus on the official party interpretation of the problem. This is why extraparliamentary Left critiques, such as those of Antonio Carlo and Edmondo M. Capecelatro, violently attack ideological Trojan horses in their "Against 'The Southern Question,' " *International Journal of Sociology* VI, 2–3 (Summer–Fall 1974), 31–84. It is interesting that the two authors cannot find *one* single quote from Gramsci to pin the official Communist position on him, and they have to settle with ascribing guilt by association in quoting from an official Communist party document written by Grieco, for whose work, as the party leader at that time, Gramsci was allegedly responsible. The most detailed and exhaustive analysis of this problem is to be found in Massimo L. Salvadori, "Gramsci e la Questione Meriodionale," in Salvadori, *Gramsci*, pp. 57–103. See also Perlini, *Gramsci e il Gramscismo*, pp. 85 ff., who reiterates the accusations of Carlo and Capecelatro in a violent polemic against other pro-Gramsci Left positions.

scian account, which is by no means a theory of imperialism and which focuses primarily on the question of southern intellectuals as the catalytic agents for the revolutionary political action needed for a socialistic resolution to the problem of underdevelopment. General economic questions are always seen as secondary and mediated through cultural lenses by Gramsci, for whom political organization and conscious human intervention is the axis around which all of social life revolves. At first sight, this approach makes him appear very similar in *intent* to Lenin. A closer examination, however, reveals that Gramsci and Lenin differed significantly also on other key notions, such as revolution, political organization, and economics.

The Theory of Revolution

This becomes even clearer through an analysis of their respective views of state and revolution. Although Lenin did not sufficiently analyze the notion of revolution and remained caught within the predominant concepts of science, technology, and organization, thus foreshadowing the mechanical reproduction of capitalist relations even after the successful overthrow of capitalism, in *State and Revolution* he did stress the importance of ousting the state bureaucrats and replacing them with new ones—armed workers—denied all special privileges. Official Communist ideology reinstated the privileges and merely altered the legitimating rhetoric. But both the Leninist and the official Communist versions are qualitatively different from what Gramsci had in mind: the coming into being of a new humanity self-conscious of its potentialities and consequently immune to any new form of instrumentalization. Gramsci, thanks to his unrelenting critique of positivism and the various guises that it took, was able to avoid the traps that repeatedly snared Lenin. There is absolutely no fetishism of science in Gramsci, for whom "it is not atomic theory that explains human history but the other way about: in other words, atomic theory and all scientific hypotheses and opinion are superstructures."[56] Society and politics for Gramsci can never be grasped adequately by an objectivistic social science: "The situating of the problem as a search for laws and for constant, regular, and uniform

56. Gramsci, *Prison Notebooks*, p. 468.

lines is connected to a need, conceived in a somewhat puerile and ingenious way, to resolve in peremptory fashion the practical problem of the predictability of historical events."[57] To prevent the occlusion of the all-important creative moment in the scientific enterprise, in fact, Gramsci avoids talking about Marxism as "the science of politics" and uses the less elegant phrase, "the art and science of politics." The stress throughout is on politics as an activity, so that prediction, far from being an extrapolation from the given or a mere extension of past regularities into the future, is primarily an act of commitment: "In reality one can 'foresee' to the extent that one acts, to the extent that one applies a voluntary effort and therefore contributes concretely to creating the results foreseen."[58] Bourgeois social sciences presuppose precisely what is in the process of historically disappearing: the passivity of the masses; "statistical laws can be employed in the art and science of politics only so long as the great masses of the population remain . . . essentially passive."[59]

None of this can be found in Lenin, who hypostatizes science above and beyond society and thus accepts its application (technology) as neutral. But early twentieth-century science and technology are primarily social relations and, moreover, bourgeois social relations. Revolution in Lenin thus turns out to be a mere shift in management. The organizational structure is retained: the party commissar replaces the capitalist boss, and throughout the revolutionary process, the proletariat remains essentially unchanged.

> For Lenin, it is a matter of accepting the proletariat *as capitalism has constituted it* in order to carry out slightly different tasks. It has been well educated and well adjusted. In other words, the basic personality created by capitalism is the one upon which socialism must rest. The construction of socialism presupposes alienation in its most profound sense: submission to authority and repression of individual possibilities of imagination, autonomy, liberty, creativity, i.e., of organization.[60]

This comes out all the more sharply in comparing Gramsci's analy-

57. Ibid., p. 437.
58. Ibid., p. 438.
59. Ibid., p. 428.
60. George, "Forgetting Lenin," p. 55.

sis of Taylorism to Lenin's. For Lenin, it was

> a combination of the refined brutality of bourgeois exploitation and a number of the greatest *scientific achievements in the field of analyzing mechanical motions during work*, the elimination of superfluous and awkward motions, the elaboration of correct methods of work, the introduction of the best system of accounting and *control*, etc.[61]

All would be well, according to Lenin, once the Taylor system is brought under socialist management. How the brutality would be eliminated remains a moot point. Ultimately efficiency and brutality are inextricably connected, and in seeking the former, the Russian Revolution wound up reintroducing the latter, with only minor variations on old patterns of domination. As Korsch noted shortly afterward (1922), no proletarian revolution is possible without the revolutionary transformation of the mode of production and of labor.[62] Far from being mere Stalinist deviations, the new relations of domination were to an extent already rooted in Lenin's partial and confused theoretical vision.

How does Gramsci deal with Taylorism? First of all, he does not approach it as a purely technological problem of efficiency, but (in "Americanism and Fordism") as a social relation inextricably connected with everyday life, prohibition, sexuality, and culture in general. Secondly, what concerns Gramsci is not primarily production, but rather what happens to the subjects who in producing commodities produce themselves as well. Far from focusing on the disciplined proletarians as human robots who, in Lenin, thanks to their discipline and docility can readily fit into the Bolshevik organization, Gramsci stresses the changes the human subject undergoes.[63] What he finds is that the degradation of the producing subject to the level of a mere mechanical function, instead of destroying that subject, actually provides conditions conducive to the overcoming of alienation. Gramsci's critics never tire of pointing out how in Gramsci no notion of

61. Lenin, *Collected Works*, XXVII, 259. As quoted in Fleron and Fleron, "Administrative Theory," p. 81.

62. Karl Korsch, *Arbeitsrecht für Betriebsräte* (Frankfurt, 1968).

63. V. I. Lenin, *Collected Works* (Moscow, 1976), VII, 391–392.

false consciousness, alienation, or reification is to be found,[64] and it is futile to search his writings for an analysis of the caliber of Lukács's "Reification and the Consciousness of the Proletariat" in *History and Class Consciousness*.

This does not mean that Gramsci did not see alienation as a problem. Neither Gramsci nor Lenin was familiar with Marx's full elaboration of alienation, since the *Manuscripts* and the *Grundrisse* were unknown to them. Yet, while Gramsci concretely deals with the substantial issues involved there, Lenin altogether ignores them.

In Lenin, the focus is always on power and on the organizational means to conquer it. Socialism tends to be seen as a solution to the capitalist problems of production, efficiency, and organization rather than the rise of a new humanity, a new civilization, and the abolition of domination (which are seen as superstructural epiphenomena automatically taken care of with the establishment of the workers' state). In Gramsci, however, the stress is always on the latter, with the former being merely the means for its achievement. Unlike Lukács, for whom the problem of alienation is located squarely in the capitalist division of labor, in Gramsci it is always a *political* problem.[65] This does not mean that Gramsci ignores the production process. When he deals with it, however, it is not as if it were a set of interacting abstract categories, as in Lukács, or an objective *thing*, as in Lenin. To the contrary, Gramsci treats the production process as a *living* activity that in capitalism reduces human beings to the level of mere animals and consequently generates a political confrontation that leads to communism. This is brilliantly captured in a long passage worth quoting in

64. Perlini, *Gramsci e il Gramscismo*, pp. 156, 177.

65. It is well known that, as Lukács himself admitted in the "Preface to the New Edition" (1967) of *History and Class Consciousness*, trans. Rodney Livingstone (London, 1971), the Hegelian identification of objectification and alienation led him to postulate the identical subject-object of history and, therefore, ultimately to pose the problem of the overcoming of alienation in unresolvable terms—which eventually led him to reject the whole problematic. But what happens if the theory of alienation is reconstructed *without* collapsing objectification and alienation? In answering this question first in his *Dialektik des Konkreten* (Frankfurt, 1967) and then in his more political work, *La Nostra Crisi Attuale* (Rome, 1969), Karel Kosik ends up by posing the problem primarily in *political* terms, i.e., along Gramscian lines. This theme is developed in Paul Piccone, "Czech Marxism: Karel Kosik," *Critique*, no. 8 (1977), pp. 43–52.

full:

The compositor . . . has to keep his hands and eyes constantly in move-ment, and this makes his mechanization easier. But if one really thinks about it, the effort that these workers have to make in order to isolate from the often fascinating intellectual content of a text (and the more fascinating it is the less work is done and less well) its written symbolization, this perhaps is the greatest effort that can be required in any trade. However, it is done, and it is not the spiritual death of man. Once the process of adaptation has been completed, what really happens is that the brain of the worker, far from being mummified, reaches a state of complete freedom. The only thing that is completely mechanized is the physical gesture; the memory of the trade, reduced to simple gestures repeated at an intense rhythm, "nestles" in the muscular and nervous centers and leaves the brain free and unencumbered for other occupations. . . . American industrialists have understood all too well this dialectic inherent in the new industrial methods. They have understood that "trained gorilla" is just a phrase, that "unfortunately" the worker remains a man and even that during this work he thinks more, or at least has greater opportunities for thinking, once he has overcome the crisis of adaptation without being eliminated: and not only does the worker think, but the fact that he gets no immediate satisfac-tion from his work and realizes that they are trying to reduce him to a trained gorilla, can lead him into a train of thought that is far from conformist.[66]

Whereas American industrialists have become aware of this process, the same cannot be said for most Leninists, who tend to deal with the proletarians as trained gorillas—even within the party! The problem with Gramsci's account, which he could hardly be expected to have foreseen, is that capitalism during the last half-century has proceeded to separate workers physically from one another by means of new political tools such as the assembly line, and also to colonize their thoughts by means of consumerism and the culture industry in a way that makes it difficult for any critical vision to emerge from the laboring process.

The notion of hegemony provides yet another example of the divergence of these two thinkers. For Lenin, what is always central is the form of revolution, which, however, uncritically retains capitalist

66. Gramsci, *Prison Notebooks*, pp. 309–310.

and domineering content, and thus paves the way for the now well-known abstract negations of the Russian Revolution. In Gramsci, the content is always in the foreground. Thus, although Gramsci's concept of hegemony has been associated with Lenin's and identified with the dictatorship of the proletariat, Gramsci's emphasis is on direction and Lenin's is on domination.[67] The Leninist concept focuses exclusively on political society; the Gramscian counterpart includes both political and civil society—and the very terms have considerably different meanings for the two men.[68] Things are further complicated by Gramsci's own claim that

> the theoretical-practical principle of hegemony has also epistemological significance, and it is here that Ilich's [Lenin's] greatest theoretical contribution to the philosophy of praxis should be sought. In these terms one could say that Ilich advanced philosophy as philosophy in so far as he advanced political doctrine and practice.[69]

Passages such as these, which abound in Gramsci, are what mislead people of the caliber of Mondolfo into locating an antinomy "between the libertarian and the authoritarian tendency that is embodied in the Gramscian concept of hegemony."[70] An examination of how Lenin theoretically articulates this notion, however, shows that, in his enthusiasm for the Russian Revolution, Gramsci may have projected onto Lenin his own concept of hegemony. As Bobbio has shown, Gramsci actually owed Lenin far less than he thought concerning the concept of hegemony.[71] In the historical Lenin, hegemony has little to do with

67. For the official Italian Communist Party view, see Luciano Gruppi, *Il Concetto di Egemonia in Gramsci* (Rome, 1972). For a restrained but accurate critique of Gruppi, see Nicola Auciello, *Socialismo ed Egemonia in Gramsci e Togliatti* (Bari, 1974), pp. 85–86.

68. Thomas R. Bates, "Gramsci and the Theory of Hegemony," *Journal of the History of Ideas* XXXVI, 2 (April–June), 357. See also Hughes Portelli, *Gramsci e il Blocco Storico*, trans. Maria Novella Pierini (Bari, 1973), pp. 3–11.

69. Gramsci, *Prison Notebooks*, p. 365.

70. Rodolfo Mondolfo, *Umanismo di Marx, Studi Filosofici 1908–1966* (Turin, 1968), p. 403.

71. Norberto Bobbio, "Gramsci e la Concezione della Società Civile," in Rossi, *Gramsci*. As Paggi has argued, Gramsci's Leninism in the *Prison Notebooks* is a function of reading Lenin as the executor of the eleventh thesis on Feuerbach: this identification "will constitute the woof of the philosophical writings in jail." Leonardo Paggi, *Antonio Gramsci e il Moderno Principe* (Rome, 1970), p. 357.

culture and refers mainly to the class domination that the proletariat exercises through the party in realizing a narrow view of socialism understood as the collective ownership of the means of production, planning, and the abolition of privilege.[72] But there is no attempt to achieve or even to provide for the genesis of a new humanity, and the unchanged old content eventually has the better of the new externally imposed social form, causing the old relations of domination gradually to reappear. In other words, what distinguishes Gramsci's notion of hegemony from Lenin's is that for Gramsci it is a theory of the *overcoming* of alienation, but in Lenin it remains primarily a theory of *domination*.

Theory of the Party

These same themes reappear in the theory of the party. For Gramsci, the process of creating a new culture in which all members participate as self-conscious subjects is to be mediated by the party as the "Modern Prince," who takes "the place of the divinity or the categorical imperative."[73] The goal is not more efficiency, or a more rational organization, but the bringing about of what is qualitatively new. Here Gramsci avoids the pitfalls of static humanism, which sees alienation as the deformation of something initially sound, and thus as a degeneration to be overcome by a return to some *status quo ante*. What he meant by the "new culture" was something qualitatively new, hitherto prefigured only in thought and expressed as negativity. Gramsci's problematic rotates around the notion of self-constitution into a new state.[74] Clearly, in this context Gramsci returns to a Hegelian notion of the state seen as the highest expression of civil

72. This has been accounted for in terms of the intrinsic differences between the two different contexts within which Gramsci and Lenin operated, the East and the West. Portelli, *Gramsci e il Blocco Storico*, pp. 163–164; and Auciello, *Socialismo ed Egemonia*, pp. 125–126. These arguments, however, are not altogether convincing.

73. Gramsci, *Prison Notebooks*, p. 133.

74. As Auciello summarizes it (*Socialismo ed Egemonia*, p. 100), in Gramsci civil society "appears as that specific level in which the state . . . educates and organizes the consensus of those that it governs through the exercise of hegemony by the social group in power; thus it appears as a primary and essential moment of that educational effort which the state performs in order to raise the cultural and moral level of the masses."

society rather than as a mere tool of class domination, as in the orthodox Marxist tradition. In this, Gramsci again radically differs from Lenin. Whereas Lenin constantly stresses the state's class character and its repressive nature, Gramsci concentrates on its cultural-hegemonic function: "Its aim is always that of creating new and higher types of civilization."[75] Even in relatively "visionary" works such as *State and Revolution*, there is not much in Lenin about qualitative changes resulting from the revolutionary process. Rather, the revolution is a mechanical transition throughout, whose changes remain purely external and involve property relations:

> We are not Utopians, we do not indulge in dreams of how best to do away *immediately* with all subordination. . . . We workers ourselves [the Bolsheviks?], relying on our experience as workers, establishing a strict, an iron discipline, supported by state power and the armed workers, shall reduce the role of the state officials to that of simply carrying out our instructions as responsible, moderately paid "managers."[76]

These differences in emphasis between Gramsci and Lenin do make a great deal of difference once they turn from abstract philosophical speculation into state policies.

In comparing Lenin's and Gramsci's theories of the party, Togliatti unwarrantedly assumes that Lenin did in fact have one such theory. But as Carlo has shown convincingly, Lenin "does not present *one*, but *a series* of complex and contradictory positions" on the question of party organization.[77] A careful study of the forty-five volumes of his *Collected Works* reveals that there is an economistic account during the 1890s, the well-known theory of *What Is to Be Done?*, a much looser account between 1905 and 1919, the bureaucratic views implicit in *Left-Wing Communism: An Infantile Disorder*, and the worried forebodings of the very last years. There is no justification for elevating the views in *What Is to Be Done?* to the level of *the* Leninist theory of the party, apart from the unfortunate fact that these views have best fit the needs of bureaucratic collectivist regimes and, it

75. Gramsci, *Prison Notebooks*, p. 242.
76. V. I. Lenin, *State and Revolution* (New York, 1932), pp. 42–43.
77. Antonio Carlo, "Lenin and the Party," *Telos*, no. 17 (Fall 1973), p. 40. It should also be added that Gramsci constantly rethought the problem of organization, and no *one* theory of the party can unequivocally be extrapolated from his works either.

should be added, generally reflect Lenin's own political practices. Ascribing to Gramsci the views of *What Is to Be Done?* becomes further suspect when it is realized that Gramsci was barely acquainted with this work.[78] But even if Togliatti is correct in locating Lenin's theory of the party in *What Is to Be Done?*, that would not put an end to the problems. Despite the superficial similarity in the emphasis on intellectuals in both Gramsci and Lenin, there is no relation whatsoever between the two. In *What Is to Be Done?* Lenin, following Kautsky, sharply differentiates between the intellectuals as historical subjects who, because of their privileged position, can generate socialist theory "as [a] natural and inevitable outcome of the development of thought,"[79] and the proletariat as the passive object, which can be activated only through the bourgeois intellectuals' donation of an otherwise unattainable revolutionary consciousness. In this view, the proletariat can spontaneously attain class consciousness only if, as individuals, some exceptional members become intellectuals! Nothing is further from this than Gramsci's claim that "all men are intellectuals" and his constant berating of those who are ordinarily referred to as such, i.e., those who think about abstract ideas.[80] His definition of organic intellectuals covers the whole group able to "be an organizer of society in general, including all its complex organisms and services, right up to the state organism."[81] Being an intellectual for

---

78. Gruppi points out that this work was not available to Gramsci even though there had been a German version published in 1903 in *Neue Zeit*. See Gruppi, *Il Concetto di Egemonia*, p. 74. Davidson reports that the only account of *What Is to Be Done?* that Gramsci might have seen during the 1920s was in some references to it made in Zinoviev's speech of 6 September 1918 (translated into French in *Vie Ouvriere*, 16 April 1920). Yet, even in this article, Zinoviev hinted that *What Is to Be Done?* was somewhat dated and, at any rate, sought to locate as "the crucial theoretical contribution of Lenin the theory of the role of the Soviets which he had supposedly developed since 1905, and his corresponding teaching on the state. . . . So, even when . . . Lenin's teaching on the party was discussed, its importance was lost in the stress that Lenin's greatest contribution to Marxism was his theory of the State." Davidson, "Gramsci and Lenin," p. 133. The footnotes to *What Is to Be Done?* in the English translation of the *Prison Notebooks* are figments of the translators' Leninist imaginations.

79. Lenin, *Collected Works*, IV, 158.

80. Gramsci, *Prison Notebooks*, p. 9.

81. Ibid., p. 5.

Gramsci thus does not merely involve abstract thinking but, more importantly, entails the *objectification* of ideas. To the extent that the revolutionary party does this, all its members, down to the lowest stamp lickers, are intellectuals. The often-quoted passage according to which "the popular element 'feels' but does not always know or understand; the intellectual element 'knows' but does not always understand and in particular does not always feel," clearly shows Gramsci's view of intellectuals in capitalist society as partial beings who can be completed only by their reintegration into the social whole.[82] Unlike in *What Is to Be Done?*, the party is not charged with manipulating passive proletarians but with integrating them with the intellectuals and thus remedying the shortcomings created on both sides by the division between mental and physical labor. The notion of the party as the Modern Prince—the collective will—is in no way reducible to Lenin's "ten wise men" pulling the strings of puppet proletarians.[83] It is, rather, the embryo of a new society constituted by people able both to think and to feel, and is based on the overcoming of social divisions.

Philosophy

Interestingly enough, Togliatti did not attempt to draw any parallels between Lenin's philosophy (or what official Communist orthodoxy has codified as Marxist-Leninist philosophy) and Gramsci's. Such a study, however, has been made by the translator of Gramsci's work into German.[84] Taking Lenin's *Materialism and Empiriocriticism* as

---

82. Ibid., p. 418.
83. Lenin, *What Is to Be Done?*, p. 116.
84. Christian Riechers, *Antonio Gramsci, Marxismus in Italien* (Frankfurt, 1970). The same author, in 1967, edited a selection of Gramsci's writings (with an introduction by Wolfgang Abendroth) in German, *Philosophie der Praxis* (Frankfurt, 1967), which has since become an example of how *not* to translate. For devastating criticisms, see José Rodriguez-Lores, *Die Grundstruktur des Marxismus Gramsci und die Philosophie der Praxis* (Frankfurt, 1971); Gerhart Roth, *Gramscis Deutung des Marxismus als Philosophie der Praxis* (Frankfurt, 1972); Peter Palla, "Gramsci in Germania," *Utopia* II, 7–8 (July–August 1972), 9–14; and Franco Fergani, "La 'Questione Gramsci': una Proposta di Reconsiderazione," *Aut Aut*, no. 144 (November–December 1974), pp. 25–38. A thesis similar to Riechers's had earlier been defended by Mario Tronti in "Alcune Questioni intorno al Marxismo di Gramsci," in *Studi Gramsciani* (Rome, 1959), pp. 305–321. For an excellent critique

his model of orthodoxy, Riechers finds that Gramsci has reduced Marxism to subjective idealism.[85] Although he acknowledges that Lenin's *Materialism and Empiriocriticism* was instrumentalized after Lenin's death to set the pace for all subsequent Soviet philosophical debate,[86] he ignores the scores of criticisms—from Marxists and non-Marxists alike—that point out how little the book has to do with Marxism, how it completely trivializes the dialectic, and, as Korsch puts it, how it *"drags the whole debate between materialism and idealism back to a historical stage which German idealism from Kant to Hegel had already surpassed."*[87] This is not the place to once again flog the dead horse of *Materialism and Empiriocriticism* with critiques of the infamous theory of reflection, mechanistic epistemology, and generally vulgar materialism. It is enough to point out, with Adorno, that although Lenin "wanted to expose the complicity of subjective positivism with the 'powers that be,' " the whole effort turned out to be an antiintellectual tirade in which this "political need turned against the very theoretical goal of knowledge."[88] Although *Mater-*

---

of Riechers, see Ray Morrow's review of the book in *Telos*, no. 22 (Winter 1974–75), pp. 174–181. Surprisingly, Perlini, *Gramsci e il Gramscismo*, pp. 156 ff., unreservedly endorses the book, not so much because of Riechers's philosophical profundity but out of an unrestrained hatred for Gramsci and everything associated with him. Marramao, who had initially also endorsed Riechers's work in the previously cited "Per una Critica dell'Ideologica," has eventually changed his mind in this matter as well. For an interesting critique, see Marramao, "Ideologia."

85. Riechers, *Antonio Gramsci*, pp. 131–140.

86. Ibid., p. 145.

87. Karl Korsch, "The Present State of the Problem of Materialism and Philosophy—An Anti-Critique [1930]," in Karl Korsch, *Marxism and Philosophy* (London, 1970), pp. 115–116. See also Korsch's favorable review of Anton Pannekoek's book, "Lenin's Philosophy," *Living Marxism* IV, 5 (November 1938), where a similar argument is developed. Korsch's excellent critique, however, is vitiated by his attempt to establish a logical continuity between Lenin's views and subsequent political developments in the Communist International. As Rusconi puts it, "To the extent that Korsch considers only negatively the development of the Bolshevik Revolution as a bureaucratic revolution, or as the bourgeois continuation of a bourgeois movement, and to the extent that he does not distinguish between Lenin and official Leninism and subsequent Stalinism, he loses the essential moment of the appropriation of 'Marxism to Marxism itself.' " Gian Enrico Rusconi, "Teoria y Praxis," in Eduardo Subirats, ed., *Karl Korsch o el Nacimiento de una Nueva Epoca* (Barcelona, 1973), pp. 67–68. What Korsch misses is the extent of the falsification that had already been carried out by 1920.

88. Adorno, *Negative Dialektik*, p. 203.

ialism and Empiriocriticism was available only in Russian (the first German translation appeared only in the late 1920s),[89] and Italian Communists learned of its existence during their Moscow visits between 1922 and 1924, no reference to it is to be found in Gramsci's writings at that time or even later. It was Bordiga who explicitly attempted to resuscitate Lenin's vulgar materialism in 1924, in his journal *Prometeo*.[90] Gramsci's journal, *Ordine Nuovo*, subsequently published Lenin's later philosophical work as well as one of Engels's long essays praising Hegel and the heritage of German idealism, and pointing out that a political man's real philosophy is in his politics and action rather than his books—something that reappears repeatedly in Gramsci's *Notebooks* as well.[91]

At any rate, Lenin's *Materialism and Empiriocriticism* was primarily a political weapon meant to eliminate a wing of the party at a crucial point in the history of the Bolsheviks.[92] It has nothing to do with Gramsci's philosophy. Far from being a deficiency, as Riechers claims, it frees Gramsci's Marxism from a philosophical provincialism usually ascribed to him but that can be more correctly ascribed to the Bolsheviks and to Marxism-Leninism.[93] Gramsci's epistemology is Hegelian and Crocean throughout: knowing is never a passive

89. Pannekoek writes that, if *Materialism and Empiriocriticism* and Lenin's notions "had been known by 1918 by Marxists in Western Europe, they would have undoubtedly considered his tactic concerning world revolution with a greater critical sense and less faith." Anton Pannekoek, *Lenin Filosofo* (Milan, 1972). (Pannekoek's essay was first written in the 1930s.) In private correspondence, however, Hedda Korsch has said that in 1922, while her husband Karl was writing *Marxism and Philosophy*, she stayed up many a night translating Lenin's *Materialism and Empiriocriticism* from Russian to German so that he could know what Lenin had to say about philosophy. The silence concerning the book in the 1920s was probably not as much the result of ignorance as embarrassment over its contents.

90. Eugenio Garin, "Discorsi," in Rossi, *Gramsci*, I, 25; and Ragionieri, "Il Dibattito Teorico," pp. 122–130.

91. For a discussion of how Gramsci selectively published some of Lenin's work emphasizing the centrality of Hegel and the dialectic, see Leonardo Paggi, "Gramsci's General Theory of Marxism," *Telos*, no. 33 (Fall 1977), pp. 27–70.

92. For an elaboration of this, see Paul Piccone, "Towards an Understanding of Lenin's Philosophy," *Radical America* IV, 6 (September–October 1970), 3–20.

93. The most outspoken author of this charge is Eric J. Hobsbawm. See his "The Great Gramsci," *New York Review of Books*, 4 April 1974, pp. 39 ff; and his "Dall'Italia all'Europa," *Rinascita*, 25 July 1975, pp. 15 ff. Nowhere, however, does Hobsbawm document his claim. Compared to whom is Gramsci "provincial"? Cer-

reflection of the given but an act creating the mediations necessary to direct life.

The Gramscian Heritage

What, then, remains of Gramsci's alleged Leninism, or of the myth of Gramsci as Lenin's footnote? Not much. That it has gained such widespread acceptance can be explained only in terms of the unresolved ambiguities concerning Leninism, the distorted knowledge of Gramsci's work, and the influence of official Italian Communist Party interpretations. The historical Gramsci, however, has very little to do with Lenin's original views or with the Leninism of official Communist parties.

Gramsci provided a new and unique reformulation of Marxian theory, and he therefore has come to occupy a special place in both Italian culture and the history of Marxism. His vision almost succeeded even in transcending the unavoidable limitations imposed by his times.

Unlike most of the international communist movement around the 1930s, Gramsci succeeded in perceiving the general trends of a profound process of transformation at a worldwide level, of the relation between the state and the economy (as produced by the new requirements and by the new phase of capitalist development) precisely because in the previous years, and with particular reference to the kinds of investigations and observations connected with the analysis of fascism, he had gradually come to develop, within his theoretical arsenal, a concept of the state and its relations to "civil society" that rejected all dichotomous schemes of a traditional type and sought, rather, to trace the "presence" of the state in that "private" and "prestate" mass reality that is civil society.[94]

Gramsci's "Americanism and Fordism"—originally written in 1930 and reworked in 1934—concludes by claiming that some of the

---

tainly not Korsch or Lukács, whose problematic during the same time is considerably more limited, or any of the English or German intellectuals who went through the ordeal of the 1920s and 1930s. The mechanical inference of Gramsci's provincialism from Italy's economic backwardness should either be argued or put to rest. Gramsci was, first and foremost, a *European* thinker not limited by the problematic of an economically backward society.

94. Auciello, *Socialismo ed Egemonia*, p. 111n.

social reforms introduced in the progressive era (and later codified as integral parts of the New Deal) did not prefigure any qualitative changes in the nature of American civilization seen as "an organic extension and an intensification of European civilization" (since "nothing has been changed in the character and the relationship between fundamental groups").[95] Still, he focuses in this essay on the very questions that in the next half-century were tackled in the effort to reconstitute a bankrupt entrepreneurial capitalism under the tutelage of a strong centralized state bureaucratic apparatus. Gramsci could hardly foresee the reconstitution of civil society by means of state intervention, which created the conditions for new intensive, as against previously extensive, modes of capitalist development. Yet, he was very sensitive to the new cultural initiatives by the most advanced exponents of industrial capitalism (e.g., Ford) to rationalize workers' life styles in line with new productive requirements.

Ford was a poor example—which partly explains Gramsci's failure to see in Fordism the potential harbingers of a new phase of capitalist development. In fact, of all the major automakers and industrial giants in the United States, Ford was one of the very last to give in to the New Deal's reorganization of capital-labor relations by institutionalizing collective bargaining as a means to reintroduce some automatic control mechanisms in the process of setting prices and wages, previously performed through market mechanisms that had been annihilated in monopoly capitalism.[96] Thus, the puritanism advocated by Ford, as well as related social measures meant to rationalize the working class into the regimented and disciplined work force required by Taylorized industry, did not become a prototype for new sociopolitical relations. In fact, with the repeal of prohibition, the liberalization of other repressive measures, and the growth of the culture industry, the working class could be consumerized through the rise of the narcissistic personality,[97] on the one hand, and, on the

95. Gramsci, *Prison Notebooks*, p. 318. The only difference between the 1930 and the 1934 drafts is that Gramsci, in the first one, talks about "fundamental classes," and in the second he discusses "fundamental groups." Gramsci, *Quaderni del Carcere*, pp. 296–297, 2180.

96. For a discussion of this, see Mario Tronti, "Workers and Capital," *Telos*, no. 14 (Winter 1972), pp. 25–62.

97. Christopher Lasch, *The Culture of Narcissism: American Life in an Age of*

other, with the cybernation of the productive process, which systematically seeks to close off any possibility of choice on the part of the abstract labor it employs.[98] Compounded with the growing automation of production, which effectively mechanized most hard manual tasks, the prototype prefigured by Ford became obsolete before it could even be generalized, to be replaced by the cretinized, narcissistic consumer producers whose political malleability allowed the implementation of the New Deal as a type of Gramscian "passive revolution."[99]

Gramsci's limited access to available information concerning developments in American capitalism led him to hypostatize a historical dead end as the predominant new model of social reorganization. Despite this, his mode of analysis of Americanism is exemplary. The emphasis is first on demographic rationalization, then on the state-bureaucratic apparatuses' possible direction of this process, and ultimately on psychoanalysis as a means of remedying the psychological disruptions such a rationalization created.[100] That Gramsci could in 1930 see feminism as the result of "the new paradoxical social position" of upper-class women generated by the demographic requirements of the new phase of capitalist development testifies to his perspicacity.[101] While he obviously could not have foreseen the explosion of women's liberation and feminist movements in the late 1960s and the 1970s, a Gramscian analysis of these phenomena, relating them to the changing character of capitalist social relations and other forms of rationalization, provides an understanding of even recent sociopolitical developments without recourse to abstract moralisms or similar ideological arguments.

More generally, the aphoristic and fragmentary character of Gram-

Diminishing Expectations (New York, 1979).

98. For a detailed account of how this process works, see David F. Noble, "Social Choice in Machine Design: The Case of Automatically Controlled Machine Tools," in Andrew Zimbalist, ed., *Case Studies in the Labor Process* (New York and London, 1979), pp. 18−50.

99. Gramsci, of course, entertained but never developed this possibility of "a passive revolution." Gramsci, *Prison Notebooks*, pp. 278−279.

100. In this case also Gramsci states his claim but never follows up with the promised analysis. Ibid., p. 279.

101. Ibid., p. 298.

sci's *Prison Notebooks*, though certainly not a matter of conscious choice, unwittingly combines an approach to social reality popularized by Walter Benjamin, Adorno, and even Michel Foucault, with the retention of an all-inclusive vision of the general social development emphasized by older generations of Marxist thinkers. In Gramsci, the logic of the whole, unencumbered by a fatalistic Marxist theory of history, can grasp the particular without reducing it to an extension of that logic and thereby suffocating its uniqueness and specificity. The concept is always limited to the instrumental role of mediation in a context where life and subjectivity have uncontested primacy and hence the dialectic does not choke on the usual Marxist or Hegelian closures. Instead, by constantly confronting the hypostatized totality with a particularity that it only partially determines, this dialectic allows for the possibility of relevant and noncircular sociopolitical analysis.

In terms of the perspective of that party Gramsci helped to found and direct for the most intense part of his active political life, his outlook occupies the emancipatory side of a political oxymoron whose survival and continued success hinges on the rapidity with which the scientific-socialist, or Leninist, side is finally abandoned. Only if translated into a political project of social modernization, continuous with the Spaventa-Labriola tradition of which it is an integral component, can the Gramscian root of the Italian Communist Party resurface as a qualitatively distinct alternative to the various strategies of capitalist rationalization now under consideration in Italy and Europe in general. The Gramscian heritage lives on as an ethical vision trapped historically in an incompatible Leninist framework that grows ever more irrelevant and counterproductive in the face of modern-day realities.

Index